THINGS A COMPUTER SCIENTIST RARELY TALKS ABOUT

CSLI Lecture Notes Number 136

THINGS A
COMPUTER
SCIENTIST
RARELY
TALKS
ABOUT

Donald E. Knuth

CSLI Publications   *Stanford, California*

Copyright © 2001
Center for the Study of Language and Information
Leland Stanford Junior University
Paperback edition
21 20 19 18 17   6 5 4 3

Library of Congress Cataloging-in-Publication Data

Knuth, Donald Ervin, 1938-
    Things a computer scientist rarely talks about /
Donald E. Knuth.
      xi,257 p. 23 cm. -- (CSLI lecture notes ; no. 136)
      Includes bibliographical references and index.
      ISBN 978-1-57586-326-9 (pbk : alk. paper)
      ISBN 978-1-57586-327-6 (cloth : alk. paper)
      1. Religion and science. 2. Science--Philosophy.
3. Computers and civilization. 4. Computers--Moral and
ethical aspects. 5. Information technology--Philosophy.
I. Title. II. Series.
    BL240.2 .K59 2001
    261.5--dc21

                                              2001025685

Internet page
   http://www-cs-faculty.stanford.edu/~knuth/things.html
contains further information and links to related books.

FOREWORD: MEETING GOD AT MIT   BY ANNE FOERST

In 1997, I started the "God and Computers" project at MIT. I had come to the MIT Artificial Intelligence Laboratory in 1995 and was working on dialog between understandings of humans in AI and in Christian theology. Many people — students and professors alike — felt quite provoked about my presence there, and we often had heated arguments about mechanistic explanations of human features and the usefulness (or uselessness) of religion. The vast majority argued in a fairly reductionistic way but, yet, a few people held religious beliefs. These people, however, were clearly a minority and usually practiced their religiosity in private and kept it completely separate from their work.

After a while, I realized that some of the heat that arose in our discussions, the passion with which people argued for their point of view, could not be explained by scientific conviction alone. Quite the contrary; these emotions stem from the very human nature that makes us ask questions for meaning. Most people search for answers in the realm they know best, and so scientists often formulate possible solutions for their own existential quests in the metaphors of their scientific discipline. This is especially true for all those disciplines where the subject is — in a broad sense — human nature; that is, cognitive science, neurology, psychology, ethology, and of course AI.

From my Lutheran point of view, to be human means to ask questions. We puzzle about the nature of the universe and ourselves. We want to understand the world around us and us in it. We want to understand our friends and ourselves. And we want to know what's going on when we think or feel or interact with the world.

Human questions tend to be anthropocentric and even egocentric, as the questioning human cannot completely abstract from who he or she is and from the quests and ideals being brought to each question. We cannot help but bring our own perspectives to the table whenever we seek answers to questions such as, "Why am I here?" "What is the meaning of my life?" "Why am I the way I am?" We all are embedded in specific cultures and worldviews that will shape the way we formulate our answers to these questions. And we all have values and preferences that we apply to our quest.

Particularly in a discipline concerned with human nature, we tend to apply our own intuitive sense of ourselves to our theories about humans; also, the theories about human features that are developed in our scientific disciplines tend to influence our intuitive sense of ourselves. Being a human being concerned with the understanding of human nature therefore places the questioning person in a circle in which culturally influenced intuitions about ourselves and scientific theories about human feature are intertwined and cannot be separated from one another.

Being in an AI lab, where people attempt to build humanoid robots in analogy to human infants, the relationship between theories about human nature and intuitive and cultural self understandings is especially pertinent. When the Electrical Engineering and Computer Science Department (EECS) offered me the opportunity to teach a course about these questions, I immediately accepted it. However, from the beginning of the planning process I realized that the point I was trying to make in the course would be supported best if I also invited famous scientists concerned with human nature, and let them speak about how they addressed questions about themselves and the meaning of their life within and outside of their research. When my course proposal won a Templeton award, I had an opportunity to invite several researchers that I either had met while I was at MIT or had heard about in the course of my studies.

In the first year, the guest speakers were Paul Penfield, Rodney Brooks, Federico Girosi, Lynn Stein, and Rosalind Picard (all from MIT); Marc Hauser, Ming Tsuang, and Bijoy Misra (from Harvard); Francisco Varela (from Paris); and MIT alumnus Ray Kurzweil. As there had been MIT-wide criticisms against this project, and since many people were very much against any combination of religion and science at MIT, the series had become widely known and was attended by many people.

Over the three years that the series took place, the consistency of the audience remained fairly constant. A third of the auditorium consisted of MIT faculty together with their former students (usually from EECS) who worked now in the Boston area. Another third were interested ministers, professors from the larger Boston community, and some laypeople who had heard about the lecture series in the *Globe* and other local newspapers. Another third consisted of MIT students, mostly undergrads. From the feedback I got, these students welcomed the opportunity to see their professors struggle with the same questions that they were struggling with. Many were grateful for these presentations and became more encouraged to ask questions themselves. They were relieved to find out that even their admired teachers did not have final solutions, but could only formulate answers and theories and suggestions out of their own life experiences and expertise.

For example, Paul Penfield, then head of EECS, outlined a concept of "God as Scientist" that pointed to different realms of questions that demand different answers. Rodney Brooks, director of the AI Laboratory, talked about being torn between his scientific conviction that humans are nothing but "bags of skin" and his knowledge that he neither wanted to be treated as such nor would he himself treat people that way. The answers from each speaker were always authentic, sometimes surprisingly open and personal, and most of the time captivating not just from an academic perspective but from the personal situation of the listeners, especially the students.

In the second year, MIT professors Robert Randolph, Steven Pinker, Sandy Pentland, and Joel Moses spoke, as well as Professor Brian Cantwell Smith of Indiana University, and the experience was very similar. It was, however, much more difficult to find speakers. The first year had been an experiment to bring questions outside of hard science into the academic setting of MIT; the invited speakers were excited about the prospect to do something new. Many of them were atheists or agnostics, but it was fascinating to see how, for example, Jewish and Protestant atheism differed from one another. No one had expected to have a large audience or so much media interest. The second year was different, because the expectations for the second series were higher, and the speakers knew that they would have less freedom to experiment. The talks were fascinating nonetheless. I had attempted to move away from a purely "cognitive science approach," and so Bob Randolph, then senior associate dean at MIT, talked about the history of religion at MIT. Stephen Pinker evaluated explanatory models for the phenomenon of religion in humans and concluded that *homo religiosus* is, in a way, the result of our evolutionary development. The other speakers had equally engaging topics. The feedback from the audience was again very positive, but an increasing number of people wished to hear one speaker several times. They felt that this would give a speaker the opportunity to develop his or her thoughts over time, and the audience could get to know their thoughts more thoroughly.

When I was thinking about a speaker for such a series of talks, after some consideration only one person seemed to be possible, and I invited Don Knuth. I had come across his book *3:16* and liked it a lot. I also had read some of his work in computer science. Having a person who is deeply faithful and simultaneously a top computer scientist was certainly attractive and fitting in the context of the series. That I liked his humor was part of my choice, and I had also heard people say good things about him as a person.

When he actually agreed to give a series of six public lectures and participate in a panel discussion, I was overjoyed — and, actually, it turned out that he was in reality even more fun than his books had suggested. So here's my sincere *schönen Dank!* to Don Knuth, who had the courage to spend a whole term at MIT talking about interactions between faith and science.

As soon as I started advertising, I realized that this third year of the "God and Computers" lecture series would again be a big hit. Dr. Dobb's Journal offered to sponsor live webcasts, which drew sometimes several thousands of people a week to their browsers. Several people in EECS told me of their surprise to hear that Don Knuth had anything to do with God, besides being a computer science icon himself. Actually, the MIT student newspaper *The Tech* featured an article about Don headlined "Computer God talks about God."

The biggest surprise, however, was the question-and-answer period after the first lecture. After all the God-metaphors had been thrown around, Don gave an introduction in which he did not talk about computer science but about himself as a person, a Christian, a scientist. He shared his experiences and talked about the turning point of his life in the 3:16 project. The questions, therefore, were not related to any theoretical point of discussion. Instead, many listeners, particularly students, used the opportunity to ask their "god" about the questions that bothered them. Don had to address questions such as, "Why is there evil in the world?" "What happens after death?" Students wanted him to give them answers about the meaning of life, and if there were any miracles. In short, they treated Don as people within a faith-community treat their minister.

It didn't help that Don was absolutely clear about having no authority to answer these questions. It was particularly upsetting for some people when Don gave his opinion that the questions have no objective, universally valuable, and applicable answers; that everyone has to try to seek answers for themselves. From the feedback, I gathered that some people were disappointed. But the vast majority of people were excited. Against all of their prejudices, here was someone religious who did not claim to own the truth. Instead, Don invited his listeners to find their own path, of questioning and reasoning about themselves and all the rest.

The text of this book certainly speaks for itself. I would like to invite the reader to follow the quest within this book. It was an exciting event at MIT, and I am convinced that the book can get much of the same spirit across. I wish the reader fun, anger, excitement, and trouble, because that is something only a deeply engaging topic such as religion and science can do for us. Don has presented a wonderful way to relate his science and his faith, and I hope the readers will enjoy it as much as the live-audience did.

Finally, I would like to thank all people who made the "God and Computers" project possible. First and most important, I would like to thank all of the speakers, and particularly Don. It took courage to speak in front of a highly educated, critical, and sometimes prejudiced community, especially when much of the time was spent responding to impromptu questions from the audience, and I am extremely happy that Don has edited the transcripts of his lectures for publication in this book.

Also, I would like to thank John Guttag, Paul Penfield, and Rodney Brooks for their support of the project early on, and for the opportunity they offered me to work on religion at MIT. I would also like to thank Jean Hwang who managed Don, me, and the whole organization.

Finally, I would like to thank our sponsors who made this event possible: Dr. Dobb's did a wonderful webcast. The Center for Theology and the Natural Sciences in Berkeley runs the Templeton Religion & Science course program that made first series possible and also supported the third year with Don. The EECS department and the AI Lab at MIT both provided crucial support and generous contributions to the entire project.

– Anne Foerst
28 February 2001

Things a Computer Scientist Rarely Talks About

LECTURE 1: INTRODUCTION   (6 OCTOBER 1999)

It's certainly overwhelming for me to see so many people here. Why did you come to this talk, when you could have gone over to hear Jesse Ventura instead? The lectures that I'll be giving during the next few weeks are entitled "Things a Computer Scientist Rarely Talks About," and the subtitle is "Interactions Between Faith and Computer Science." I'm here because computer science is wonderful, but it isn't everything. So today I want to go beyond technical stuff to consider other things that I value.

In this series I'm going to be giving six talks that are more or less independent of each other. Anne Foerst asked me to deliver between five and ten lectures, and I settled on six because I could only think of six jokes. (And that was the first.) I have to tell jokes once in awhile to see if you can really hear me.

The first reaction that I had when I was invited to give these lectures was to say, "No way, this is impossible. The whole subject of faith and science is much too deep for me." I've given lots of talks at universities during the past 40 years, but they were always to present solutions to problems, to prove some math theorems, to make precise analyses of computational tasks, to propose general theories, or to organize bodies of knowledge — things like

that. Things that I suppose I'm reasonably good at. But surely I can't come before you today and pretend to be an expert on faith or God, much less to claim that I have any solutions to problems that have challenged and baffled the best human minds for thousands of years.

So it is especially terrifying for me to see so many of you here; I hate to disappoint you. I have a Ph.D., which makes me a Doctor of Philosophy, but it doesn't make me a philosopher — the Ph.D. was in math. I can do math and computer science okay, but my formal training in religious studies is basically nil since high

1

school. I've done a lot of reading in my spare time, but why should I expect you to listen to me talk about one of my hobbies?

When I read what other people have written about matters of faith, it's quite clear to me that my own ideas don't measure up to those of world-class philosophers and theologians. I'm not too bad at reacting to other people's notions of religion, but I'm not too good at introducing anything that is fundamentally new or important in this area.

In other words, as far as theology goes, I'm a user, not a developer.

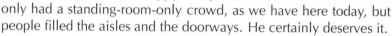

A week and a half ago, I went to Memorial Chapel at Harvard and was in the audience when Billy Graham came. I'm happy to say that he not only had a standing-room-only crowd, as we have here today, but people filled the aisles and the doorways. He certainly deserves it.

Turning things around, however, what if an eminent theologian were to give a series of lectures about computer programming? Would I go out of my way to go to hear them? Would I find them of value afterwards? I'm not sure.

On the other hand, all computer people present here today know that discussions of computer science are not totally different from discussions of religion, especially when we consider languages for computer programming. In the 60s, people would often talk about "Algol-theologians"; these were people who were skilled in the exegesis of obscure texts passed down by international committees. Programmers could use all the analogies of religious studies when we were discussing computer languages. Over the years numerous high priests of programming have expounded one language or one methodology over another with religious zeal, and they've often had very fanatical disciples. Thus everyone knows that the world of computer science is full of cults. In this sense religion and computer science are not completely separate; they share a fair amount of common ground.

We are all familiar with C. P. Snow's famous metaphor of the two cultures that divide educated people into two camps, humanists and scientists. Last month I was in England and I visited the new British Library in London, a magnificent building that has been built to last at least 200 years. And I learned that it actually enshrines the notion of two cultures permanently in stone. The new British Library has two separate sections with two separate reading rooms, one for the humanities and one for the sciences. It turns out that there are good reasons for this from the librarians' standpoint: The humanists tend to work with a small number of books from the historic collections, while the scientists tend to work with lots of books from current periodicals. So the architect gave the humanists a big room with lots of desks in the middle, surrounded by reference works on the four walls; the scientists got a room with lots of journals in the middle, surrounded by desks on four sides. You see, he gave the one-dimensional thing to the desks for the scientists and the two-dimensional thing to their journals, but he switched the dimensions for the humanists.

Actually this week Stanford is dedicating its own new library. Henceforth in Stanford's University Library we're going to have not two cultures but three: humanities, sciences, and social sciences. And everybody knows that engineering is yet another culture.

The truth in fact is that C. P. Snow got it wrong by at least an order of magnitude — there are many more than two cultures. I think a lot of you know the Apple Macintosh ads telling us to "think different," but people already do. From my own corner of the academic world, I know for example that physicists think different from mathematicians; mathematicians who do algebra think different from mathematicians who do geometry; both kinds of mathematicians think different from computer scientists who work on algorithms; and so on and so forth. People often decry this lack of unity in the knowledge of the world, but let's face it: People *are* different. *Vive la différence.*

Even if people did think alike — and they don't — we in universities would have to cope with a vast growth of knowledge. In my own field, for example, it once was possible for a grad student to learn just about everything there was to know about computer science. But those days disappeared about 30 years ago. Nowadays the subject is so enormous, nobody can hope to cover more than a tiny portion of it. I receive on the average at least one copy of a journal every day; the actual total is more like eight or nine per week. These are just the ones I subscribe to, not the ones that I find in the library. They're filled with good stuff, yet they represent only a fraction of my own small part of the field. Growth is relentless. So a constant trend towards more and more specialization is inevitable. Scientists have to concentrate on a small part of the world's knowledge if they want to have any hope of continuing to advance it.

There might be some light on the horizon, however. I predict that in the not too distant future, people in academic life are going to define themselves not by one specialty area, but by two sub-specialties that belong to two rather different main specialties. This means that we'll have a web of interests, in which each person will serve as a bridge between different parts of the overall structure. You can see that this is much better than having a tree hierarchy that branches out further and further, with nobody able to talk to the people on other sub-branches. We'll have people that each belong to two areas, in two different parts of the overall structure. Then we'll be able to have some hope of coping with new knowledge as it comes along. Maybe after 50 more years go by, people will carry this process further and have three sub-sub-sub-specialties; I don't know.

But in any case, besides the specialties and sub-specialties that people will have in such a future scenario, we'll also want to know something about other people's main areas of interest, just as we do today. And in future years, just as today, we'll want to know about our own place in the universe and about our relationship to God, even if we aren't specialists in cosmology or theology.

From this perspective it is surely not forbidden for people like me to grapple with questions of religion, nor for theologians to grapple with questions of computation. And people who are like me can better understand my own explanations of such grapplings than they can understand the explanations of a person who has a different mode of thinking. For similar reasons I am clearly not the best person to explain computer programming to my mother, nor even to teach her how to use Lotus 1-2-3. She needs someone who thinks like she does, in order to explain the ideas of that software, even though I'm supposed to know more about computers. Conversely, my thoughts about religion might be useful to computer scientists.

Thus I'm here now to discuss "Things a Computer Scientist Rarely Talks About." In my Stanford classes, of course, I have never spoken about any of the topics that I plan to discuss in these lectures. At Stanford I did have a tradition of setting aside the last day of every course for a special Q&A session, at which I promised to answer any question that the students had on any subject — *except* questions about religion or politics. Religion is taboo in Stanford classes outside of the department of Religious Studies, although other kinds of knowledge are not, and I guess that makes sense.

On the other hand, I remember reading a letter to the editor of the Caltech alumni magazine many years ago. The writer said that during the first ten years after he graduated, he wished he'd had more training in his major field. Then during the next ten years, he wished he'd had more training in management. During the next ten he wished he had more training in business planning. Then for another ten, he wished he'd learned more about medicine and health. During the next ten he wished he'd learned more about theology.

I've been concerned for a long time, in fact, about the lack of material about theology that is written for people like me. There are plenty of books for other kinds of people, it seems, but not very much for a computer scientist. I can remember once going into a large so-called Christian book store and realizing that almost all of my professional colleagues would find it extremely oppressive just to be in that room. I'm disturbed by the notions of religion that many of my academic friends have; but I understand that their notions have been formed quite naturally, in reaction to the things that they see in the media, aimed at different subcultures. From my point of view, the way they perceive religion is strange and totally distorted from the kind of religion that I grew up with. Therefore when I was asked to give a series of lectures in the God and Computers program at MIT, my first reaction — "No way can I contribute anything of quality" — was tempered by second thoughts that maybe I could say a few things that might be helpful to some of the people in this audience because such things are so rarely discussed.

Naturally I never agree to give a talk unless I think I have something to say. In this case I realized that there is one important message that I can bring to you that no theologian could ever do, precisely because of my amateur status. Namely, I can give testimonials that theologians have basically done a good job. After looking at hundreds of their books, I can report, as an essentially disinterested observer, that a lot of their work has been both interesting and valuable to me as I continue to seek to know more about God. Therefore I can explain, to other people who share my own peculiar way of thinking, what I've learned by reading works outside my own field of expertise.

Please realize that these lectures don't represent a career change for me! This is a once-in-a-lifetime excursion, after which I'm going to go back home and continue working on the stuff I do best. I want to use this opportunity to say things about which I feel deeply, even though other people could say them better, partly in an effort to inspire those other people to come forward and advance the discussion. And given that I'm glad to attempt this, just once, what place to do it could possibly be better than here at MIT?

Of course it's impossible to talk about religious issues without any bias, so I have to explain to you where I'm coming from. I was born in Milwaukee, Wisconsin. I grew up as a member of the Lutheran Church, and I went to kindergarten through 12th grade in Lutheran schools. My father devoted his lifetime to Christian education in the Lutheran school system. I attended church regularly, but Sunday morning was a separate compartment of my life. I had a kind of cozy relationship with the church; I didn't feel a need to explore any alternatives. I had several excellent pastors, but I didn't know much or think much about other people's faith. I was plenty busy with computer science and mathematics, more than six days per week.

An important change for me began in the fall of 1978, when I decided it would be interesting to learn more about the Bible by applying some of the techniques that I'd been using to understand large computer programs, techniques that had also helped me learn about other complicated subjects. In that year, for reasons I'm going to explain to you next week, I decided to amuse myself by going to the library and finding out as much as I could about several dozen verses of the Bible. This became what I called the "3:16 project," because I decided to focus on the sixteenth verse of the third chapter of each Biblical book. (That was perhaps a strange thing to do, but next week in my second lecture I'm going to explain why it makes perfect sense; meanwhile please trust me.) The main point was that in this way I could read what people of all different religious persuasions and people from many different periods of history had written about those verses.

To my surprise I learned so much from this exercise that I began to think I really ought to share the experience with other people. Eventually it became clear to me that I should look at the history of those verses even more closely, and that I should try to write a book about them. Perhaps, I thought, such a book would appeal to a few of my colleagues, who are by nature turned off by almost all the other books that deal with religion. The title of the book that I should write was also clear: It had to be called *3:16*.

I began to write *3:16* during the 1985–86 academic year, when I happened to be living in Boston. In fact the Boston connection is another big reason why I've succumbed to the temptation to come here again and give these lectures. It seems that this is the part of the world where I've had the best opportunity to study religious issues. That period in 85–86 was a very special time in my life: It was the 25th year of my marriage to Jill, and I had promised her that she could at last have a sabbatical year. I promised to do all the shopping and cooking and cleaning, so that she could have a chance to write books of her own.

Well, on some days after finishing the household chores, I did have a few extra hours to kill, so I went to the Bible Museum to copy down the 3:16 verses in dozens of different translations; I also spent many, many days at the Boston Public Library looking at hundreds of Bible commentaries. I came over several times on the Red Line to the Andover–Harvard Library for books that weren't at Boston Public. Eventually when it was time to return to California I had drafted about twenty chapters of the proposed book; it turned out that I wrote the chapters about Ecclesiastes and the Song of Solomon while I was staying a few days in Cambridge, at the home of my publishing partner Peter Gordon, who lives a few blocks from Harvard Square. (That was one week before Harvard's 350th anniversary, when Harvard gave an honorary doctorate to Ronald Reagan — some of you might remember that occasion. Ah, 1986.)

I like a phrase that I learned from Joseph Sittler, who was a guru for many Lutheran pastors in the Midwest a generation or so ago. Sittler said he was especially pleased to have been raised in the Lutheran tradition because it taught him that he didn't need a "cerebral bypass operation" in order to approach God. Martin Luther was a great scholar — a man who used his head and his heart simultaneously. The 3:16 project was a turning point in my life because it opened my eyes to what other scholars have written. I learned to appreciate the way God is present in the lives of people from many different cultures. I learned that there were deep connections between Christianity and other world religions. I no longer lived Sunday mornings in a different world from the world that I occupied during the rest of the week.

During that year in Boston I attended an ACM conference on computer science education. Well . . . , I didn't actually go to the conference; I went only to the reception. But anyway, when people at the reception asked me, "What have you been doing lately, Don?" I had to say sheepishly, "I've been writing a book about the Bible." Wow, what a conversation stopper! At least you would think so. I distinctly remember feeling that I was somehow coming out of the closet, and that everybody would think I'd really lost it. (In those days it was okay to be religious if you were Jewish, or practiced certain other faiths, but not if you were Christian.) To my surprise, however, several people gave me lots of encouragement, and they expressed an interest in reading drafts of the book before publication.

In summary, to make a long story not too long, I finished writing *3:16* during weekends after returning to Stanford, and it was published in 1990. I'm not here today to sell copies of that book; a good book is going to find its audience without any hype, and a mediocre book is going to die a quiet death even if it has wonderful advertising. But I have to tell you something about the *3:16* book, because the experiences I had when writing it are what informed much of what I'm going to be talking about in the next lectures; that's when I had the most time to think about religious issues. Basically that book discusses what great theologians of many different persuasions and different ages have said about chapter 3 verse 16 of Genesis, and about Exodus 3:16 and Leviticus 3:16, and so on through Revelation 3:16.

My conservative friends think the book is too liberal. My liberal friends think it's too conservative. Everybody agrees, however, that the artwork in the book is spectacular. I commissioned different artists to create special calligraphy for each of the 3:16 verses, and I'm going to be talking about that in the fourth lecture of this series. The book . . . ; how can I summarize it? It's not a preachy book where I say, "Here's what I believe and I'm real smart so you better believe it too." Rather, it's a book where I say, "Here are some important issues and some different perspectives. What do you think about them?"

I've thought of a few dozen things to say in the remaining lectures of the series that might not be entirely trivial. Lately I've gotten a sense that people are developing a craving for better understanding of the relations between scientific work and faith. Contributions of physicists, biologists, cosmologists, and theologians that I've read with respect to this topic have been extremely valuable, but I do feel that a computer science perspective can add several things that have been missing so far from these important discussions. A lot of computer scientists have no doubt come up with similar or better ideas than the ones I'm going to be discussing in the next few weeks, and other people will no doubt be able to explain the ideas better than I can. Still, now that I have this once-in-a-lifetime opportunity, I want to put the ideas on the table and give them my best shot. I certainly hope that these lectures are going to prove to be helpful to you as you continue to ponder the mysteries of life.

You might have noticed that I have been reading from notes while speaking today. That brings up an interesting fact about C. P. Snow's two cultures: Have any of you ever been to a convention of English professors? Do you know that they actually *read* their papers to each other, word for word, relishing each and every literary nuance? It blew my mind when I first learned that — because of course computer scientists do the opposite, we always just stand up and talk. But I know that my pastor always reads his sermons, and so here today I didn't know whether I should read or just talk. I thought I'd better play it safe and try to read, since my subject has a little bit to do with faith.

On the other hand, I'm actually only half prepared today. I mean, my plan for these lectures is that they should be about 50 percent planned in advance and about 50 percent improvised. Thus these lectures are not only about interaction between faith and science, but also interaction between you and me.

So starting at this point, or whenever I happen to get to it in the other lectures, I'd like to open everything up for discussion. My only preparation for the second half of each lecture will have been to live 60 years in order to get here and meet you. I hope many of you have questions, because that way I can focus on what you really want to hear. Who wants to speak first?

Q: The Bible has so many verses. Why did you choose to study chapter 3, verse 16, and what significance could that have?

A: I guess you're wondering if I chose 3:16 because the square root of 10 is 3.16, or something like that. The answer is, "Come next week."

Q: What Bible did you use?

A: As I said, I went to the Bible Museum to look at every Bible I could get my hands on. In the Boston Public Library I found many Bibles that I hadn't seen anywhere else; the Bible Museum also has a room full of Bibles and I found a wide variety there. New Bible translations were also coming out during the time I was doing this project. I studied the Bishops' Bible of 1568, which was the chief English translation before the famous King James Version of 1611, and I also went back to Tyndale's original translation of 1525. Altogether I had about 25 different versions. It took much longer than I'd expected to write everything out in longhand, but I carefully copied 25 translations of each 3:16 verse and I got writer's cramp in the process. The third lecture in this series is going to be about translating the Bible; I finally decided to make my own translations, and I'm going to explain in the third lecture why that turned out to be one of the best decisions I ever made.

Q: I wonder about your colleagues, who you had related to only from the point of view of scientific culture in earlier years, the people who knew you only as a computer scientist. How do they relate to you now that you've published this book in which you discuss your faith and your religious feelings?

A: Let me try to explain that in a couple of different ways. First of all, my colleagues seem to approve. (To my face, at least; I don't know what they're saying to each other behind my back and in emails.) After publishing the book, I expected negative reactions, but what happened was exactly the opposite; I've gotten amazingly positive mail and a lot of positive feedback.

I don't particularly flaunt my faith; I generally wait for people to ask me about it, if they're interested in such things. For example, let me tell you a little story. I don't like to wear suits, but every once in awhile I like to wear something that's a little bit dressed up. (I have a special shirt on today. Did any of you notice?) About twenty years ago my wife presented me with a wonderful Christmas present, a beautiful shirt based on an old Egyptian pattern called a "galabiyah," and embroidered by a Laotian refugee named Maria Keovilay who had been sponsored by our church. This woman had been the best embroiderer in her village, and she made an absolutely gorgeous decoration on top of the plain black base. I wore this shirt once to Brown University when they dedicated their new computer science building, and my wife was sitting in the audience. She heard people saying, "Oh, here comes the high priest of computer programming."

The main reason I mention this story is that my fancy galabiyah looked much more like a high priest's robe when I first received it than it did when I wore it at Brown, because Maria had embroidered a great big cross on the back. She undoubtedly thought this was the ideal way to express friendship, because she knew me only as a member of our church. But I couldn't feel right wearing that cross, because it was too much of an in-your-face thing. I'm certainly not ashamed of the cross as a symbol, yet I'm not the kind of person who explicitly emphasizes my Christianity and implicitly asserts that the people I meet had better believe in God the same way I do. So I decided that the cross should be de-embroidered from the shirt.

In general, the reaction to my having published the 3:16 book has been warm as far as I know, and in fact much warmer than I would ever have predicted.

Q: Are there any ways in which your study of theology has informed your work with computer science?

A: As far as I know the effects have only been indirect. The theological studies have given me more of a sense of history, helping me better understand the development of ideas in science, because science and religion have not always been so separate as they are now. For example, it turns out that Isaac Newton once wrote a 20-page essay about 1 Timothy 3:16, and I would have never looked at that before. This gave me a little bit more feeling for Newton's personality, but it's a historical connection. As a scientist, I'm quite interested in how ideas get started in the first place, so the more source materials I read, the better. Theological study has helped in that way. But otherwise such studies have been relevant mostly to the other aspects of my life, to the parts of me that want to understand something about my own place in an ongoing system.

Q: You've referred several times to a computer scientist's perspective. How do you distinguish that from other points of view?

A: I have kind of a radical idea about this, but I've had it for 30 years now and still haven't found anything wrong with it. Namely, suppose someone asks, "Why did computer science jell so fast during the 60s, all of a sudden becoming a department at almost every university in the world?" I answer that the reason is not to be found in the fact that computers are so valuable as tools. There's not a department of Electron Microscope Science at every university, although electron microscopes are great and powerful tools.

I'm convinced that computer science grew so fast and is so vital today because there are people all over the world who have a peculiar way of thinking, a certain way of structuring knowledge in their heads, a mentality that we now associate with a discipline of its own. This mentality isn't sharply focused, in the space of all possible ways of thinking; but it's different enough from other ways—from the mentalities of physicists and mathematicians that I spoke of earlier—that the people who had it in the old days were scattered among many different departments, more or less orphans in their universities. Then suddenly, when it turned out that their way of thinking correlated well with being able to make a computer do tricks, these people found each other.

I believe it was this way of thinking that brought computer scientists together into a single department, where they met other people who understood the same analogies, people who structured knowledge roughly the same way in their heads, people with whom they could have high-bandwidth communications. That's what I meant when I referred to a "computer science perspective."

I didn't choose to be a computer scientist because my main mission in life was to advance computation. I chose computer science simply because I was good at it. For some reason, my peculiar way of thinking correlated well with computers. Moreover, I'm sure that people had this way of thinking hundreds of years ago; when I read old publications I think I can recognize the authors who would have been computer scientists if they had lived in the time of computer science departments. There was a time when physicists were called natural philosophers, and there was a time before chemists belonged to departments of chemistry. From considerations like this I believe that computer science will eventually take its place on essentially the same level as every other field of study, say 100 years from now; the fact that this mode of thinking never had a name until quite recently is just a historical accident.

One of the main characteristics of a computer science mentality is the ability to jump very quickly between levels of abstraction, between a low level and a high level, almost unconsciously. Another characteristic is that a computer scientist tends to be able to deal with nonuniform structures — case 1, case 2, case 3 — while a mathematician will tend to want one unifying axiom that governs an entire system. This second aspect is sometimes a weakness of computer science: When we encounter a situation that can be explained by one axiom, we might still give it five, because five different rules are no sweat for us. But we're at our best in circumstances when no single principle suffices; then we can handle the discrepancies between different cases very nicely.

One of the first people to receive a Ph.D. in computer science was Renato Iturriaga de la Fuente, who graduated from Carnegie Institute of Technology in 1967. When I met him in Mexico City in 1976, he was head of the Mexican equivalent of our National Science Foundation. He told me then about his conviction that an ability to shift seamlessly between levels of abstraction and to deal fluently with nonuniform models helped him greatly to deal with scientists of many different backgrounds. In his job, he said, a computer scientist's way of thinking tended to be more effective than that of other scientists, even though he wasn't doing any computer programming or computer science research himself at the moment.

So that's what I think tends to be different about computer scientists. Experience shows that about one person in 50 has a computer scientist's way of looking at things.

Q: Do you have any comments on other religions?

A: When I said briefly that I find deep connections between Christianity and other world religions, I didn't mean to imply agreement in terms of specific doctrines but rather in terms of attitudes. I see aspects of Buddhism, Taoism, Zen, Islam, and other faiths that appear essentially Christian to me; conversely, I encounter other things that so-called Christian preachers say on the radio that I don't think are Christian at all. Of course I'm just one person, and other people are entitled to their own opinions.

In the later lectures I'm going to try to get a little further into questions like this. Ask yourself what you would do if you were God and you wanted to deal with people on the earth; how would you present yourself?

Q: Earlier you said you thought that your colleagues would be put off when walking through a Christian reading room in a book store. What was it about such an environment — the book titles, or whatever it was — that you think would put them off? Does your book *3:16* address this in any way?

A: I can't explain it; I just felt like the ceiling was about four feet lower, I don't know why. There was a certain heavy atmosphere, an overpowering aura that was very much attuned to people who already consider themselves enlightened.

But that's a cop-out; I'll try to explain. There is a certain kind of art that looks kitschy, but it can be very meaningful to people who traditionally associate it with worship. To other people it looks like the kind of art that — well, the kind of art that "those people" like.

It seemed to me that book after book in the store was saying, "Close your mind." But as I said before, the tradition that I grew up in encouraged me to look at religion with an open mind, as Luther did. Although I didn't have much motivation to check out the works of writers from other traditions until I  wrote the 3:16 book, in fact I was never told that it was dangerous to read other stuff. The vast majority of the books in this store seemed to be of a much more prescriptive and restrictive kind, saying "Here's the orthodoxy. Learn rules 1, 2, 3, . . . , 10."

I guess that's the best way I can express my feelings now. My own book doesn't address the problem especially well, since its full title *3:16 Bible Texts Illuminated* implies that it "illuminates" the Bible. Still, it might be appealing to my colleagues if they look for it on the Web instead of in a bookshop.

Q: Is it possible to somehow quantify how the process of writing your book affected your faith in the Lutheran tradition specifically? Did it perhaps bring about a stronger faith, or did it possibly weaken your faith with respect to the traditions in which you had been brought up?

A: In general, I think my faith was greatly shored up by the 3:16 project, because it survived the attacks of so many writers who hold diametrically opposite views. On the other hand the experience did weaken my faith in certain specific things, such as some of the stories about miracles that I was brought up with. At present I don't think those stories are necessarily true, although I still believe they could have happened. My current attitude is that many specific details in the Bible might not be historical, because I know now about what can happen to manuscripts over long periods of time, and because I often find significant discrepancies in newspaper accounts of events that I have witnessed in person.

I can't quantify the change in my thinking to the extent of putting a number on it. I can say that I was extremely happy two months ago when the Lutheran Church voted to have full communion with the Episcopal Church. Our national convention needed a two-thirds majority to pass that motion, and it passed; that was very good news for me. I've become much more ecumenical in my approach and not specifically Lutheran. I'm also glad that the Lutherans and Catholics will be signing a so-called Concordat later this month in Augsburg, Germany, resolving the major differences that split the church in the sixteenth century.

Q: You spoke of a free-for-all day at the end of the courses that you teach. Why did you exclude religion, and do you still exclude religion? Furthermore if you do, why do you still?

A: I see, you've given me a metaquestion there. Actually I'm retired now, so that was one scenario you didn't consider. And the truth is, I excluded from consideration not only religion and politics but also the final exam.

But when I was teaching and actually running such sessions, I felt that religion was different and special, an intensely personal thing, where scientific method and normal standards of proof don't apply. I wouldn't avoid talking about chemistry, for example, because chemistry is something that people are sort of paying tuition for to learn about. But the students weren't paying tuition for some professor to tell them what he thought their religion should be, or even what he thought his own religion was. I could naturally talk to interested students about anything outside of class, but class time seemed to be in a different category.

Maybe now there's a different attitude, at least at some universities. And probably if I had been at another place, like say Luther College, I would have had a different policy. I guess I was primarily influenced by local tradition; Stanford has its traditions. One of the traditions at Stanford is that you don't use Stanford budget money for research — only for teaching. I never understood why Stanford itself shouldn't be interested in expanding the world's knowledge; but I went along with Stanford's tradition, according to which all support for research comes strictly from government grants, never from the endowment. The Stanford endowment goes for teaching. My thoughts about bringing up religion during class hours were similar in spirit; somehow religion seemed to be off the chart.

Q: What do you think about the rate of the growth of computer science? And what expectations do you have for the future?

A: Ah, if only the growth in computer science would slow down so that I could finally finish my books! I sort of keep hoping that red herrings will steadily come along, to keep people busy; I get secret satisfaction when bad ideas take hold and suck a lot of people in … like Java. (Just teasing.) But computer science keeps getting bigger and broader and deeper.

I can't predict that it's going to continue expanding at this rate. Moore's Law certainly can't go on indefinitely. But will computer science still be growing 50 years from now? It's hard for me to say that with confidence.

On the other hand I can say quite confidently that biology will still be growing 200 years from now. Biology is a much deeper subject than computer science; just by its nature, biology has much more to deal with. Nobody needs a crystal ball to predict an enormous future growth of biology. Yet even in the considerably more limited field of computer science we still have no indication of any slowdown whatsoever.

Q: Can you mention some of the theologians you've read that you find compatible with your own culture?

A: Well, I tend to be a detail-oriented person, as you can guess, and so are a lot of theologians. So I have often felt an instinctive kinship when picking up a new commentary. In fact, my experiences as I was writing the 3:16 book weren't that different from writing computer books, although I wasn't using integral signs as much. The processes of abstraction and generalization and interpreting texts were much the same. Really I would say there wasn't that much difference in mentality between the detail-oriented theologians and myself, except for their substantial expertise in languages; languages have lots of nuances that I don't understand. With respect to linguistic matters I can only believe what I read.

My fifth lecture will be about what I learned about God during this project, and what I learned at the same time about theologians; I prefer to discuss such ideas in detail at that time.

Q: Can you say something about your thoughts on the value of prayer?

A: Prayer . . . I should probably be praying now that somebody will ask me an easier question! I believe there's great value to prayer, but I don't know why.

One of the things I want to do before this series of lectures is over is put up on the Web a wonderful parable that helps explain my feelings, although the parable itself—called "Planet Without Laughter"—has nothing to do with prayer per se. It's a little short story by Raymond Smullyan, which appeared in a book that's now out of print. When you see that short story, I think you'll get an idea about how I might "know" sometimes that prayer is important without understanding why. Some things are beyond rationality and proof, and I don't think God wants them to be analyzable or provable.

Q: What sorts of analysis that you run across in computer science proved to be most useful in doing this research?

A: Obviously there wasn't much quantitative stuff in the religious texts for me to analyze as a mathematician. But it turned out that Numbers 3:16 (of all things) was about numbers, so there was some interesting mathematics in there. The most quantitative aspect of this work was the study of randomness, and so next week in Lecture 2 I will talk about that at length.

There also are qualitative things that are implicitly informed by analysis. So, for example, the knowledge that I could in principle prove a program correct helps me to write a program, even though I'm not actually going to prove the program correct. I don't have the time to go and check that the program for TℰX is actually 100% correct. Furthermore, I don't even know how to formulate the concept that a METAFONT program draws a beautiful letter A, so I couldn't possibly prove the correctness of such a program. But still, somehow, the theory that I've learned while doing computer science gives me more confidence in the programs that I have written.

Working on the 3:16 project was kind of similar: Although I didn't have a direct connection between numbers and the study of Bible verses, the methodology that I had gradually developed by working with numbers turned out to be useful when I worked with less quantitative material.

Q: Do you have any comments or conclusions regarding the existence or the nature of evil?

A: The question is, for example, why are people killed in wars? I'll be getting to this topic later on, but I don't have any new insights that I haven't picked up from other people.

The Book of Job discusses this problem at length and tries to come to a conclusion. And if you look at ten different commentaries on the Book of Job, each one says that the conclusion was different. This proves, I think, that it's really a tough problem.

But still there must be something there, and we ought to ponder it. What would the world be like if there was no evil? I will be trying to get into this question more deeply in the fifth and sixth lectures.

Q: What do you think of the hypothesis that the human brain is a giant computer program?

A: Such a hypothesis will obviously be very hard to confirm or deny. I tend to believe that recently proposed models of the brain, which are based on the idea of continuous dynamic evolution of symbolic signals instead of on processes that resemble today's computing machines, have good prospects for helping to explain the mysteries of consciousness. If so, a lot of randomness must be involved in that, and I'll be talking a little bit more about such things also in the lectures to come.

(I guess I'm using the future lectures too often as an excuse for dodging your questions. I'm glad you're interested in all of these topics, but I don't want to get ahead of my story or I'll have nothing left to say. Please bear with me.)

Maybe the brain uses random elements; maybe the universe does too. Maybe all these things are controlled somehow by prayer or whatever; who knows? We might only be perceiving three dimensions of some higher-dimensional reality. I'm going to try to explore these questions from my limited viewpoint later on, but of course I don't have any definitive answers.

Q: You were asked earlier about how the quantitative, analytic aspects of computer science might relate to theological studies. But a large part of your own work on such things as literate programming deals with things that are *very* hard to quantify, like maintainability of programs and ease of use. I'm wondering if you found parallels between that work and the work that you've done reading the theologians.

A: Yes, thank you for the reminder that quantitative considerations are only one aspect of computer science. You're saying that much of my work is not about theorem proving and so on but more about methodology, where I write a computer program and I feel happy about it — not because I've proved that it was correct but because I enjoy its elegance or something like that. There's a strong aspect of aesthetics, which I'll be discussing in my fourth lecture. (Again, I don't want to steal any thunder away from that lecture by dwelling on such topics today.) I believe that all the non-quantitative things probably carry over almost completely from one culture to the other.

Q: What influence might computers have on future developments in theology?

A: The simple answer is that Web-based resources have recently appeared that make it much easier now to approach the vast theological literature. You can click on a word and find out what the original Greek was; you can find out where the same Greek word was used elsewhere; and so on. Many aids to self-exploration will surely continue to appear because of technology. Already there are home pages for the Gospel of Mark and other books. Soon this will extend to every part of the Bible and to the canonical texts of other religions. There will be surveys that people can refine and make much more accessible than ever before, for people who want to explore their own chosen topics in their own way.

Could advances in computer technology actually influence the manner of divine revelation? That is a really interesting question, but I haven't thought about it much. There's a general notion of so-called process theology, which says that over the centuries God has been revealing Himself/Herself in different ways. When I first heard about process theology, it sounded to me like nonsense because

I had always been taught that God was the same yesterday, today, and forever. But then the more I thought about it, the more I realized that God would best be able to communicate sensibly by sending messages that were appropriate for the current time.

For example, we know now that proteins are molecules made up of atoms; but 2000 years ago, people didn't know what molecules were, so Jesus didn't talk about them. Thus it only makes sense that different kinds of revelation are appropriate as the people in the world change. It's a very good question, whether the rapid developments we are experiencing will lead to valid and trustworthy new insights about God.

I'm worried that somebody will start a new religion based on fractals. What I mean is, religion has a certain power that charlatans can take advantage of. So if you come up with something that makes a little bit of sense and has a little bit of mystery to it, you can fool a lot of people. I also have that in mind as a possible danger.

Q: If you were asked to give a lecture for an audience of theologians on the subject of computer science, what would you talk about?

A: A lecture for an audience of theologians? Let me tell you that the amount of terror that lives in a speaker's stomach when giving a lecture is proportional to the square of the amount he doesn't know about his audience. Once I gave a series of lectures to biologists at Caltech about computer science, and that was one of the hardest tasks I ever had to face.

I guess, however, that I could explain something to the people whose writings I've read. I could explain to them some interesting ideas about infinity that they might be able to explore better than I. In fact I hope to go into some of that in Lecture 6.

Q: You've talked about a computer science perspective. Do you see any danger in that perspective, considering that computer scientists like to abstract things and say "Okay, I've got a handle on this." With religious matters such an approach may not be possible. You can't think of prayer as a black box, where you put something in and get something else out. So I wonder if you see danger ahead, when people think they've got a handle on stuff that they really don't.

A: Absolutely. That's a significant point. For example, I mentioned an essay that Newton wrote about 1 Timothy 3:16; I admire it a lot. He studied quite a few manuscripts of Greek papyri in order to analyze where a deliberate change had been made by someone copying this passage and trying to "improve" it; he nailed the manuscript where the change was introduced, and this was an original contribution made by Isaac Newton to theology.

But Newton also wrote other essays about religion, where he considered the Book of Daniel and the Book of Revelation. He took these very mystical, symbolic books and treated them as if they were mathematical formulas and axioms; he tried to say, "Assuming X, then Y must be true," and so on. I felt *so* sorry for him!

Similarly I'm sure that I also tend to make mistakes like that. Even so, I have a right to my mistakes.

Q: In your announcement of today's lecture you describe writing *3:16* as a turning point in your life, as if some part of you that was going in one direction is now going in another. Can you say more about that? What's the change?

A: Well, my work on the 3:16 verses didn't lead to a 180-degree turn, but it certainly opened my eyes to many things that I hadn't had a motivation to look at before: the way other people practice their religion, the history of different strains of Christianity, the intellectual challenge of Biblical criticism, the lack of simple answers.

Perhaps it was, in fact, too much of a turning point, in the sense that I became over-confident. Before embarking on the project, I hadn't read much, so I could only feel that maybe I was missing something. Afterwards I had read enough that I tended to feel that I knew everything, which of course I didn't. The reading gave me substantially more confidence, and maybe that was a better or worse thing.

When I pursued the project there were no holds barred on what I was going to look at. I wanted to explore whatever had been said by everybody, letting them shoot their ammunition whichever way it would go. After I had done that and still come through with what I felt was a strong enough faith to get through the rest of my life, this gave me a confidence that I couldn't have had before I did the experiment.

Thank you all very much for asking such excellent questions, and for laughing at the right times.

Notes on Lecture 1

Page 2, Snow's famous metaphor: C. P. Snow, *The Two Cultures and the Scientific Revolution* (London: Cambridge University Press, 1959); *The Two Cultures: And a Second Look* (London: Cambridge University Press, 1964).

Page 2, new British Library: See Colin St. John Wilson, *The Design and Construction of the British Library* (London: The British Library, 1998).

Page 3, Stanford's University Library: See the article by James Robinson, "Phoenix Rising: Restored Bing Wing respects past, present, future," in *Stanford [online] Report* (6 October 1999), `www.stanford.edu / dept / news / report / news / october6 / libbingwing-106.html`. Also Michael A. Keller et al., "Reconstructing the heart of the university," *Imprint* **18**, 2 (Stanford, California: The Associates of the Stanford University Libraries, Fall 1999).

Page 7, title of the book: Donald E. Knuth, *3:16 Bible Texts Illuminated* (Madison, Wisconsin: A–R Editions, 1991).

Page 7, Joseph Sittler: I heard his comment on a videotaped interview by Robert M. Herhold, *Theological Reflections: Spirituality Explored* (Minneapolis, Minnesota: Video Publishing, 1981), 28 minutes. Copies of this video are currently available from Seraphim Communications, `www.seracomm.com`. (The comment occurs about 20:40 minutes into the tape.) Herhold had previously assembled a number of Sittler's memorable remarks in the book *Grace Notes and Other Fragments* (Philadelphia: Fortress Press, 1981). Sittler's implicit reference to an essentially *complete* cerebral bypass should of course be distinguished from the cerebral *arterial* bypass operation that was once believed to help prevent strokes. To me it means, "Respect the limitations of your brain, but don't abandon logic altogether."

Of course Lutherans do not have a monopoly on the idea that one's mind need not be switched off when approaching God. For example, the former pastor at Harvard, George Buttrick, once put it this way: "The church has sometimes forgotten one word in the Great Commandment: 'Thou shalt love the Lord thy God with all thy ... *mind.*' [Deuteronomy 6:5, Luke 10:27] ... The rigor of logical positivism, though it is all too small to cover man's pilgrimage, lays on every man the requirement of stringent honesty. It is a great gift that higher education should keep saying: 'Face the facts. Be honest. Do not beg the question. And make the doors of a church high enough so that a worshiper need not leave his head on the sidewalk.'" [*Biblical Thought and the Secular University* (Baton Rouge: Louisiana University Press, 1960), 54–55.] I thank Peter Gomes for bringing this quote to my attention.

Page 8, ACM: The Association for Computing Machinery has been the leading professional organization for computer specialists in America since 1947.

Page 11, Isaac Newton: See *Isaaci Newtoni Opera Quæ Exstant Omnia*, edited by Samuel Horsley (London: J. Nichols, 1779–1785), volume 5, pages 531–550.

Page 13, one person in 50: See Donald E. Knuth, *Selected Papers on Computer Science* (Stanford, California: Center for the Study of Language and Information, 1996), Chapter 4, especially page 94.

Page 16, Moore's Law: In 1965, Gordon E. Moore gave a talk in which he observed that chip capacity was doubling every year; this remarkable trend continued until the late 1970s, after which doubling has continued to occur every 18 months or so.

Page 17, Raymond Smullyan: See the end of Lecture 4.

Page 17, TEX and METAFONT: See my book *Digital Typography*, cited in the notes to Lecture 4.

Page 19, home pages for the Gospel: Michael Spencer's *Gospel of Mark Homepage*, currently `www.geocities.com/~eutychus`, was established in 1997 and has links to many other sites. The central reference for the Gospel of Mark is now, I think, *Kata Markon*, `metalab.unc.edu/GMark`.

Page 21, Newton also wrote: Isaac Newton, *Observations Upon the Prophesies of Daniel, and the Apocalypse of St. John* (London: Darby and Browne, 1733); critical edition edited by S. J. Barnett, with notes by Mary E. Mills (Lampeter, Wales: Edwin Mellen Press, 1999).

LECTURE 2: RANDOMIZATION AND RELIGION (13 OCTOBER 1999)

Most of you know that my work in computer science is primarily focused on computational methods, also called algorithms. If somebody would ask me to name the most important trend in the study of algorithms during the past ten years, I would have to say that the increased significance of *randomized algorithms* was a clear winner.

Already in the 1940s people had invented the Monte Carlo method, which was heavily used for calculations related to such things as nuclear physics. A technique called hashing was introduced in the 50s to improve the speed of information retrieval. In the 60s we played around with the randomization of data. In the 70s we applied randomization to factorization and a few other problems. And then all of a sudden the notion of randomization got a big boost because of a series of discoveries made during the 80s, when the ideas were applied to a host of combinatorial and geometric problems, including such things as load balancing and approximate counting.

Now we have reached a point where textbooks devoted to the subject have come out; college courses devoted entirely to the study of randomized algorithms have become part of the computer science curriculum, typically taking either a half year or a full year. We now can prove that randomization allows us to solve certain problems faster than any method that doesn't use random numbers: Any deterministic method for such problems has to run significantly slower than a method that takes advantage of randomization.

Yesterday I was at Harvard to celebrate the dedication of their new computer science building, and I spoke to Michael Rabin, who I think everyone considers to be the "father" of randomized algorithms. To my great surprise, here he is in the audience today! I asked him yesterday for some advice on what I should talk about in a lecture about randomization and religion, and his first reaction was that I should discuss the question, "Do random numbers really exist?" This leads directly to the notion of free will, and to the question of whether the universe is deterministic. But that's one of the questions I'm *not* going to talk about today; that's for lecture number 6. In Lecture 6 I do plan to discuss topics such as free

25

will and the omnipotence of God, and I hope I'll have something interesting to say at that time.

Today, however, I want to emphasize a quite different aspect of the subject, based largely on some of my personal experiences with randomized algorithms. In 1975 I published a paper that explained a method I'd been using a lot during the 60s to estimate the running time of backtrack programs. The computer scientists present here today will all understand what I mean by backtracking, because one of the standard exercises that we use in introductory programming courses is to solve the classic problem of placing eight queens on a chessboard so that no two of them attack each other; in other words, no two queens are allowed to be in the same row, the same column, or the same diagonal. More generally, we ask students to write a program that finds all ways to place N nonattacking queens on an $N \times N$ board. The only decent way to solve this problem, if N isn't extremely large or extremely small, is probably to carry out a process of trial and error: First you put one queen on the board, then you try placing the second queen on a square not attacked by the first, and so on. If you get stuck, you backtrack and reconsider one of the previous placements.

When you have a trial-and-error algorithm like this, experience shows that the backtrack process sometimes runs lickety split and finishes in a second or two. But sometimes you start the program and wait and wait and wait, only to learn that many centuries are going to be needed before the program finishes. And it's not easy to tell the difference between those two vastly different behaviors.

So I worked out a way to predict the efficiency of backtrack applications. It's an extremely simple method, based on rolling dice and following a random path. For example, in the N queens problem the idea is to put the first queen down in a random place and write down the number of possibilities that you chose between. Then put down the second queen in a random place consistent with the first, and again write down how many choices you considered. Keep on going until getting stuck. Finally, you need to multiply all those numbers that you wrote down, and add the products in a certain way; it turns out that the expected value of this quantity is the expected number of computations needed to solve the N queens problem.

As I said, I published that method in 1975 after having had lots of experience with it; it actually works amazingly well. In 1976 I gave a survey talk at the meeting of the American Association for Advancement of Science, which took place in Boston that year. In that talk, which had the title "Coping with finiteness," I used the estimation method for the following problem: "How many ways are there to get from one corner of an 11 × 11 grid to the opposite corner, following a path that doesn't cross itself?" For example,

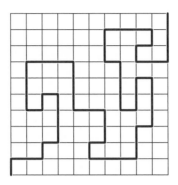

is such a path. If you take a random walk on this grid, you sometimes have three choices for the next step, and sometimes you have two, but sometimes you have only one. You can multiply the numbers together and add the products appropriately to get an estimate for the total number of paths. I used a computer to try this a few thousand times, and when I gave the talk in 1976 I estimated that the total number of paths from corner to corner would be $(1.6 \pm .3) \times 10^{24}$.

I didn't believe that I would ever in my lifetime know the exact answer to that problem. It seemed to me that such a number was much too huge. Computers keep getting faster and faster, but 10^{24} is way, way out there; the world will have to go through a lot more Y2K crises before a computer can count up to 10^{24}. (Incidentally, if you think Y2K will be bad, wait until the year 9999; that one will be considerably worse—and the year 999,999 will really be problematic! But even if we process one path per nanosecond, more than 31.6 million years will go by before 10^{24} paths have been enumerated.)

I was wrong. A couple of years later, Richard Schroeppel, an illustrious MIT alumnus whom many of you know, pointed out that there was in fact a feasible way to calculate the number of such paths exactly. Nowadays we know that his discovery is a special case of an important general principle, from which it follows that such a simplification is possible because the problem has small "treewidth." In fact we can now do the calculation on a PC in two or three seconds, and the exact number turns out to be

$$1{,}568{,}758{,}030{,}464{,}750{,}013{,}214{,}100\,.$$

To my great relief, this number is indeed $(1.6 \pm 0.3) \times 10^{24}$. I don't know, maybe I was just lucky; but in any event this is the way I got started in randomization.

Such techniques are clearly a win for quantitative problems, but I began to use randomization also for *qualitative* things. For example, when teaching at Stanford, I often used randomization when I was grading papers. (Yes, I'm sure students sort of suspected this all the time.) Let me explain why I'm not ashamed to admit the fact. Suppose a student has presented me with a 200-page listing of a computer program — a term project, say — and I don't have time to read all 200 pages. So I turn to a random page and I look very closely at what's on that page; what I find there suggests other pages that I should look at. (The program might invoke a subroutine, for instance.) The parts I do look at, I check over very carefully; for example, maybe I'll have to check out what that subroutine does. But I don't have to read all 200 pages. And the student doesn't know what pages I'm going to look at. So I can get a pretty good idea about the quality of the program by using this approach. And in fact, all kinds of theories have recently been developed about things like "zero knowledge proofs" by which people can convince you that they know how to solve a problem without revealing how they do it. Randomization has therefore turned out to be useful in ways we didn't expect at all.

Another thing I tried to do in the 70s was to consider an age-old question: What is mathematics? The age-old answer is, of course, that mathematics is what mathematicians do. But what do mathematicians do? More precisely, I wanted to have some idea about what I would need to teach a computer in order to be able to say that the computer understood mathematics. The way I approached this was to take nine books that I felt were typical of things mathematicians do, and I looked at page 100 of each book. And I asked myself, "How would I have to program a computer so that it would be able to create or at least to understand the mathematics that's on page 100 of these nine books?" In this way, you see, I wasn't calculating any formula that would yield an estimate plus or minus a standard deviation. Yet the study of an essentially random page still gave me a better insight into the nature of mathematics than if I had asked a bunch of mathematicians to define their subject.

At about the same time I decided to do a similar thing with the Bible. I wanted to study verses of the Bible, and the Bible has about 31,000 verses altogether. So one way to study them — similar to the approach I had taken with student grading, and similar to the way I tried to find out the nature of mathematics — would have been to take the 31,000 verses and put them onto little slips of paper. Then I could put all the little slips into a big urn, stir the urn thoroughly, and draw out random slips. Looking at those slips of paper would give me an idea about what's in the Bible.

My earlier experience with backtrack calculations showed that I could actually do a bit better. Suppose, for example, that I wanted to choose 66 Bible verses for study. The Bible has 66 books, and I can get a better result if I choose one verse out of each book instead of choosing all 66 verses from the same big urn. Statisticians call this the technique of *stratified sampling*; it helps us make sure that things haven't been lumped together into the same place. I thought, "Hey, it would be neat to try this, and see what I get." (In those days we said "neat" instead of "cool.")

I was asked at that time to teach a Bible class at my church. For years I had been sitting in on Bible study classes, but never as a teacher. People told me that it was now my turn to get up in front of the group. So I said, "Okay, I'll do it, provided that you're willing to go through an experiment with me. We're going to look at *random* verses of the Bible."

I decided that one interesting way to choose a fairly random verse out of each book of the Bible would be to look at chapter 3, verse 16. I'll explain a little bit more about that in a minute. But basically, for the first class everyone was asked to look at Genesis 3:16, Exodus 3:16, and Leviticus 3:16 — namely chapter 3, verse 16 in each of the first three books of the Bible.

I hadn't read those verses yet myself. It's important that if you're working with a random sample, you mustn't rig the data. However I did rig it, of course, in one place: A lot of you surely know that the most famous verse in the whole Bible, by its number, is found in the book of John, chapter 3, verse 16. And the truth is that I rigged it in this way because I didn't want the pastor of my church to complain that my class was a dud if we didn't get to anything interesting. With my rule we were guaranteed to hit at least one good verse.

John 3:16 is even more famous than I knew at the time. Later on when I wrote a book about my experiences, the book's title was simply *3:16*, as you can see. The book was printed in Singapore, and all the correspondence we had with the printers in Singapore referred to it by this  short title. But after it had been printed and shipped to America, we discovered that the boxes were all identified with the title "John 3:16." In other words, even in Singapore — where fewer than 10% of the population is Christian, and where the people I dealt with at the printing house were Muslim and Hindu — somehow people knew about John 3:16. Maybe they had been watching American football on television or something, I don't know.

Many people continue to refer to my book by the title "John 3:16" although the word "John" is nowhere to be seen on the title page, simply because that verse is so famous. For me, "3:16" was primarily a catchy number that people in my class would know, a number they'd be able to remember easily. They wouldn't have to look it up.

We could have rolled dice. True randomization clearly leads to a better sample than the result of a fixed deterministic choice like chapter 3, verse 16. On the other hand, there's no reason to think that there's anything unusual about chapter 3, verse 16 except in the Book of John. And I didn't like the idea of rolling dice, for several reasons. One reason was that we would have to roll the dice in advance if people were going to prepare for the class. But then if a person missed a class they wouldn't know what to do for next time. The other reason was that when you roll dice there's a temptation to cheat. You get a bad roll and you say, "Well I didn't really mean that . . . the dice slipped, or bumped into the edge. Let's try again." Thus my 3:16 rule actually couldn't be rigged.

Let me give you another example. If I were an astronomer, I would love to look at random points in the sky. I would like to make a really exhaustive survey of different parts of the sky; and I would try to choose them without any other astronomer telling me where to aim my telescope. But before I looked anywhere I would announce in advance how I was going to do this, by some rule that couldn't be rigged. For example, I think I would base it somehow on the digits of pi (π), because π has now been calculated to billions of digits and they seem to be quite random. We could get astronomical coordinates by starting say at digit positions 1000, 2000, 3000, . . . , continuing for as many positions as we want. (This would be pi in the sky.) I really believe such a survey would be quite informative.

Yet another example was suggested by my son-in-law, Greg Tucker, last Sunday. He said he was inspired by the 3:16 book to start up the "H-20 project," which is designed to answer the question "What is Massachusetts?" Greg is in civil engineering here at MIT. He and my daughter have a book of maps of Massachusetts at a large scale; they live fairly near the campus, at coordinates H-20 in the relevant map of Cambridge. So they're going to try to visit H-20 on all the other pages of their book. That should give terrific insights into the real nature of Massachusetts.

Most of you know that Cambridge will be having an election for city council next month. If I were mayor of Cambridge, I would do the following. First I'd mentally divide the city into, say, 50 sections with about 2000 people in each section. (Or maybe I'd choose sections with roughly equal area instead of equal population.) Then I would find some way to select one person at random in each of those 50 districts. And I would set aside each Wednesday afternoon or evening to meet one of those people, inviting them to my house so that I could get to know them pretty well. After a year I would have gotten a pretty good idea about what 50 typical people of Cambridge want the mayor to do and how I could help them best. I think this would be *way* better than just listening to the people who paid the most for my campaign. Right?

And you see, I'm doing the same kind of thing with the Bible. At least, you'll see in a minute that I try hard to get fully acquainted with the verses that I've chosen to sample.

When I'm in a book store nowadays, or when I'm at a conference looking at a table full of new books, I try to gauge how good the books are by picking them up and — yes, I guess it's okay to reveal the secret — I turn to page 316. I try to read that page rather carefully, and this gives me an impression of the whole book. (Often the book is too short; then I use page 100. Authors, take note if you expect me to buy anything you've written.) This system works quite well, I think.

It's something like the Gallup Poll, where the pollsters go out and interview 1000 people, after which they tell us what Americans are thinking. Although such a sampling method is not guaranteed to work at all, it really has an amazing power in making fairly good use of your time while giving you substantial insights into any complicated subject.

So that's why I tried the 3:16 rule when I began to lead a Bible study group at my church in 1978. However, I had to debug the rule. After the class got going, I soon realized that some books of the Bible don't *have* three chapters. In fact, I had to leave out seven books, because they didn't get as far as 3:16. Instead of 66 books, I was therefore down to 59. There was, in fact, a close call: The Book of Titus ends at chapter 3, verse 15.

After a few more class sessions I realized that I'd have to go back to the drawing board yet again, because sometimes there's a chapter 3 but it doesn't have 16 verses. In such cases I decided to go into chapter 4. The official rule, more precisely, was to look at the 16th verse after the beginning of chapter 3, provided that such a verse exists.

Now we had 58 pretty random verses of the Bible, together with John 3:16 (which was known to be exceptional). The poster that I brought with me today displays each of these 59 verses, which fit nicely in a 10 × 6 matrix if we include the 3:16 logo as well. I've had this poster in my office for ten years now, and it's kind of amazing because I don't get tired of it. I often look up and see something new, partly because the artwork is so good, but also because the poster is kind of a map of the themes of the Bible. In fact, some people have called this method of Bible study "the way of the cross section."

That experimental Bible class of 1978 turned out to be remarkably successful. Starting with about a dozen people the first week, it went on for about half a year, and interest continually was build-

ing. We soon had to move to a larger room. And the final verse, Revelation 3:16, turned out to be a fitting climax.

Last week in my first lecture I promised to explain why the idea of studying chapter 3, verse 16, makes perfect sense, and I hope you now agree.

Why did it seem to work so well? I think there are two main reasons for its success. The first reason you can understand if you think of the traditional definition of a liberal education: I don't know where I heard it first, but a liberal education is supposed to teach you "something about everything and everything about something." And here was a good case in point, where I was only half educated. I mean, I knew something about all parts of the Bible, because I had been going to church and to Lutheran schools in my early years; but there was no part of the Bible that I knew thoroughly. Although I had a vague knowledge about many things, I couldn't point to any particular topic that I had surrounded, a topic about which I had found out just about everything that I could. These 59 verses filled that gap for me, because I tried to study them exhaustively.

I didn't just look at each verse casually and say "oh, how great it is"; instead, I tried to scour the best theological libraries of the world to find out what everybody has written about the verses in question. Fortunately it's not difficult to do a pretty good job of this with respect to the Bible, because books about the Bible are very often indexed by the verses that they discuss. Thus I could go through shelf after shelf in the library stacks, looking at the indexes at the back of each book; that told me what pages to look at. There also are "reader's guides" to theological journals, which cover the periodical literature and point to papers that emphasize particular verses in nontrivial ways. And of course Bible commentaries are organized by verses. So a good library provides lots of resources with which a person can get up to speed fairly quickly on any one Bible verse. In this way my chance to learn "everything about something" was essentially my opportunity to get the missing half of a liberal education about the Bible.

Such an approach is no good if you want to try to learn all 31,000 verses and everything about all of them. But for a few isolated verses, especially in cases where the verses aren't especially famous, it was pretty easy. I could rapidly become a world authority on Leviticus 3:16, because nobody else would have done all the homework about that particular text. And even though I was studying only 59 verses, thus dealing in detail with less than 1/500th of the Bible, it was amazing how many different subjects came up, sending me to other verses. (I'll say more about that later.)

The really big win for this method, however, is not what it teaches about the Bible itself. The Bible isn't that long a book; you can easily read it all the way through. For instance, my great grandfather Knuth was a blacksmith, and I've been told that he had a copy of the Bible in German, which he read several times from beginning to end although he was not an educated man. But nobody can possibly read all the *secondary* literature about the Bible. There are tens of thousands, maybe hundreds of thousands of books about the Book of Books; the task of covering them all is so daunting that a non-theologian like me tends not to open *any* of them, since there are so many. Or if I do crack one open, my choice is probably biased by what other people have told me to read. And that is unsatisfactory to me, as a scientist; I don't feel comfortable with just reading the top ten best-sellers, concentrating only on what is popular or reputed to be great. I need to know something about the ordinary parts of the Bible before I have any confidence that I might be able to assess what it is really about.

When I first based a Sunday morning class on the 3:16s, I didn't do anything like an exhaustive study. I would go to Stanford's Library on Saturday and spend a few hours in preparation, reading say five commentaries and a few translations of the verses that we were going to consider on the following day. But later on — after the class had worked out so well and I had decided that this approach was sufficiently interesting that I ought to write a book about it — I began to take the job much more seriously, and I would typically work on each verse for about three solid days. My usual routine was to start Friday afternoon and work intensively until Monday noon on each one. And by going to the best libraries and checking the best resources I could find, I was able to read books that spanned many centuries, written by authors with many different viewpoints.

Of course I made use of the classical commentaries on the Torah by the most famous rabbis. I also read things like the mystical literature from St. Bernard of Clairvaux; I read Thomas Aquinas and the scholastics; I read Calvin's commentaries. (As a Lutheran I wouldn't ordinarily be motivated to look at John Calvin's writings because, you know, I've been told that they're a bit subversive. But in fact, Calvin wrote a commentary on nearly every book of the Bible, and even though those commentaries fill a large shelf I only had to read roughly 59 pages. And I found that they were great; I was surprised and pleased to see a number of significant insights that I didn't find in any other books.) I also read Luther, of course, and commentaries from the 17th, 18th, and 19th centuries. I read many dozens of commentaries by Catholic, Protestant, and Jewish theologians of the twentieth century, from ultra-conservative to ultra-liberal. In this way I could kind of surround those 59 verses and get to know them pretty well.

In fact, I now think of the 59 verses in the poster as if they are pegs on which I can hang a knowledge of the Bible. After having completed this study, every time I hear something about the Bible it reminds me of something that's close to something that's close to one of the 3:16s. Before the 3:16 project began, I didn't have any solid points of reference, I just had a lot of wishy-washy approximations to knowledge; but with this "map of the Bible" I have some solid pegs on which I can attach other stuff. That's why I claim that this method turned out to be a smashing success.

On the other hand, sampling can be ineffective or misleading if you don't understand the limitations of the method. I have to confess that when I was working on this project, sometimes I would wake up in the morning and wonder if I just wasn't being totally insane by studying the Bible in this way. Then I would remind myself, "Well, maybe no. It's okay."

There's an obvious danger of confusing my approach with numerology. In fact, I was surprised to learn that when a lot of people first heard that I was studying the 3:16s, they jumped to the conclusion that I must believe there's something magical about those verses. The number 3 represents the Trinity, and 16 is a perfect square: Wow! And 3.16 times 3.16 is 9.99.

So people would send me letters trying to cure me of this delusion. They would say, "Don, don't you realize that the chapter and verse numbers were added to the Bible long after the material was written?"

Of course! That was precisely my point — that there *couldn't* be any special meaning associated with whatever happened to appear as the 16th verse of chapter 3. I simply wanted to focus on plain old ordinary nonspecial verses that aren't known to be exceptional in any direction — except, of course, in the case of John 3:16. In fact, when I wanted to get a better insight into the Gospel of John,

I actually studied John 16:3 for my own edification. I had to put John 3:16 into the published book only because people were looking for it; I myself got more out of a random verse.

History is full of misguided attempts to read the Bible as a book of mathematics, because it's so easy to find fortuitous patterns in numerical data. I think a lot of you know that Hebrew and Greek letters were traditionally associated with number representations, before Hindu–Arabic numerals came along. According to these ancient rules, every word in the Bible also has a numerical significance. A lot of people study what's called *gematria*, where the idea is to find great hidden significance in the numbers that are represented by words in the Bible.

The most famous recent example of this kind is the book called *The Bible Code*, which was a best seller two years ago. It started when several excellent mathematicians in Jerusalem happened to notice some numerical patterns among the Hebrew letters in religious texts, and they couldn't understand why this pattern should be present. Another man heard about it and decided to write this book, *The Bible Code*, in which he has the Bible prophesying things that are going to happen in the future. So I looked it up on the Web today, and I learned about some really interesting developments. Not only have the patterns been explained by statisticians, but also Don Steinberg at CNET.com has found prophesies foretold in the Microsoft Access Developers Tool Kit 2.0 license agreement. And on "Yahoo! Internet Life" you can discover coded references to Bill Gates in the Book of Revelation. Several Web sites have been started where you can look in texts of your choice and make your own discoveries and predictions.

I checked Amazon.com this morning to find out if *The Bible Code* is still selling well. Two years after publication, it's ranked 3967 among all Amazon.com's books; that puts it somewhere between Volume 1 and Volume 3 of *The Art of Computer Programming*. Of course it's way ahead of my 3:16 book, which has rank 54,042 today. *The Bible Code* has 207 customer comments; they're quite fascinating. Everybody gives it either five stars (the highest ranking) or one star (the lowest).

Numerology is fun, and it can lead to endless amusement if you know what you're doing. I'm reminded of the time in the early 80s when I was writing *The TEXbook* (the user manual for TEX) and I was looking for quotations to put at the end of the chapters. I forget exactly why, but I was led somehow to John Wesley's writings and I found the following in Volume 5 of his *Collected Works*:

> At some rare times, when I have been in great distress of soul, or in utter uncertainty how to act in an important case which required a speedy determination, after using all other means that occurred, I have cast lots, or opened the Bible. And by this means I have been relieved from that distress, or directed in that uncertainty.

The amazing thing is that these words appear on page 316! You can look it up.

Now in this instance Wesley is using randomization for a different purpose: He's using it for divine guidance. There are cases in the Bible where people "cast lots," which in those days meant rolling bones to find out how the bones would land. For many centuries in China, people have used a pattern of six binary codes called the I-Ching with randomization as a source of guidance. When I visited Shinto temples in Japan, I learned about a similar custom there called *omikuji*, the "divine lottery," which uses a really neat randomizing device: You shake a box and out comes a long stick, and the stick has some kind of marks on it directing you to another place where you can obtain your fortune for the day.

Maybe God *does* force the way the dice are rolling, or sends a message in some other way; people everywhere have a craving to find out. There might be something to that, and I don't have any way to know for sure, but I do know that my own methods are completely different. I'm not using random numbers because of any assumption of magic or supernatural activity; I'm just trying to be systematically unbiased.

I have to tell you another story that I decided not to put in the book because I didn't want to mislead anybody. Six days before I was scheduled to begin teaching my Bible class beginning with

Genesis 3:16, I found myself in Stanford Hospital needing emergency surgery. It wasn't serious, but after I woke up and was feeling kind of rotten I wondered whether I should maybe postpone the first class meeting. But then I noticed a curious thing: My hospital room number was 316! So maybe God was smiling on the project after all.

And I've got yet another story to tell you. Lloyd Waner was a famous baseball player for the Pittsburgh Pirates. He was born on March 16 in 1906. Now that's the third month and the 16th day — 3/16/06; and his lifetime batting average was .316. Could that be purely coincidental?

Of course the answer is, "Yes, absolutely." I took a big book of statistics down from my bookshelves and I knew that I would almost surely find something about 316 in there, in order to make up this example. When you have a number in mind you'll run into that number frequently; other numbers will go in one ear and out the other, but you will remember a number that resonates with your thoughts. For example, if you live in Arlington, look at the road signs as you drive home tonight; you'll see the turnoff for US route 3 and state route 16, although you've driven past that intersection many times before without seeing any significance in those numbers.

Richard Feynman once told an interesting story from his days as an MIT student. He was sitting in his fraternity house when the idea came into his head "completely out of the blue" that his grandmother was dead. And immediately afterward the phone rang. But the phone call was for somebody else, and his grandmother turned out to be in perfect health. He decided to remember the incident, "in case somebody told me a story that ended the other way." He knew how to understand coincidences.

But the main danger to avoid, when you're using an approach like I did for the sampling, is different; it has nothing to do with numerology or coincidences. The mistake you don't want to make is to close your eyes to everything except the verse that you've selected for study. I mean, it would be wrong for me to pick a slip of paper out of a well-stirred urn and just look at the one verse written on that slip. Even if I sat and meditated for a long time on that verse, I'd miss most of the point if I didn't also take the context of that verse into account.

For example, I can't imagine anybody learning much if they tried to pore over a random sentence of one of my own books in that way. What if somebody were to take a sentence on page 316 of my book and hang on every word of that one sentence, blocking out all the other words? Maybe a psychology major could write a Ph.D. thesis about what I had in mind when I composed that sentence. People now examine the Bible with such an intense magnifying glass, you can't help but think that the original authors couldn't possibly have intended it for that level of scrutiny; surely they were thinking of a flow of many verses.

Thus I couldn't fully understand the thrust of the 3:16 verse just from the 3:16 verse itself. But I did try to put a very intense light on that verse. For example, I tried to study all the problems that might have occurred in transmission; the Bible is thousands of years old, and manuscripts were repeatedly recopied over the years, causing many changes to creep in. I was amazed to learn that almost every verse of the Bible has textual problems, where the scholars who collated these manuscripts have had to make a call on what readings are original. In each 3:16 verse, I checked the records of what different manuscripts say, in order to get some idea about how much variation there was. I also looked at 3:15 and 3:17, the neighboring verses, but without turning the light on as strongly: I didn't take time to study all the details of those verses, I simply accepted the majority opinion about the proper way to resolve any textual problems they might have. Similar considerations applied to verses 14 and 18, which got even less scrutiny.

In much the same way, when I was grading student papers, the page I chose would lead me to a few other pages, but the further I got from my selected page the less time I would put into actually checking every detail.

I generally had the best results interpreting a 3:16 verse when I tried to let the Bible interpret itself. I would look first for other verses that used the same vocabulary, in order to understand the meaning of the words. I'd also look at other verses that treated the same topic. This process led me to considerably more than 59 verses of the Bible. In fact, my book has an index of the Bible verses that it cites, and this index extends over quite a few pages. Consider the Book of Isaiah, for example; the index lists verses 1:20, 1:26, 2:2, 2:3, 2:4, 2:7, 2:11, 3:4, 3:14, and so on through 64:1 and 66:14. Verses in chapter 3 are naturally expected, but in fact the references extend throughout the Bible. Almost every part of the Bible helped to shed light on the 59 verses that were the chief focus.

The number of topics that those verses led to also proved to be amazingly diverse. I'll try to prove it to you: If somebody will call out a random letter of the alphabet, I can read you some entries out of the index of the book ... D for Don? Okay, let's see: "Daniel, Dante, David, Day of Jehovah, Dead Sea, Dead Sea Scrolls, death, Delitzsch, depression, Deutero-Isaiah, Deuteronomic history, Deuteronomy, dice, disarmament, disciples, divorce, domination, doubts, dove." These are the D-topics and the D-people that occur in the discussion of the 3:16s.

I found out after publishing this book that other people had independently come up with a similar idea. Pastors in New Hampshire and Missouri both wrote to me that they had preached some sermons about the 3:16s, before hearing about my work. A man in Pennsylvania had also used them independently for study, and he sent me a copy of his notes. In that case, I was disappointed in what he sent me, because it seemed that he was only looking at the 3:16 verses in isolation; after quoting a verse, he would summarize it in a rather simplistic way, to my way of thinking, and then go onto the next one. Everybody has personal preferences, but for me the really important thing is to go into a study strongly enough to get a feeling of completeness, so that you learn as much as you can out of the parts that you do choose to study.

But does this rule of 3:16s give a decent sample? My experience in computer programming has taught me that truly random numbers are often unnecessary, in the sense that convenient approximations to randomness usually turn out to be good enough for practical purposes. The 3:16 rule does have a little problem, however, because chapter 3 is near the beginning of a book; the book has started to get underway, but the verse being studied tends to deal with the early part of a story. In fact, chapter 3 often turns out to be about the notion of "calling": The 3:16s discuss the call of Moses, the call of Samuel, the call of Ezekiel, and the call of Jesus. In all four Gospels, chapter 3 is about things that occur early in Jesus's ministry. So we don't get as much variety as we would in a truly random sample. But that didn't really seem to matter too much.

A more serious problem might be that some books of the Bible are oversampled while others are undersampled. Consider, for instance, the Book of Psalms: There are 150 Psalms, but I only get to look at one. The Book of Isaiah has a big break at the beginning of chapter 40, where quite a different author apparently begins to speak; I'm not giving due weight to those other parts. On the other hand, the Hebrew Bible has a single Book of Prophets, which our English Bibles have subdivided into twelve books of so-called minor prophets. We have Hosea, Joel, Amos, Obadiah, Jonah, Micah, Nahum, Habakkuk, Zephaniah, Haggai, Zechariah, and Malachi all as separate books, while the Hebrew Bible has them all together in one book. My sampling procedure caused me to learn a lot more about minor prophets than I did about Isaiah.

A similar phenomenon occurs in the U.S. Senate, where Rhode Island and Massachusetts have the same number of senators because every state is equal. Nevada and California are equal. My sample is somewhat misleading for that reason.

But overall, I have to say that after avoiding the most dangerous pitfalls of sampling and deciding to live with the other problems, I think this methodology worked quite well — except in one respect. Namely, it worked *too* well: It gave me the illusion that I knew much more about the Bible than I actually do. I still have to keep telling myself that I've only looked at less than 1/500th of the Bible. The fact that I was able to surround a few verses in a reasonably complete way, and to solidify a few pieces of knowledge, has tempted me to become overconfident. Thus, the final danger of the approach I have taken is that people who practice it must remember that they have seen only a small part of the full story.

I've spoken about these things longer than I had planned for today, but fortunately there still is plenty of time for you to ask questions.

Q: You devised a straightforward "brightline test" with respect to which verse you studied: verse 3:16. But when you started to expand outwards, did you have any means of making somewhat objective decisions as to what subsidiary verses you'd look at?

A: You're right; I started with 3:16, but then it was up to me to decide what would interest me about the context. How could I keep my own prejudices from significantly influencing the outcome of the experiment?

I was systematic in one sense, which I'll talk about in some detail in Lecture 3 with respect to translation. Namely, I always checked the vocabulary, especially the rarer words, looking at the other places where those words were used in the Bible, hopefully by the same author. Similarly I followed standard cross references about the ideas treated in the 3:16 verse; many Bibles and commentaries provide a rich network of cross references.

I couldn't use a fixed rule in every case when I was exploring the context, because sometimes a story begins say at verse 1 and proceeds through verse 16, but sometimes the relevant story begins at the 16th verse and goes on from there. Therefore verse 16 didn't always lie at the midpoint of my search.

Once in a while the direction of my search would just be based on a quirk. For example, I found out by chance that Ruth 3:15 had a very interesting history because of a typographic error in the original printing of the King James Bible. And Boston Public Library owns copies of both the first and second printings, which I could examine in the rare book room. I couldn't resist exploring that, because I'm into typography; there definitely was a subjective bias.

I guess I also went far afield in Numbers 3:16, because that verse led to a topic in which I could use my mathematical training. That was certainly a case where somebody else would probably have chosen a different direction. It turns out that the numbers reported in the census mentioned in Numbers 3:16 have some very peculiar properties, and those properties can be explained by understanding the linguistic basis for number systems. Consequently there's good reason to believe that the numerical data are quite ancient, coming from a time whose conventions had already been forgotten when the Book of Numbers was compiled in its final form. Again, I couldn't resist that bait; once in awhile I got tempted by some such intriguing tidbits, slightly off the general methodology.

But primarily I had a system, and you can judge for yourself whether I was sufficiently objective while following supposedly scientific instincts. Although I wanted to understand the context properly, my main goal was really to zoom in on all the things that were directly interesting about the verse in position 3:16.

Q: In your sampling, did you ever encounter the situation that different editions of the Bible numbered different verses as 3:16?

A: Yes. I didn't know it beforehand, but in fact some Bibles have different verse numberings than others. For example, in the Vulgate, the Psalms appear with a different numbering scheme; the Psalm I've always known as Psalm 23 is Psalm 22 in the Vulgate. Hebrew Bibles give a verse number to the title of a psalm, but such texts are unnumbered in English Bibles; thus Psalm 3:2 in Hebrew is Psalm

3:1 in English. When I learned about such discrepancies, I decided to stick to the numbering scheme that is used in virtually all English Bibles, because it is by far the most commonly used convention.

Most of the newer translations reorder some of the verses, because there's good scholarly evidence that the original text occasionally got mangled. Sometimes parts of one chapter will even move into other chapters, for example in the Book of Job. But in such cases, the new Bibles still retain the old numbering scheme; they don't renumber the verses.

I think the discrepancies between numbering systems would have affected only two or maybe three of the verses I considered to be in position 3:16.

Q: When coming up with the final 59 books that you selected, did you use only the Protestant canon or also the Catholic and Orthodox canons?

A: The 59 I have treated are all from the main canonical books common to all three traditions, namely the Hebrew canon plus the New Testament.

By the way, I should say something about the seven books that were left out because they were too short—the ones that didn't have enough verses to reach 3:16. I had no qualms about leaving them out, since each of them is similar to books that I did include. Thus Obadiah is like Jeremiah and Joel; Haggai is like Zechariah; Titus is like Timothy; Philemon is like Colossians; 2 John and 3 John are like 1 John; Jude is like 2 Peter.

If I were to study the Apocrypha, the so-called deuterocanonical books, I would of course use my favorite method: I'd study Tobit 3:16, Wisdom 3:16, 1 Maccabees 3:16, and so forth. The same would apply if I went on to consider additional books like Esdras in the Orthodox canon. But so far I haven't done this; I've tried to keep the project down to a reasonable size.

Q: I have a question regarding whether you felt you caught the major themes of the Bible. There's a famous anecdote about a man who was depressed and randomly opened the Bible and found the verse that said, "and Judas went out and hung himself." That wasn't very helpful, so he opened another one and it said, "go out and do thou likewise"; and that was even more depressing. Then he went on to find "whatever thou doest, do it quickly." So my question is, with the dangers of sampling and randomization do you feel you really got a sense of the message of the Bible by doing this?

A: You know, in computer science studies I've never been much of a fan of worst-case estimates.

I've heard that famous anecdote too, and it's fun, but I doubt if it's a true story because you have to work pretty hard in order to find such an example. Of course there are some very depressing verses, if you look hard enough. And you could find examples at the other extreme as well.

I have no way to know for sure that I've captured the essence of the Bible without doing a lot more reading. When I studied the numerical problem of paths on a grid, I did a few thousand tests to estimate their number. Here I've done 59 tests. I have a gut feeling that the standard deviation of what I ran into was small enough that the experiment was reasonably successful. But of course I really don't know. As I said, overconfidence in the results was probably the greatest flaw I encountered.

However, I would say that, given the amount of hours I put into this project, the approach I took beats any other method that I know. I surely couldn't have been anywhere near as satisfied if I had embarked on a reading program devised by somebody else who told me to "read this, this, and this." I would have to wonder if that person had been leading me astray, for example by giving me those three verses that you mentioned.

Q: The historical time frame represented by New Testament samples is much smaller than the time frame of Old Testament samples. Did you notice any effects from that? What was the ratio of Old and New Testament samples in this study?

A: The Old Testament has 37 of the sample verses and the New Testament has the other 22. So the testaments are related to each other in my study by something like the golden ratio.

In the New Testament, not only do you have a relatively short time frame but you also have the fact that Paul wrote a lot of epistles. So I had to deal there more often with a single author, although the Deuteronomic history in the Old Testament also has a fairly consistent style.

I would say that the sampling method allows you to see exactly how time influences things. It gives you a pretty good insight into such similarities and differences.

Q: Out of all these 59 verses what was the least interesting? With which one did you have to really struggle?

A: The least interesting verse is hard to say. People told me that I was bound to run into a genealogy, and it was true: 1 Chronicles 3:16 was part of a genealogy. But it turned out to be a really interesting genealogy! I came to the conclusion that if I were the pastor of a church, I could speak on any one of those 59 on a Sunday morning and give a sermon that would not be a dud.

I mentioned this to the pastor of University Lutheran Church at Stanford, and he took me up on it. Along came a time when the appointed reading was Malachi 3:16, so he invited me to preach the sermon that day. Well, I did it; but, being a college professor, it turned out that I spoke for 50 minutes, as if giving a classroom lecture, before I realized how long I had been going on. So he didn't ask me to do it again. Still, I don't think I wasted any of those 50 minutes on unimportant or uninteresting material.

When writing the book, I think I had to stretch the most on Numbers 3:16, for which the text is simply the following: "Moses enumerated the sons of Levi as he had been commanded by God." In order to get a reasonable story, I had to go and figure out what the enumeration was all about; that's where I think I had to push a little bit.

In almost every other case I had to cut. You see, my book sticks to a very tight format, with exactly four pages devoted to each of the 59 books of the Bible being studied. The first of those four pages is an introduction to the particular book, so that the reader can understand something about its author, its context, the period of time it's coming from, and a summary of its contents. For example, let me open to a random page ... here's an introduction to the Book of Zechariah. The facing page has calligraphy of Zechariah 3:16; then come pages that summarize everything I was able to find in the libraries about Zechariah 3:16 (which actually turns out to be Zechariah 4:6). Furthermore there's a fixed number of lines on each page. I had to use TEX to typeset everything, making sure that there were no widow lines or other typographic anomalies to spoil the appearance. In order to get down to the desired number of lines, my manuscript included a lot of discretionary phrases or discretionary paragraphs, which I could omit if I didn't have enough space, and I had to leave out a lot.

Thus, to my surprise, I didn't run across much deadwood where there was a shortage of things to discuss. Only in Numbers 3:16 do I recall having to go out into the context before getting a good story.

Q (Michael Rabin): There are many instances where this will apply. For example, I would suspect that if you took a completely unmanageable text like the tax code of some country, say the U.S. tax code, and if you would sample it this way, I think you could probably get a pretty good idea of its direction and purpose.

But do you see application in other areas? For example, could you take genes—DNA sequences that code for proteins, minus the nonsense—and do some kind of sampling of the stretch, and then for example distinguish between a gene or a set of genes with respect to plant life or animal life?

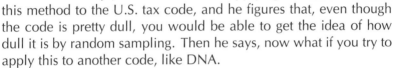

A: Was everyone able to hear Michael Rabin's comment? He says, consider first of all applying this method to the U.S. tax code, and he figures that, even though the code is pretty dull, you would be able to get the idea of how dull it is by random sampling. Then he says, now what if you try to apply this to another code, like DNA.

Of course this is an enormously complicated biological problem, and there's lots of DNA code that doesn't get expressed in proteins. People are wondering what it is there for. Could we tell perhaps by random sampling whether or not plants are a lot different in this respect than animals? (Don't take me seriously, but I have a hunch that when the unknown parts of the DNA are decoded, the so-called sequences of junk DNA, they're going to turn out to be copyright notices and patent protections.)

Rabin: I was referring to the genes.

A: Oh, to the parts that are expressed and not the parts in between. Yes, that really ought to be done. I think if somebody would work on a few of these and try to do an exhaustive understanding of a few things taken at random they would get a better idea about how to solve the whole problem. Of course people already do that, in some sense. They look very closely at a gene that seems to be correlated with, say, multiple sclerosis. But a random method would give a better picture of the whole system of genes, not only information about a specific one. Those are very good points.

Closing time is near, but I still see many people raising their hands, and it's hard for me to make an unbiased choice. Anne, can you help me select the last two questioners?

Q: How much do you think the success of your method is the result of its being applied to a product that was made by humans? I'm not sure it would work as well with things like genes, because they occur in nature. The Bible and such things as the texts of William Shakespeare would seem to be rather different in terms of such things as redundancy.

A: I don't believe random sampling is inapplicable to nature; as I said, I think it would work quite well in the sky. I really think you get a balanced understanding of just about anything when you look at random parts of the whole.

This approach has worked extremely well in many other cases. For example, by studying a little bit of a problem in computational geometry you can figure out properties of constructions that certainly weren't created by human beings. Purely mathematical patterns, or things that arise in ways unrelated to human intelligence, all seem to support the method of randomization.

No matter what complicated thing you have, I think there's a fairly good chance that random sampling will give insight. Of course if you start with purely random data, then random sampling is going to tell you that it is purely random data.

Q: I just wonder if you feel that your qualitative analysis would have been better if you'd chosen a purely random sampling method as opposed to the sort of human heuristic that you ended up choosing for ease of determination in your course.

A: I don't think it was a bad idea to get only one verse out of a long book that had a single author, but I think it was unfortunate to get only one verse out of a book like the Psalms that had many authors.

Even though the Book of Ecclesiastes is very short, I think it's a very important part of the Bible. So I wouldn't want it to be underrepresented by a method that treats every verse equally. Whatever rule I used, I would definitely want it to be stratified by authors or something like that.

I suppose I could have gotten slightly better qualitative results if I had used a more random method of selection. But then nobody would have known if I'd done it fairly. I didn't start out writing this book with the idea that anybody was going to check whether I was being fair or not; I started out with the class, and wrote the book after discovering that the class was successful. But after the fact, it turned out to be more interesting to have obtained qualitative insights by using an approach that was clearly not rigged. I plan to say more about this in the fifth lecture, because there was another potential source of bias that I didn't have time to discuss today.

Notes on Lecture 2

Page 25, We now can prove: See, for example, Rajeev Motwani and Prabhakar Raghavan, *Randomized Algorithms* (Cambridge University Press, 1995), Section 4.2.

Page 26, a way to predict: Donald E. Knuth, "Estimating the efficiency of backtrack programs," *Mathematics of Computation* **29** (1975), 121–136. Reprinted as Chapter 6 of *Selected Papers on Analysis of Algorithms* (Stanford, California: Center for the Study of Language and Information, 2000).

Page 27, "Coping with finiteness": The notes for Lecture 6 below contain the complete publication history of this paper.

Page 27, Y2K: When these lectures were given in 1999, there was good reason to worry that flaws hidden in computer programs would lead to serious problems all over the world when the year (Y) changed to 2000 (2K), because year numbers were often abbreviated to two digits. Therefore I was careful to return from Massachusetts to California well before December 31.

Page 28, the exact number: See *Selected Papers in Computer Science*, as cited in Lecture 1, page 57.

Page 29, what mathematicians do: See Donald E. Knuth, "Algorithms in modern mathematics and computer science," *Lecture Notes in Computer Science* **122** (1981), 82–99. A revised version entitled "Algorithmic thinking and mathematical thinking" [*American Mathematical Monthly* **92** (1985), 170–181] was reprinted with corrections as Chapter 4 of the book *Selected Papers on Computer Science*, cited in Lecture 1.

Page 29, page 100: I learned recently that this approach is far from new. My colleague Francis Everitt found the following passage on page 513 of Ford Madox Ford's book *The March of Literature* (New York: Dial Press, 1938): "The above passage—though chosen purely at random according to a habit of this writer, of turning to page ninety of any edition of an author (in this case the 1927 Edinburgh edition of Browne edited by Charles Sayle) and then quoting the first paragraph of reasonable length that he comes upon — the above passage, then, has almost no interest of content, yet for the lulling nature of its cadences, the surprise and vivacity of its illustrations, and the composure of its writer, it will stand beside any passage of prose the greatest in the world."

Page 30, American football: Aggressive Christians often hold up signs that say "John 3:16" when they think a TV camera will spot them. (Maybe it makes them feel virtuous, but I don't know of any non-Christian who has been led to a better understanding of Christianity by seeing such a message.)

Page 30, there's no reason: I actually challenge this hypothesis in Lecture 5.

Page 34, something about everything: A similar quotation is frequently attributed to Thomas Henry Huxley; and indeed, the commemorative plaque near Huxley's birthplace in Ealing includes the aphorism "Try to learn something about everything and everything about something," which his biographer Cyril Bibby said was a favorite saying [*T. H. Huxley on Education* (Cambridge: University Press, 1971), page 10]. However, Bibby typically gives citations to original sources of Huxley's own words, so this phrase is probably due to someone else. It is attributed to Lord Henry Brougham (1778–1868) on the Web site of the venerable BBC radio show "Quote. . . Unquote," where query Q695 currently asks for an explicit reference; see `www1c.btwebworld.com/quote-unquote`.

Page 34, "reader's guides": *New Testament Abstracts*, published since 1956 by the Weston School of Theology in Cambridge, Massachusetts; and *Old Testament Abstracts*, published since 1978 by the Catholic Biblical Association in Washington, D.C. Both publications include annual indexes of Scripture references, and I found those indexes quite helpful.

Page 37, Another man: Michael Drosnin, *The Bible Code* (New York: Simon & Schuster, 1997).

Page 37, looked it up on the Web: Pete Aitken's survey "Torah! Torah! Torah!" at `www.postfun.com/pfp/bible/code.html` was especially good.

Page 38, "cast lots": For example, in Leviticus 16:8–9; Numbers 26:55–56; Joshua 7:14–18, 13:6, 18:6; 1 Samuel 10:20–21, 14:41–42; Nehemiah 11:1; Esther 3:7; Jonah 1:7; Matthew 27:35; Acts 1:26. See also Proverbs 16:33, "The lot is cast into the lap, but the decision is wholly from God." And Proverbs 18:18, "The lot causes disputes to cease." Other aspects of probability in sacred texts have been considered by Oscar Sheynin, "Stochastic thinking in the Bible and the Talmud," *Annals of Science* **55** (1998), 185–198.

Page 38, the I-Ching: See Martin Gardner, *Knotted Donuts and Other Mathematical Entertainments* (New York: W. H. Freeman, 1986), Chapter 20.

Page 39, Lloyd Waner: See www.baseballhalloffame.org for a biography; also sportsillustrated.cnn.com / baseball / mlb/all_time_stats/players/w/45347.

Page 39, Richard Feynman: *"Surely You're Joking, Mr. Feynman!"* as told to Ralph Leighton (New York: W. W. Norton, 1985), page 130.

Page 43, Numbers 3:16: I was primarily inspired by the comments of George E. Mendenhall, "The census lists of Numbers 1 and 26," *Journal of Biblical Literature* **77** (1958), 52–66.

Page 43, the Vulgate: The Latin version of the Bible prepared by St. Jerome near the end of the 4th century. This translation was normative for Roman Catholics until recently.

Page 44, "and Judas went out": Matthew 27:5b.

Page 44, "do thou likewise": Luke 10:37b.

Page 44, "do it quickly": John 13:27b.

Page 45, worst-case estimates: See, for example, Chapter 1 of *Selected Papers on Analysis of Algorithms*, cited above.

Page 45, golden ratio: $(\sqrt{5} + 1)/2 \approx 37/22$. (This ratio has been the subject of a lot of crank literature; see George Markowsky, *College Mathematics Journal* **23** (1992), 2–19.)

Page 46, Along came a time: 22 November 1992.

LECTURE 3: LANGUAGE TRANSLATION   (27 OCTOBER 1999)

All of you who are old enough to recall the early days of computing will remember that one of the very first "killer applications" envisioned for computers was that they were going to translate automatically from other languages into English. In the 1950s, people predicted that by the 60s all documents would routinely be translated by computer. In those days, of course, people didn't realize how hard some of the problems were. But the desire for language processing was so great that AI meant artificial intelligence and MT meant machine translation.

I thought I'd start out today by showing you the current state of the art. This morning I looked at the home page for the 3:16 book on Netscape, and I translated it into French using an automatic service called "Babel Fish." Here [*Example 1*] is the original English as it appears in the online file:

3:16 Bible Texts Illuminated, by Donald E. Knuth

The text found in chapter 3, verse 16, of most books in the Bible is a typical verse with no special distinction. But when Knuth examined what leading scholars throughout the centuries have written about those verses, he found that there is a fascinating story to be learned in every case, full of historical and spiritual insights. This book presents jargon-free introductions to each book of the Bible and in-depth analyses of what people from many different religious persuasions have said about the texts found in chapter 3, verse 16, together with 60 original illustrations by many of the world's leading calligraphers.

The result is a grand tour of the Bible — from Genesis 3:16 to Revelation 3:16 — a treat for the mind, the eyes, and the spirit.

Some have called Knuth's approach "the way of the cross section."

"This book is ingenious, provocative, and wonderfully informative. A more imaginative and effective passageway into the Bible I have yet to see. Jews and Christians of all stripes — in fact, nonbelievers too — will read 3:16 with profit and delight." –William Sloane Coffin, Minister Emeritus, Riverside Church, New York City

"It is difficult to think that a totally new approach to the Bible could be found — at least one that is sane. Donald Knuth has found one, and produced a book that is physically beautiful and intellectually and spiritually stimulating." –Raymond E. Brown, Professor Emeritus, Union Theological Seminary

EXAMPLE 1.

And here [*Example 2*] is how the machine renders the same text in French:

textes de bible de 3:16 élucidés, par Donald E. Knuth

Le texte trouvé en chapitre 3, le vers 16, de la plupart des livres dans la bible est un vers typique sans la distinction spéciale. Mais quand Knuth a examiné ce que les principaux disciples tout au long des siècles ont écrit au sujet de ces vers, il a constaté qu'il y a une histoire fascinante à apprendre dans tous les cas, complètement des perspicacités historiques et spirituelles. Ce livre présente les introductions jargon-libres à chaque livre de la bible et des analyses détaillées de quelles personnes de beaucoup de différentes persuasions religieuses ont dit au sujet des textes trouvés en chapitre 3, le vers 16, ainsi que 60 illustrations initiales par plusieurs des calligraphes principaux mondiaux.

Le résultat est une excursion grande de la bible—de la genèse 3:16 à la révélation 3:16—un festin pour l'esprit, les yeux, et l'esprit.

Certains ont appelé l'approche de Knuth "la voie de la coupe."

"Ce livre est ingénieux, provocateur, et merveilleusement instructif. Un passage plus imaginatif et plus pertinent dans la bible que j'ai voir encore. Les juifs et les chrétiens de toutes les raies—en fait, des nonbelievers trop—liront 3:16 avec le bénéfice et le plaisir." –Le Cercueil De William Sloane, Ministre Honoraire, Église De Rive, New York City

"Il es difficile de penser qu'une approche totalement nouvelle à la bible pourrait être trouvée—au moins une qui est raisonnable. Donald Knuth a trouvé un, et a produit un livre qui est physiquement beau et intellectuellement et religieux stimulant." –Raymond E. Brown, Professeur Emeritus, Union Theological Seminary

EXAMPLE 2.

I don't know much French; but I'd say this isn't terribly bad as a first crack, considering that it was done by computer in a fraction of a second. Of course the machine didn't catch the double entendre in the "way of the cross section" joke. And mechanical translations are funny when proper names like William Sloane Coffin are translated. But Riverside Church is translated *Église De Rive*; this is impressive, except for the capital D.

Babel Fish works with many languages besides English and French. For example, it produces similar results in German; Anne will be able to tell us whether the German here [*Example 3*] is any good.

My own training in languages was quite limited: I learned a little Latin in high school and then I learned a bit of Russian and German in college. (In the 60s you could not get a Ph.D. without having some sort of minimum competency in two foreign languages.) To pass my German language requirement, I was supposed to translate several

3:16 Bibeltexte belichteten, durch Donald E. Knuth

Der Text, der in Kapitel 3, Verse 16, der meisten Bücher in der Bibel gefunden wird, ist ein typischer Verse ohne spezielle Unterscheidung. Aber,
als Knuth überprüfte, was führende Gelehrte während der Jahrhunderte
über jene Verses geschrieben haben, fand er, daß es eine faszinierende
von den historischen und geistigen Einblicken auf jeden Fall, voll zu
erlernende Geschichte gibt. Dieses Buch stellt Fachsprache-freie Ein-
leitungen jedem Buch der Bibel und der eingehenden Analysen von dar,
was Leuten von vielen unterschiedlichen frommen Überzeugungen über
die Texte gesagt haben, die in Kapitel 3, Verse 16, zusammen mit 60
ursprünglichen Abbildungen von vielen der führenden Schreibkünstler
der Welt gefunden werden.

Das Resultat ist eine großartige Tour der Bibel — von Enstehungs-
geschichte 3:16 bis Enthülling 3:16 — eine Festlichkeit für den Verstand,
die Augen und den Geist.

Einige haben genannt Knuthannäherung "die Weise des Querschnitts."

"Dieses Buch ist scharfsinnig provozierend, und wundervoll informativ.
Ein phantasiereicherer und wirkungsvollerer Durchgang in die Bibel, die
ich, schon zu sehen habe. Juden und Christen aller Streifen — tatsächlich,
nonbelievers auch — lesen 3:16 mit Profit und Freude." –Sarg Williams
Sloane, SIND Emeritus, RiversideKirche, New York City

"Das es schwierig ist, zu denken, daß eine total neues Annäherung an die
Bible gefunden werden könnte — eine mindestens, die gesund ist. Donald
Knuth hat ein gefunden und ein Buch produziert, das ist physikalisch
schön und intellektuell und Angelegenheiten anregend." –Raymond E.
Brown, Professor Emeritus, Anschluß Theological Seminary

EXAMPLE 3.

chapters of a math book, converting them into smooth English equivalents. That was my first serious experience with language translation; of course the translation of mathematics is pretty easy, since
mathematicians tend to stick to a vocabulary of only 50 words or so.

I never was very good at speaking other languages, but over the
years my input mechanism has gotten reasonably good. The output
process has always been my main source of problems. But as I
work on *The Art of Computer Programming* I frequently need to
understand some article in French or German or Russian or Spanish
or some other language; therefore I must often spend a lot of time
with a dictionary. It would have been a lot easier if I had been able
to use a computer system like Babel Fish.

As a computer scientist, of course, I have considerably more
experience with formal languages than with natural languages. The
study of programming languages is one of the most important sub-
fields of computer science, and the aspect of computing that at-
tracted me most during my student days was the writing of software

routines called compilers. A compiler takes a program expressed in some formal algebraic language and translates it perfectly into a machine language, retaining exactly the true meaning of whatever the programmer had said in the formal language. The methods that I learned for dealing with formal languages are, however, only partially adequate for the languages of the real world, because natural language is much more difficult. And my lecture today is about natural language translation, not about formal language translation.

In the previous lecture I spoke about the advantages of randomization for getting insight into complex subjects. When I began the 3:16 project in 1978, I knew that lots of new translations of the Bible had been coming out. So my first instinct was to think, "This 3:16 idea is good because I'll get to compare several dozen translations on random verses. I'll be able to find out which is the best translation, and I'll buy it for my library at home."

Well, my first surprise was that there is a tremendous variability between the different translations. I was expecting the translations to differ here and there, but I thought that the essential meaning and syntax of the original language would come through rather directly into English. On the contrary, I almost never found a close match between one translation and another. (I'll show examples shortly.)

The other thing that I noticed, almost immediately when I had only looked at a few of the 3:16s, was that no translation was consistently the best. Each translation I looked at seemed to have its good moments and its bad moments; there were many cases in which one version would shine over the others for a particular verse and then it would be the worst in the next verse.

Several years later, when I started to work on the idea of a book called *3:16*, I went to the Boston Public Library and to other places like the Bible Museum and found as many different translations as I could get my hands on. I copied down more than two dozen translations of each verse, as I mentioned last time; and the additional translations gave me still more variations than I had seen before.

My next idea was to run a sort of competition between the various translations, in my own mind at least. For each 3:16 verse, I was going to choose the translation that seemed to be the best, of all the translations I had found; then I could give credit to whichever translation had been chosen in each case. But soon I started to worry about copyrights and the possibility that I would need to obtain official permission to use each text. I would have to write a whole bunch of letters and wait for the replies, and maybe pay fees and get into other complications. That sounded bad.

So I thought, "Could I possibly translate the verses myself? No, such an idea is preposterous, since I don't know any Hebrew and I don't know any Greek." Unfortunately for me, the Bible wasn't written in English; it was written in Hebrew and Greek, and a little in Aramaic.

A few days later, however, I thought the problem over again and came to a different conclusion. "Look, I have these 25 translations and I've also got other resources to look at. I only have 59 verses to worry about. That's less than 1/500th of the Bible, so I can afford to put three or four hours into each verse. No problem. The vocabulary in this small sample isn't too large. I should be able to look everything up in the references I have. Besides, I can check my ideas against the translations that I've already seen; then I'll be sure that any mistakes in my own version have also been made by at least two experts."

Let me show you some of the resources that were at my disposal in 1985. First I had a hefty book by James Strong of Madison, New Jersey, called *The Exhaustive Concordance of the Bible*, a work that had fascinated me ever since I first saw it. It's a cross-index to every single word in the Bible. The original printing was made in 1890; I own a copy of the 31st printing, made in  1973. It contains more than 1800 large-format pages. This book includes absolutely every word, including common words like "the"; but for a few such words it doesn't show the context, it just tells you how many times "the" occurs in each verse. (For example, it's found in Genesis 1:1^2, 2^6, 4^3, 5^5, 6^4, and so on through Revelation 22:19^5 and 21.)

You can get the idea of the main part of Strong's Concordance by looking at this excerpt [*Example 4*], which shows the word "count." (I chose this word because it comes closest to the concept of computing.) Here you can see every place the word "count" appeared in the famous King James translation of the Bible, in context.

I just couldn't resist buying this book when I first saw it in the 1970s. I guess I'm the kind of a guy who likes complete things. And I'm also interested in sorting, so I tried to find out how Strong actually did the sorting for his project, but I've never been able to

count See also ACCOUNT; COUNTED; COUNTETH;
COUNTING; RECOUNT.
Ex 12: 4 shall make your *c'* for the lamb. 3699
Le 19:23 *c'* the fruit thereof as uncircumcised:
    23:15 *c'* unto you from the morrow   5608
    25:27 *c'* the years of the sale thereof,   2803
    52 then he shall *c'* with him,   * "
Nu 23:10 Who can *c'* the dust of Jacob,   4487
1Sa 1:16 *C'* not thine handmaid for a   5414
Job 19:15 my maids, *c'* me for a stranger: 2803
    31: 4 see my ways, and *c'* all my steps? *5608
Ps 87: 6 The Lord shall *c'*, when he writeth "
    139:18 If I should *c'* them, they are   "
    22 I *c'* them mine enemies.   1961
Mic 6:11 Shall I *c'* them pure with the   *
Ac 20:24 neither *c'* I my life dear unto   *2192
Ph'p 3: 8 I *c'* all things but loss for the 2233
    8 do *c'* them but dung, that I may   "
    13 Brethren, I *c'* not myself to have 3049
2Th 1:11 God would *c'* you worthy of this 515
    3:15 *c'* him not as an enemy, but   2233
1Ti 6: 1 *c'* their own masters worthy of   "
Ph'm 17 If thou *c'* me therefore a partner, 2192
Jas 1: 2 *c'* it all joy when ye fall into   2233
    5:11 we *c'* them happy which endure. *3106
2Pe 2:13 as they that *c'* it pleasure to riot 2233
    3: 9 as some men *c'* slackness; but is "
Re 13:18 hath understanding *c'* the number 5585

EXAMPLE 4.

discover it. Maybe some day I'll find a contemporary account in which he was interviewed by a newspaper or something. It was certainly a huge job to be done with 19th-century technology.

Q: Perhaps he used graduate students?

A: Right. I do know how James Murray accomplished the sorting for the Oxford English Dictionary. He and his wife had eleven children; he put all the data on slips of paper and trained his kids to put the slips in order.

Anyway, Strong compiled and sorted a massive database. During the 80s his work was redone by computer and very few errors were found.

Q: Why did he undertake it?

A: Evidently he liked complete things too. According to his preface, "The present work is entitled *The Exhaustive Concordance* ... because it is the only one hitherto constructed that gives all the words of [the English Bible] and all the passages where they are found; and in this respect no Concordance can ever be made more perfect."

I want to emphasize especially his greatest innovation, represented by the numbers at the right-hand side of Example 4—the numbers 3699, 5608, 2803, and so on. These are very important, because they point to the original Hebrew word that was translated

2802. חֶרֶת **Chereth,** *kheh'-reth;* from 2801 [but equiv. to 2793]; *forest; Chereth,* a thicket in Pal.:—Hereth.

2803. חָשַׁב **châshab,** *khaw-shab';* a prim. root; prop. to *plait* or interpenetrate, i.e. (lit.) to *weave* or (gen.) to *fabricate;* fig. to *plot* or contrive (usually in a malicious sense); hence (from the mental effort) to *think, regard, value, compute:*—(make) account (of), conceive, consider, count, cunning (man, work, workman), devise, esteem, find out, forecast, hold, imagine, impute, invent, be like, mean, purpose, reckon (-ing be made), regard, think.

2804. חֲשַׁב **châshab** (Chald.), *khash-ab';* corresp. to 2803; to *regard:*—repute.

2805. חֵשֶׁב **chêsheb,** *khay'-sheb;* from 2803; a *belt* or strap (as being interlaced):—curious girdle.

EXAMPLE 5.

into the English word "count." At the back of the book, Strong prepared a Hebrew and Aramaic dictionary in which every word is given a number. For example, 2803 is *châshab,* a word with many meanings; it not only stands for my favorite subject, "computing," it also means "think, regard, value, forecast, invent." [*Example 5*] When people are doing mathematics they tend to do some such reckoning.

My point is that I could use Strong's Concordance without having to know anything about Hebrew; I only had to know about numbers like 2803. I didn't have to know the Hebrew alphabetic order. I didn't even have to know the Hebrew alphabet. Actually, I've had several chances in recent years to go to Israel, and there I could see Hebrew letters on highway signs, in advertisements on buses, and so on; I've gotten to know almost all of them by now. In 1986 I didn't know anything but Aleph. But 2803? That I could handle.

Example 4 indicates that 2803 corresponds to "count" in Leviticus 25:27, Leviticus 25:52, and Job 19:15; but other Hebrew words were translated "count" elsewhere. For example, in Numbers 23:10, "Who can count the dust of Jacob," the Hebrew original was 4487, a word that means "to weigh out."

If I want to go the other way, to find all verses in which the Hebrew word 2803 appears, the dictionary entry in Example 5 tells us to look in the main concordance under the English words "ac-

3048. λογία **lŏgīa,** *log-ee'-ah;* from *3056* (in the commercial sense); a *contribution;*—collection, gathering.

3049. λογίζομαι **lŏgīzŏmai,** *log-id'-zom-ahee;* mid. from *3056;* to *take an inventory,* i.e. *estimate* (lit. or fig.):—conclude, (ac-) count (of), + despise, esteem, impute, lay, number, reason, reckon, suppose, think (on).

3050. λογικός **lŏgīkŏs,** *log-ik-os';* from *3056; rational* ("*logical*"):—reasonable, of the word.

3051. λόγιον **lŏgīŏn,** *log'-ee-on;* neut. of *3052;* an *utterance* (of God):—oracle.

3052. λόγιος **lŏgīŏs,** *log'-ee-os;* from *3056; fluent,* i.e. an *orator;*—eloquent.

3053. λογισμός **lŏgīsmŏs,** *log-is-mos';* from *3049; computation,* i.e. (fig.) *reasoning* (*conscience, conceit*):—imagination, thought.

EXAMPLE 6.

count," "conceive," "consider," "cunning," ..., "think." Usually there's only one word to look under, but in this case there are quite a few. As I was doing a translation and came across a Hebrew word whose usage I needed to understand, I could find all occurrences of that word in the Bible without great difficulty.

Nowadays the task is even easier, because quite a bit of software is available to do the job quickly on today's PCs. Using a hypertext Bible, you can simply click on an English word to find the original Hebrew word, and from that you can move to the next occurrence of the same Hebrew word, and so on. But in 1985, I had only Strong's.

The italic numbers *2192, 2233,* ..., *5585* on the later entries of Example 4 have a similar function, but they refer to Greek words instead of Hebrew. When you get into the New Testament, you can use Strong's dictionary of Greek words, again operating entirely by number. (The Greek word for "count" that corresponds most closely to Hebrew 2803 is, I think, *3049,* namely *lŏgīzŏmai;* see Example 6.) I learned some Greek letters in college, because I was in a fraternity; and I became quite familiar with most of them later, because mathematicians make frequent use of almost every Greek letter. But again, I wouldn't have had to know the Greek alphabet or its alphabetical order, because Strong's numerical codes made it easy to find anything in his Greek dictionary.

If I hadn't known about Strong's concordance I would never have had the gumption to undertake my own translations of Bible verses. But I also ran across another very important type of resource

EXAMPLE 7.

in the library, namely an *interlinear Bible*. Such a Bible reprints the original Hebrew together with English, in a sort of literal translation written above or below. [*Example 7*] And, in fact, this one not only has the literal equivalents but also Strong's numbers. For example, the Hebrew word in the upper right corner here is Strong's number 1638. I can look it up and find out exactly what it means.

Even though I can't read Hebrew, I like to see the order in which the words occur, so that I can sort of get a feeling for the flow of ideas. I'm sure you all know that Hebrew is written from right to left; in this interlinear Bible the English goes backwards too. For example, the literal English corresponding to the first word of Example 7 is "And He broke"; the English rendition of this whole passage, when you unscramble it, says

And He broke / with gravel / my teeth / He has covered me / in the ashes. / And You cast off / from peace / my soul; / I have forgotten / goodness. / And I said, / Gone / is my strength / and my hope / from Jehovah.

The quotation is from Lamentations, chapter 3, verses 16–18; I'll come back to those verses later. Interlinear Bibles for the New Testament, in Greek and English, are available too.

(I can't help mentioning that I always grit my teeth when I use this particular interlinear Bible, because I can't stand the typography. But I have to admit that it is a valuable resource.)

There is also a tremendous scholarly work, a set of twenty volumes begun in 1932 under the editorship of Gerhard Kittel and nearly complete today, which contains signed articles about essentially all the words of the Bible. Each article assesses the historic usage of that word in detail, discussing not only where it appeared in the Bible but also where it appeared in other ancient literature. Thus whenever I ran into a tough case where it was important to learn about the nuances of a particular word and to understand what leading scholars have dug up about its historical development, I could turn to Kittel. There are ten volumes for Greek and ten volumes for Hebrew, but I mostly made do with a one-volume condensation of an English translation of the Greek portion. In fact the Hebrew volumes were less than half complete when I did my work; they are expected to be fully complete next year.

At any rate, you can see that many resources have been prepared by scholars. And these reference books are actually designed so that it's not only possible for amateurs to do their own translation, it's also fun. It is really interesting — at least for a person like me — to play around and learn a little bit about these languages. And it would have been even more fun if I could just have done the translations for myself, with no obligation to publish them and to take responsibility for any errors. But as I said, I could be sure that even if I made mistakes, somebody else would have made them too.

I don't like to talk abstractly, so let me now show some concrete examples. Let's take Genesis 3:16, the first verse I had to tackle. Immediately when I started the 3:16 project I got into meaty stuff, beginning with issues of women's liberation: [*Example 8*]

EXAMPLE 8. GENESIS 3:16   (KING JAMES VERSION)

> Unto the woman he said,
>> I will greatly multiply thy sorrow
>>> and thy conception;
>>> in sorrow shalt thou bring forth children;
>> and thy desire *shall be*
>>> to thy husband,
>>> and he shall rule over thee.

This is the King James translation, which came out in 1611 and was almost universally used in English Protestant churches for the next 350 years. You can compare it to the New English Bible of 1970, one of the first major new translations into English after the 17th century. [*Example 9*]

EXAMPLE 9. GENESIS 3:16   (NEW ENGLISH BIBLE)

> To the woman he said:
>> 'I will increase your labour
>>> and your groaning,
>>> and in labour you shall bear children.
>> You shall be eager
>>> for your husband,
>>> and he shall be your master.'

Take a look also at the New Jerusalem Bible. [*Example 10*] There was a Jerusalem Bible, from which I learned a lot in the late 60s, and then there was a New Jerusalem Bible. (The New Jerusalem Bible came out shortly before I left Boston in 1986, when I had already completed my draft translations.)

EXAMPLE 10. GENESIS 3:16 (NEW JERUSALEM BIBLE)

To the woman he said:
I shall give you intense
pain in childbearing,
you will give birth to your children in pain.
Your yearning will be
for your husband,
and he will dominate you.

Still another important example is the New Revised Standard Version [*Example 11*]. It's the latest in the long Tyndale–King James line, which tends to be a fairly literal rendition of the original texts; this was a major revision of the Revised Standard Version of the 50s. The Revised Standard Version was essentially a cleaning up of the King James after centuries of change, while the New English Bible took a completely new approach. Here, for example, the phrase "greatly increase your pangs in childbearing" is an updated version of the corresponding phrase "greatly multiply thy sorrow and thy conception" in the King James.

EXAMPLE 11. GENESIS 3:16 (NEW REVISED STANDARD VERSION)

To the woman he said,
"I will greatly increase your
pangs in childbearing;
in pain you shall bring forth children;
yet your desire shall be
for your husband,
and he shall rule over you."

Q: Do you have a feminist version?

A: The interesting thing, of course, as I got into this verse, is the history of how people have misinterpreted the idea of domination through the years; the relevant Hebrew word refers to influence and power but does not imply subjugation. The phrases "rule over you" and "be your master" are not great translations. Indeed, the same Hebrew verb appears in Genesis 1:16, where the sun dominates the day and the moon dominates the night. Even more interesting is Genesis 4:7, where we read that "sin yearns for you, and you can dominate it" — the construction is exactly the same as in Genesis 3:16, with the object of yearning becoming dominant. But I refer you to my book for further discussion, because I don't want to get into such emotional topics right now actually.

As far as I know, there has never been a specifically feminist translation of the Bible, although there are some excellent commentaries going back more than 100 years. The New Revised Standard Version is extremely careful about gender-specific terminology, and generally quite admirable in this respect, but I don't think it is optimum here.

EXAMPLE 12. GENESIS 3:16

> *Turning to the woman, God said,*
> *"Great will be your troubles*
> *during pregnancy,*
> *and your labors during childbirth;*
> *yet you will be filled with desire*
> *for your husband,*
> *and he will dominate you."*

It's time now to show you my own translation, just for comparison [*Example 12*]. In my book I wanted each 3:16 verse to stand on its own, so I sometimes added a few words. Here, for example, instead of simply saying "to the woman he said," as the three modern translations all do, my version is longer in order to set the scene: "Turning to the woman, God said." The concept of turning wasn't really in the Hebrew text, but the point is that this verse continues a story, so I added a word. I also identified the pronoun, saying "God" instead of "he," so that we know who's talking when we see verse 3:16 in isolation. I decided early on that such context-setting amendments would be reasonable if used carefully. In the remainder of the verse I naturally have quite a few words in common with the other translations, but I tried to choose each word carefully — selecting from the best ideas that I found among some two dozen candidates.

The very first verse that I had to translate was not actually Genesis 3:16 but John 3:16 — the familiar words traditionally rendered "For God so loved the world" in the King James Bible. The reason I had to translate it first is that my first priority was to send the English text to Hermann Zapf, who was the calligrapher for this verse. Hermann had to get his work done first, because my plan was to make prints of his work and send them to all the other people who were going to be artists for the book. This verse had to be put into the pipeline first because I wanted Hermann to have plenty of time to work on it.

Here [*Example 13*] is the translation of the verse that I came up with at the time. In this case my goal was a little different: I tried to make the translation maximally different from the familiar text, because the familiar text was so familiar that people couldn't understand it anymore. Oft-repeated phrases eventually tend to go in one ear and out the other. So I chose different words, even though the familiar words might have been more accurate.

EXAMPLE 13. JOHN 3:16

> *Yes, God loved the world so much*
> *that he gave his only child,*
> *so that all people with faith in him*
> *can escape destruction, and live forever.*

As I said, this was the first verse that I translated. And after the book was published I realized that it was by far the worst translation in the book. I made at least two significant errors, but I didn't become aware of them until after going through the exercise of translating all the other verses and then learning a lot more about the Bible during subsequent years.

The first error that I made is when I said "God loved the world so much that . . . "; I didn't realize that the author of this Gospel has a kind of peculiar way of writing sentences that point ahead instead of backwards. So the actual meaning is not that God loved the world so much but that He loved it *so*, in this way. Once you get used to the Gospel of John and the letters of John, you see that this style comes up all the time: The first part of a sentence points to the last part, or to the next sentence.

The other mistake I made here is at the end of the verse, when I said "live forever" where the King James said "have eternal life." I had always thought that eternal life meant to live forever, and in fact it does have that significance in Matthew, Mark, and Luke. But in John's gospel we find other places where it tells us "this is what eternal life means"; and when you actually start to understand the phrase "eternal life" as used in the Gospel of John you find that it is very much analogous to what the other gospels call "the kingdom of God" or "the kingdom of heaven." About 30 years ago, Clarence Jordan published some wonderful paraphrases of the gospels, where he speaks of "the God movement"—a really superb way to translate the idea of "the kingdom of God" into contemporary American English.

After coming to Boston this fall I learned that Paul Tillich spoke about John's concept of "eternal life" in one of the sermons he gave in the 40s. He observed that

... eternal life is a *present* gift: He, who listens to Christ, has eternity already. He is no longer subject to the driving of time.

In later works Tillich developed these thoughts further, speaking of "The Eternal Now." The idea that you can be living in eternal life today, and that it's an ongoing process—essentially a timeless thing—is really what the fourth gospel means by the phrase "eternal life." It doesn't only mean "by and by," it implies "now" as well.

Several years went by after my 3:16 book had appeared, and I kept thinking about these two errors in the translation of John 3:16. Finally I couldn't stand it any longer, and I decided to try again and make a better translation. I wrote to Hermann Zapf, the calligrapher and book designer. He had originally said I could keep the artwork that he gave me for the book. This, of course, was very special because my understanding with the other artists was that the illustrations remained their property; I was paying only for the right to reproduce them. But Hermann said I could keep his original artwork.

To make a long story short, the collection of all artwork for my book traveled around the world, and all the calligraphers eventually decided to donate their contributions to the permanent calligraphy archive at San Francisco's Public Library, thereby keeping the collection intact. This decision pleased me, of course, except for the fact that I would no longer be able to keep Zapf's original piece. So I wrote and said, "Hermann, I'd like to make a new translation of this verse. Do you have time to do the new illustration for me?" And the outcome was perfect, because he sent me a beautiful calligraphic interpretation of the new translation as a surprise for my birthday in 1996. Here then is my new version [*Example 14*]: It might not be optimum, but anyway it's better than it was before.

Notice that I had carefully planned the translation so that Hermann could highlight the word GOSPEL as a sort of acrostic. At the

Yes, this is how God
loved the world :
He Gave his
Only Child ;
So that all
People with faith in him
can Escape destruction and
Live a full life,
now and forever.

EXAMPLE 14.

beginning of the new version I say "Yes, this is how God loved the world: "; and at the end, I explain John's meaning by saying not that people "live forever" but that they "live a full life, now and forever." This I believe is a much better translation than before. And the new artwork is actually downloadable on the Web: If you go to the 3:16 home page that I mentioned earlier, you can click and get a PostScript file that will print this image, and you can paste it into your copy of the book.

As I said, every mistake in my translations was partly excusable because it had been made also by experts. The same is true of the mistakes I made in translating John 3:16. But there is an exception to that statement: There's a case where my translation of one of the 3:16 verses is different from any other, in any Bible that I've ever seen. What's more, I can't believe that any other Bible will ever come out with the same translation that I have. And when I show you, you'll understand why. This is Mark 3:16. [*Example 15*]

EXAMPLE 15. MARK 3:16

> *Jesus chose Simon, and gave him*
> *a new name: 'Rock'.*

All other translations of the Bible naturally use the name "Peter" instead of "Rock." But the fact is, at the time when Jesus called him Rock there was no such name as Peter. Nobody else living had such a name. In fact, nobody is known to have had the Greek name *Pétros*, outside of the Christian community, before 278 A.D.; and the equivalent Aramaic name *Kephâ'* is known only in an isolated legal document from the fifth century B.C. Thus it was shocking for somebody to be called "Rock" at the time of Jesus, or at least it must have raised eyebrows. (Of course we do have a few Rockys nowadays.) I figured that the only way to convey the impact that this verse had, when the gospel was written, was to avoid the name "Peter" which has now become so common. I also think it's helpful to think "Rock" in every other place that the name "Peter" appears in the Bible.

Next I'll show you a translation of Jonah 3:16, which is actually Jonah 4:6 because you've got to go into chapter 4 for this one. [*Example 16*]

EXAMPLE 16. JONAH 4:6

> *Then God made a plant spring up*
> *over Jonah's head, to give him some shade*
> *and to calm him down.*
> *This plant made Jonah very happy.*

When I studied this verse I learned an interesting story about an argument between Saint Augustine and Saint Jerome, concerning how this verse should be translated into Latin. The Hebrew name of Jonah's plant, *qîyqâyôwn*, had almost certainly been translated incorrectly in the Greek Bible that was used in the churches at that time. Saint Jerome was living in the area where this ivy-like plant was common, so he knew the correct word to use. His choice, however, led to riots in some churches; people said, "It must have been a gourd plant, not an ivy plant, because the Greek translation called it a gourd plant. If the Greek translation had been wrong, surely Jesus would have *told* us so." Saint Augustine wrote a stern letter to Saint Jerome, telling him to change the Latin word, because the Greek translation was the Bible known to the Holy Apostles and people were accustomed to it. Augustine said, "Let's not upset the flock of Christ with a great scandal by publishing anything new." Jerome, however, refused to budge.

I sidestepped the whole issue by simply saying "a plant." And I also tried, in this case, to write the translation in the style of a children's story or a fable, because the Book of Jonah has that general character.

Now I would like to talk a little bit about Hebrew poetry, because that led to some of the most interesting aspects of translation. The psalms are poems, and the prophets often spoke in poetic oracles. The convention in Hebrew poetry is to have rhymes of sense instead of rhymes of sound. The more you read such poems, the more you come to understand how they tend to repeat each idea from two different points of view. It's like hearing or seeing something in stereo. In my translations I tried to retain this parallelism together with appropriate English-style parallelism. Here, for example, is a sample of Amos's prophecy: [*Example 17*]

EXAMPLE 17. AMOS 4:1

> *Listen to this, you fat cows of Bashan,*
> *   you women who live on the hill of Samaria:*
> *You, who squeeze the powerless*
> *   and crush the penniless;*
> *you, who order your husbands*
> *   to bring lots of drinks!*

By the way, it's a strange coincidence that three of the 3:16 verses deal with relations between men and women. Many of you know Peter Wegner at Brown University; his wife Judith teaches courses about women's issues in Hebrew culture, and when she learned about my book she was amazed that three of the key verses in her area of study happened to all fall in my sample. Genesis 3:16 is one of them; Isaiah 3:16, which we'll see in a moment, is another; and Amos 3:16 (actually Amos 4:1) is the third. As you can see from Example 17, Amos was a guy who really said it like it is. Up in Samaria there was a lot of exploitation, and he came from more rustic parts of the country.

Here now is Habakkuk 3:16: [*Example 18*]

EXAMPLE 18. HABAKKUK 3:16

> *I heard this and my body quaked;*
> *   my pale lips quivered at the sound.*
> *My bones began to totter, and*
> *   I shook in terror where I stood.*
> *I calmly wait for days to come*
> *   when plunderers will meet with grief.*

When I was translating poetry, I tried to incorporate English poetic elements whenever that could be done in the spirit of the original text, so that the words would sound poetical to people of today. I didn't emphasize this point in the book, but I did actually pay attention to things such as the rhythm of the words. "I HEARD this AND my BOD-y QUAKED, My PALE lips QUIV-ered AT the SOUND, My BONES be-GAN to TOT-ter, AND I SHOOK in TER-ror WHERE I STOOD. I CALM-ly WAIT for DAYS to COME when PLUN-der-ERS will MEET with GRIEF." It scans, anyway. I did that intentionally, although I never intended to read it aloud; one could set it to music. I tried to retain poetic meter if possible, while being faithful to the nuances of the text.

Another thing that occurs in about a dozen places in the Bible is the idea of an *alphabetic poem*. People disagree about why this was done, but the pattern is unmistakable. Chapter 3 of the Book of Lamentations is one such poem. The first three verses start with the letter Aleph, the next three verses start with Beth, the next three with Gimel, and so on; verses 16 through 18, which I showed you in Example 7 above, all start with the sixth letter of the Hebrew alphabet, Vav. Chapter 3 consists of 66 verses altogether, and the Hebrew alphabet contains 22 letters.

Michael Rabin told me about other cases where the first letters of each verse would spell the name of the author. In my book *Concrete Mathematics*, coauthor Oren Patashnik told me he wanted to rewrite the second paragraph of my preface so that its 14 lines would actually begin with the same first letters as the initial letters of a sonnet that he once wrote for his wife. I insisted that such a thing was impossible, but he did it — with great ingenuity, in fact, because he had to hyphenate in one place. I guess I've never revealed his secret to anybody else before today. The idea is that everybody is supposed to read our preface and think that it is perfectly ordinary English, not at all contrived.

Maybe people wrote alphabetic poems for the Hebrew Bible because they wanted their work to be easy to memorize; or maybe they did it because they wanted to express their love for God by working harder than usual. Such poems are not often translated into alphabetic poems in English, although there are a few such cases in the New Jerusalem Bible. The most elaborate examples known to me occur in the translation by Ronald Knox, who was the main Roman Catholic scholar at Oxford during the 30s and 40s. (He is known also as the author of several mystery novels.) His highly original translation of the Bible, published in the 40s, deserves to be better known; I had difficulty locating it in Cambridge last week, although I finally found a copy at Radcliffe Library. (His translation of the New Testament has recently been reissued in paperback, but his translation of the Old Testament has long been out of print.) Wherever Knox found an alphabetic poem in the Hebrew Bible, he translated it into a poem whose first letters were A, B, C, . . . ; in a case like Lamentations 3, the first letters were A, A, A, B, B, B, C, C, C, and so on. Example 19 shows how he rendered verses 15 through 19.

> **Entertainment of bitter herbs he gives** 15
> **me, and of wormwood my fill,**
>   **Files all my teeth with hard gravel-** 16
> **stones, bids me feed on ashes.**[5]
>   **Far away is my old contentment, hap-** 17
> **pier days forgotten;**
>   **Farewell, my hopes of long continuance,** 18
> **my patient trust in the Lord!**
>   **Guilt and suffering, gall and worm-** 19
> **wood, keep all this well in memory.**

EXAMPLE 19.

Incidentally, Knox wrote a charming little book called *On Englishing the Bible*, which is even harder to find than a copy of his Old Testament translation. In this book he captures the joys and griefs of a translator in a better way than I've ever seen elsewhere. He explains the important differences between a *literal* translation and a *literary* translation. And he writes in a delightfully British way, saying for example that "You have to play cat's cradle with almost every sentence in the New Testament, if you want to decide how an Englishman would have said the same thing." He describes beautifully the goals that I also had when I tried to put Bible verses into American English, retaining the sense and feeling of the original as well as I could understand it and express it.

Sometimes it's quite impossible to achieve such goals — and of course a strictly perfect translation is impossible almost by definition — but amazing things are possible. For example, I think some of you will have heard about a famous novel in French by Georges Perec, called *La Disparition* ("The Disappearance"), written entirely without the letter E. The hero of this story is named "Anton Vowl." Perec was a member of a group of Frenchmen called Oulipo, who systematically use constraints to enhance creativity. The amazing thing is that Perec's novel has recently been translated into English — well, more properly, into Anglo-Saxon, because the letter E is forbidden — while totally preserving the alphabetic constraint. The translated novel is, appropriately enough, entitled *A Void*.

Another story from my personal experience illustrates a similar point. In Appendix B of my TEX manual, I worked very hard to prepare a sample English text that would illustrate most of the basic ideas of TEX all on one page. And on the right-hand page you can see exactly what is typeset from the commands shown on that left-hand page. One of the difficulties I faced was the fact that each line could be at most 66 characters long, because of the page size. The Russian translators of this book did an incredibly brilliant job. Although Russian words tend to be 15% longer than English words, they were able to translate the entire example so that it still presents a one-page summary of all the essential features of TEX.

In the case of Lamentations 3, I didn't have to translate all 66 verses, so I decided to start verse 16 with the letter V (corresponding to the Hebrew Vav). Then, just to prove that I could do it, I went on to verses 17 and 18, which are the other verses that start with Vav in the original. My translation [*Example 20*] was also designed to follow another constraint, namely to use a "dirge" meter (which was also present in the Hebrew Lamentations): three metric feet followed by two metric feet. Fortunately such a meter wasn't impossible to achieve.

EXAMPLE 20. LAMENTATIONS 3:16–18

> *Viciously he ground my teeth on gravel,*
>   *trampling me in dust and ashes.*
> *Villainy destroyed the peace I long for;*
>   *memories of joy soon vanished.*
> *Very soon my life will be concluded;*
>   *all my hope in God seems wasted.*

Obviously the message of these verses is sort of a "downer"; the city of Jerusalem was destroyed, and this is a lament. The picture does get brighter, however, later in the chapter.

The Isaiah verse [*Example 21*] is another case where the transition from Hebrew to English worked out reasonably well. The words have kind of a ring that just sort of falls out naturally from the original Hebrew.

EXAMPLE 21. ISAIAH 3:16

> *God says:*
> *"The women in this city are so haughty!*
> *They strut around with heads held high,*
>   *flirting with their eyes;*
> *they mince along with dainty steps,*
>   *jingling with their feet."*

And in the psalm [*Example 22*] it was even possible to make the words rhyme. I believe this is a faithful translation of the Hebrew poem, although it sounds almost as if it were composed in English.

EXAMPLE 22. PSALM 4:8

> *I'll lay me down in peace, and go to sleep;*
> *for you alone, O God, my safety keep.*

The next verse I want to show you is the one that probably fell together the best. It comes from the prophecy of a man I used to call "NAY-hum," but now that I have friends in Israel called "NOKH-um" I pronounce it differently. Anyway here is Nahum 3:16: [*Example 23*]

EXAMPLE 23. NAHUM 3:16

> *Your merchants outnumbered the stars in the sky.*
> *Grubworms strip, then off they fly.*

The reason I'm happy about this is that Nahum's prophecies were terse and enigmatic, something like the sayings of ancient Chinese philosophers. I wanted to preserve his terse style, and I also wanted to preserve the ambiguity of his phrase "grubworms strip." That phrase can be understood in two senses: You can say that these baby locusts are stripping the plants, or you can also say that the locusts shed their skin, thus stripping in a different sense. Fortunately the word "strip" works in English for both meanings. And I could even rhyme "sky" with "fly."

Let's turn now to the New Testament. 1 Timothy 3:16 is one of the most amazing verses in the whole Bible, and I have to show it to you in Greek because it's a poem in Greek. But it's a different kind of poem than we're used to. My English translation [*Example 24*] starts with a few words about the mystery of true religion; then comes the poetic part, in six short lines:

EXAMPLE 24. 1 TIMOTHY 3:16

We know that true religion
is a great mystery: Christ was
*   revealed in body,*
*   justified in spirit,*
*   witnessed by angels,*
*   proclaimed to pagans,*
*   trusted on earth,*
*   glorified in heaven.*

And the Greek for those six short lines looks like this:

ἐφανερώθη ἐν σαρκί,
    ἐδικαιώθη ἐν πνεύματι,
ὤφθη ἀγγέλοις,
    ἐκηρύχθη ἐν ἔθνεσιν,
ἐπιστεύθη ἐν κόσμῳ,
    ἀνελήμφθη ἐν δόξῃ.

The pattern starts with a word that ends with θη, theta-eta; then comes ἐν — or, in the third line, ἀγγ, which sounds almost the same. (An interesting thing about Greek is that double-gamma is pronounced "ng"; thus ἀγγέλοις is transliterated *angélois*, not *aggélois*.) Clearly this is a poetic construction in Greek, probably a fragment of a hymn. None of the English translations I studied were quite able to retain the original spirit. I worked hard to make my translation a fairly good match. Of course I couldn't also make it rhyme.

Then I had to decide how I was going to punctuate the phrases, because the Greek original had no punctuation. Some authors break these six lines into three plus three, while others say it's two plus two plus two. I prefer two plus two plus two — kind of like my lectures in this series, two lectures and a break, then two more and another break, then two to finish. The main reason for preferring a 2+2+2 breakdown of 1 Timothy 3:16 is the pairing of body/spirit, angels/pagans, earth/heaven: something supernatural is always being paired with something natural in this poem. The Greek original was so finely constructed, I wanted very badly to capture its essence properly in English.

2 Timothy 3:16 is another very famous verse, and in fact endless battles have been waged over exactly what it means. [*Example 25*]

EXAMPLE 25. 2 TIMOTHY 3:16

> *All Scripture, inspired by God, is beneficial:*
> *for principles, for persuasion, for correction,*
> *and for education about what is right.*

This verse is ambiguous in the Greek. Does it say that all scripture is inspired by God, or does it say that all of the scripture that happened to have been inspired by God is beneficial? Here I was careful to make a translation that would be equally ambiguous. In other words, if the original is ambiguous, the best translation into English will be ambiguous too; then you can discuss the ambiguity.

The hardest verse of that kind in my sample was 1 Peter 3:16. Here I saw no way to retain the ambiguity that is present in the Greek text. If you look at a dozen translations of this verse, you'll find slightly more than half of them disagreeing with me and about 30 or 40 percent agreeing with the interpretation I decided to favor.

EXAMPLE 26. 1 PETER 3:16

> *Maintain good will.*
> *Then, if people denounce you as criminals,*
>   *they will be ashamed of themselves*
>   *for slandering your Christian conduct.*

In other translations, the Greek that I've translated "maintain good will" is rendered by another phrase like "keep your conscience clear." The Greek word συνείδησις, *syneídēsis,* can mean "conscience" as well as "consciousness." The first meaning refers to the little voice that talks to you sometimes when you're doing something wrong. The other meaning, equally likely in Greek discourse, refers to the sense that you have with respect to a community, the way you relate to others. I couldn't think of any English word to express both meanings simultaneously, so I had to take a stand on what Peter meant in this verse. I studied all the other occurrences of *syneídēsis* in 1 Peter, and I looked carefully at the context of 1 Peter 3:16, and I decided to cast my vote with the second possibility: He wasn't saying "Keep your conscience clear," he was saying "Maintain good will" to others. Still, I know that the majority of translators have voted the other way. So that was the hardest verse of all that I had to translate.

I'll finish now by showing you the easiest verse, the one from Paul's second letter to the Thessalonians:

EXAMPLE 27. 2 THESSALONIANS 3:16

> *May the Lord of peace himself give you*
> *peace, at all times and in all ways.*
> *The Lord be with you all.*

This verse was easy because I had almost no choices to make. I told you earlier about how surprised I was at first to find tremendous variety when I compared different translations of the Bible. The multiplicity of different ways to render an idea in English is a phenomenon that people who work on search engines for the Internet have begun to notice too; they call it "verbal disagreement." But in the case of 2 Thessalonians 3:16 there was almost total verbal agreement. For example, the King James Bible [*Example 28*] says "Now" instead of "May" and it has a few other variations, but mostly it uses the same words as Example 27.

EXAMPLE 28. 2 THESSALONIANS 3:16 (KING JAMES VERSION)

> Now the Lord of peace himself give you
> peace always by all means.
> The Lord be with you all.

Here's the New English Bible:

EXAMPLE 29. 2 THESSALONIANS 3:16 (NEW ENGLISH BIBLE)

> May the Lord of peace himself give you
> peace at all times and in all ways.
> The Lord be with you all.

("Hey, I added a comma!") And the New Jerusalem Bible:

EXAMPLE 30. 2 THESSALONIANS 3:16 (NEW JERUSALEM BIBLE)

> May the Lord of peace himself give you
> peace at all times and in every way.
> The Lord be with you all.

You can see that "The Lord be with you all" is common to every translation. Well, the New Revised Standard Version had to be slightly different:

EXAMPLE 31. 2 THESSALONIANS 3:16 (NEW REVISED STANDARD VERSION)

> Now may the Lord of peace himself give you
> peace at all times in all ways.
> The Lord be with all of you.

Clearly, in this case Saint Paul was pretty much writing in English.

The decision that I made to do my own translations, even though I knew neither Hebrew nor Greek, was one of the best decisions in my life. For I learned that the absolute best way to find out what you don't understand is to try to express something in your own words. If I had been operating only in input mode, looking at other translations but not actually trying to output the thoughts they expressed, I would never have come to grips with the many shades of meaning that lurk just below the surface. In fact, I would never have realized that such shades of meaning even exist, if I had just been inputting. The exercise of producing output, trying to make a good translation by yourself, is a tremendous help to your education.

So I tried an experiment with groups of people; I've done it twice now. I don't make a career of this, but maybe every five years I'll do it again. On the first occasion I went with about 15–20 people to a retreat center in the Santa Cruz Mountains. We arrived on Friday night and we left on Sunday noon, and we brought about 100 reference books with us. We brought concordances, interlinear Bibles, and a variety of translations and commentaries. We had decided in advance that we were going to study a verse from the Book of Luke; so we gathered up all the commentaries on Luke that we could find, in all the church libraries in Palo Alto, and we took them to the hills above Santa Cruz.

On Friday night we rolled dice to choose the verse that we would translate. I cautioned people in advance that this rolling of dice wasn't magic. If the verse turned out to be so good that people fell in love with it, fine, but everybody should realize that we could have done a similar thing with other verses too. The only purpose of the dice roll was to make sure that nobody, including me, could have planned the activities in advance; we were going to learn by osmosis, by absorbing a fresh experience instead of by listening to a canned demonstration. So we rolled the dice and then we went to sleep. I didn't know if our choice was going to be a terrible dud or not; but since the 3:16s had turned out okay for me, I was confident that a random verse would probably be okay too.

Lo and behold, on Saturday when we woke up, I found out that Luke 17:10 was a very interesting verse indeed. We studied it by looking at the helps we had brought along, learning the meanings of the individual words, comparing different translations, and so on. Then we broke into groups, with about four people in each group, and each group made its own translation. One group wanted to make a fairly literal translation, another wanted a modern paraphrase. One of the groups decided to render the words in poetry and make the verse into a hymn; we actually wrote some music for that hymn afterwards, and performed it in our worship service on Sunday morning.

The benefits that I had noticed from my own experience with Bible translation carried over in the same way to everybody in this retreat. We found out that we learned a lot when we tried to put a small part of the Bible into our own words; we agreed that this exercise was an ideal way to get into the real meaning of the original. After this experience we were, in fact, glad that the Bible was *not* written in English; we even felt a bit sorry for Greek-speaking people, who don't have the opportunity to translate the Bible into their own language. We were able to do this sort of thing with the Bible in spite of the fact that we were untrained in Greek, because the experts have made their scholarship available in convenient reference works.

I did a similar thing once again, this time with Stanford grad students, where we had only about ten people and we spent only one day on the exercise. Again it was a very positive experience. My rule when I rolled the dice was that I wasn't going to allow the examination of anything in chapter 3, because I had already been there and done that; I wanted to learn a different part of Luke. Also, I said in advance that if the verse didn't have at least 16 words in it, we would take two verses. I didn't want to get a real short one.

Thus I have a strong recommendation to anyone who wants to get into the Bible: Don't simply read what other people have said about the meaning of a verse; put the verse into your own words, by using the resources that are available. You can do this even though you have just an ordinary, nontheological education.

This morning at breakfast I was reading a book by Peter Gomes called *The Good Book*, which is an introduction to the Bible. At the beginning he said something that I want to repeat to you:

> The notion that [the texts of the Bible] have meaning and integrity, intention, contexts, and subtexts, and that they are part of an enormous history of interpretation that has long involved some of the greatest thinkers in the history of the world, is a notion often lost on those for whom the text is just one more of the many means the church provides to massage the egos of its members.

I hope that some of these personal experiences help you understand why I don't think I was wasting my time looking closely at the Bible. Also, I'm sorry that my sense of timing is off, but I'm ready for questions now.

Q: Professor Hofstadter's most recent book, *Le Ton Beau de Marot*, is devoted to similar issues. I wonder if you are familiar with it and if you have any comments?

A: It sounds quite interesting, but unfortunately I'm not familiar with that book. Thank you for mentioning it. Ask me next year, perhaps.

Q: Are the original Greek and Hebrew words absolutely certain?

A: No. I should have emphasized that. In essentially every one of the 3:16s, I learned that there are quite a lot of differences amongst the extant manuscripts. Scholars have had to collate hundreds of manuscripts and they've tried to reach a consensus about which texts are most reliable. Errors in copying have occurred inevitably, because it's very easy for things to change over the centuries, considering the primitive technology that was available in ancient times. (Even today, with modern computers, we suffer from so-called "software rot," when old programs mysteriously fail to work as they should.) So these so-called textual problems appear everywhere.

Bible translations have occasional footnotes that say "Hebrew obscure" or "Some witnesses read X," where "witnesses" are parchments (manuscripts). And I used to think that textual problems were confined to those places where such footnotes appear in the translations I read. But if you look at 20 different translations, you'll find that different translations have such footnotes in different places — only where the translators themselves thought that the evidence was debatable. The fact is that the footnotes represent only a small tip of a large iceberg; a lot of judgment needs to be made throughout, in essentially every verse, in order to reconstruct a reasonably authentic text.

The first scholar who worked on this, I think, was Erasmus, who did the major preliminary studies in the sixteenth century. His work has been continued by many, many generations of scholars and they have some excellent ideas. Therefore when a footnote appears in a modern translation, it mostly concerns issues where there is still a lot of question about which really is the best available manuscript.

I said last time that when I studied the 3:16 verses, I looked at all of their textual problems in order to see what scholars were saying. For example, there was one case, in Joshua 3:16, where the Dead Sea Scrolls had a better reading than all other extant Hebrew manuscripts. But when it came to verses 3:17 and 3:15 and the rest of the context, I didn't look directly at the textual problems, I just accepted the majority opinion.

Q: You've used the word "better" for comparison, but you really haven't told us what your standard was.

A: That's true. There is no best translation, because it depends on what your standard is. It's the same as saying that there is no best computer program. We'll talk about aesthetics next week, but for now let's just say that there are different kinds of beauty, or at least different kinds of goals that you're shooting for. For instance, a translation for a child will be different from a translation for an adult or for a theologian. When I prepared the translations for my book, I mainly had my children in mind, and they were about 20 years old at the time. My primary goal was to produce a translation that my son and daughter would enjoy and understand.

Like any writer, a translator has to have a target audience clearly in mind. I'm sure that the people who prepared these other trans-lations aren't going to look at my book and say "Oh gosh, I should have done it that way." (Well, some of these aren't bad.) I figure that at the rate I did these translations I could have finished the whole Bible in 65 years. Maybe I would have gotten a little better at it after awhile. But translation is a really serious and difficult job, and these people might very well believe that their translations are much better than mine. Of course they didn't have nearly as much time to work on their versions as I did, because I was only doing a few verses.

Q: You mention that quite a few textual problems are present. How many of those textual variations actually lead to radically different senses of the verse, in your opinion?

A: I don't think radical differences occur very often, but in the book I do discuss maybe three or four cases where different manuscripts will give you a different impression of the meaning. So the odds are something like 20 to 1 that those random verses are affected by textual problems; still, the differences weren't radical.

In 1 Timothy 3:16 there is a big textual problem, however, not in the poem but at the beginning of the verse before the poem starts. In this case some manuscripts had been rigged to give an extra proof of the Trinity; I mentioned the other day that Isaac Newton had studied this carefully, and all scholars have debunked the faulty sources by now.

Q: This is somewhat a nebulous question and I don't know what you can do with it, but it seems like many of the things you've been talking about tell us a lot about humans. Like the transcription errors, what people wanted in the poetry, or the different languages that people speak as they try to convey the same ideas. I'm trying to get a sense of what this process has maybe told you about God.

A: Right; the translation is done by humans but we also have to ask, "Well, what does this have to do with God?" I will try to summarize my thoughts about that in the fifth lecture, but today I should mention the fact that Bible is also an icon. There's a word "bibliolatry," which means "worship of the Bible." Sometimes the Bible can be your God, if you consider it to be too sacred, not realizing the human context in which it came from. This error is what caused the disagreement between Augustine and Jerome that I mentioned earlier. Ronald Knox relates similar events in his book about Englishing the Bible: His translation was prepared for a Catholic church that was very sensitive in those days to any change in the meaning of the Latin text, since their Douay version (unlike the King James) had been translated from Latin instead of from Hebrew and Greek. (Knox used a clever ploy to get his translation accepted through friends in Wales and Scotland.)

At a personal level, I consider that my main goal in life is to do what God wants me to do, so I try to understand what God wants me to do. And I believe that by understanding the Bible I get very good clues about this; in other words, that's what the connection with God is for me. But I don't treat the Bible as a magical thing, as something for which I might just close my eyes, fall down on my knees, and say "I'm going to repeat these blessed words over and over."

I understand a little bit of how the Bible can be meaningful in such ways to other people, but I personally regard it as a medium through which God has been sending messages. And I try to remove as much as possible of the noise that might have accumulated in this channel.

Q: Is it possible to reconstruct original texts by detecting differences and understanding the motivation that people had for making such changes?

A: The problem is that all such assumptions about underlying motivation lead to circular reasoning. The fact that people do edit texts as they copy them allows us to "prove" just about anything we want, if we assume a particular mode of reconstruction. Bible translation is much more difficult than most people realize, because of the imperfect manuscripts and their textual problems.

But after studying these verses, I came to the conclusion that I'm glad the Bible is so challenging. If it all were cut and dried — if everything had been dictated directly by God in imperishable digital form together with check sums and unambiguous authentication — I believe people would soon get tired of it. It would be boring, and I'm convinced that God doesn't want it to be boring. Fortunately, the Bible isn't boring; in fact, it's continually interesting.

Q: With respect to the theme of challenge, you spoke about how a writer has to work harder if there's a constraint such as A, A, A, B, B, B, and you mentioned that the French group Oulipo has explored ways in which constraints affect literature. Since you know a lot about the way constraints operate in computer science, and since you've worked with linguistic constraints in both the original and a translation, do you have thoughts about the different ways in which constraints operate either for the artist or for the general public?

A: I mentioned the author Georges Perec, who was the leading member of Oulipo during the 70s. I believe his works amply demonstrate the thesis that constraints, when properly used, can bring out a writer's creativity. For example, I consider his masterwork *Life A User's Manual* to be one of the greatest monuments of 20th century literature. (Actually I once had the great honor of being invited to a meeting of the Oulipo — in fact, it's easy for me to remember the exact month and day, because it took place on March 16. Claude Berge and Pierre Rosenstiehl are members, so I knew some mathematicians in the group.)

If I look back at my own life and try to pick out the parts that were most creative, I can't help but notice that they occurred when I was forced to work under the toughest constraints. For example, 1967 was surely the most hectic year of my life, but that was the year when I was lucky enough to come up with several ideas that are now considered important, like "attribute grammars" and "Knuth–Bendix completion" and "LL(k) parsing." I actually had no time to do research that year, because *The Art of Computer Programming* was nearing publication, and my wife and I had two babies to take care of, and I needed to be hospitalized briefly, and I gave lectures in five countries on five different subjects, in addition to the classes I was teaching at Caltech. Yet I stole time to look at new things whenever I could; for example, at one conference I remember that I skipped most of the lectures so that I could sit on the beach and do research. I often wonder whether I would have been more productive or less productive if my life had been more stable that year.

My experiences suggest that the optimum way to run a research think tank would be to take people's nice offices away from them and to make them live in garrets, and even to insist that they do non-researchy things. That's a strange way to run a research center, but it might well be true that the imposition of such constraints would bring out maximum creativity.

Notes on Lecture 3

Page 53, home page for the 3:16 book:
`www-cs-faculty.stanford.edu/~knuth/316.html`

Page 53, "Babel Fish": `babelfish.altavista.com`; "Expect Babel Fish to allow you to grasp the general intent of the original, not to produce a polished translation. Machine translation produces reasonable results in many cases. But you should not rely on it." (Incidentally, the Babel Fish is a mythical animal introduced by Douglas Adams in his *Hitchhiker's Guide to the Galaxy*; see `www.h2g2.com`.)

Page 57, The original printing: *The Exhaustive Concordance of the Bible*, by James Strong (New York: Eaton & Mains; Cincinnati, Ohio: Methodist Book Concern, 1890).

Page 58, sorting for the Oxford English Dictionary: See the wonderful book *Caught in the Web of Words* by K. M. Elisabeth Murray (New Haven, Connecticut: Yale University Press, 1977).

Page 58, his work was redone by computer: *The New Strong's Exhaustive Concordance of the Bible* (Nashville, Tennessee: T. Nelson, 1984).

Page 60, almost every Greek letter: For some reason a mathematician almost never needs an "upsilon," and we don't use a differently shaped sigma at the end of a formula.

Page 61, grit my teeth: Example 7 comes from *The Interlinear Bible, Hebrew–Greek–English : With Strong's Concordance Numbers Above Each Word*, by Jay P. Green, Sr., general editor and translator (Peabody, Massachusetts: Hendrikson, 1986). I usually consult *The NIV Interlinear Hebrew–English Old Testament*, edited by John R. Kohlenberger III (Grand Rapids, Michigan: Zondervan, 1979), which is much more pleasant to read although it does not contain Strong's code numbers.

Page 61, tremendous scholarly work: *Theologisches Wörterbuch zum Neuen Testament,* edited by Gerhard Kittel and Gerhard Friedrich (Stuttgart: W. Kohlhammer Verlag, 1932–1979), 10 volumes. Also *Theologisches Wörterbuch zum Alten Testament,* edited by Gerhard Johannes Botterweck, Helmer Ringgren, and Heinz-Joseph Fabry (Stuttgart: W. Kohlhammer Verlag, 1970–2000), 10 volumes.

Page 62, one-volume condensation: Geoffrey W. Bromiley, *Theological Dictionary of the New Testament, Abridged in One Volume* (Grand Rapids, Michigan: William B. Eerdmans, 1985).

Page 62, New English Bible: The NEB New Testament was published in 1961; the full New English Bible in 1970. See *New Light and Truth* by Roger Coleman (Oxford and Cambridge University Presses, 1989), for detailed historical information about this project and the subsequent Revised English Bible (REB) of 1989.

Page 63, New Jerusalem Bible: The Jerusalem Bible had been published in 1966, as an English translation of the French *Bible de Jérusalem* (1956). The success of this translation together with further advances in Bible scholarship led to the *New Jerusalem Bible* of 1985, a direct translation from the original Hebrew, Aramaic, and Greek into English.

Page 63, New Revised Standard Version: Published in 1989, it thoroughly revised the existing Revised Standard Version (New Testament, 1946; Old Testament, 1952; Apocrypha, 1957; New Testament, Second Edition, 1971), and its Web site today still solicits suggestions for further improvement. When I was a student in elementary school, the imminent appearance of this new translation was big news; I made a special effort to purchase a copy on 30 September 1952, the first day it was available in Milwaukee, Wisconsin.

Page 64, some excellent [feminist] commentaries: See Elizabeth Cady Stanton et al., *The Woman's Bible* (New York: European Publishers, 1895, 1898); Carol Ann Newsom and Sharon H. Ringe (editors), *The Women's Bible Commentary* (Louisville, Kentucky: Westminster/John Knox Press, 1992), expanded in 1998; and Elisabeth Schüssler Fiorenza (editor) *Searching the Scriptures,* 2 volumes (New York: Crossroad, 1993–1994).

Page 65, sentences that point ahead: See, for example, John 3:19; John 15:8, 12, 13, 17; 1 John 3:1, 10, 11, 16, 19, 23, 24; and dozens more. John 15:11 takes a possibly more profound meaning if we interpret it in this way.

Page 65, what eternal life means: See especially John 17:3.

Page 66, Clarence Jordan: See his *Sermon on the Mount* (Valley Forge, Pennsylvania: Judson Press, 1952), and especially his "Cotton Patch Versions" of Luke and Acts, Matthew and John (New York: Associate Press, 1969 and 1970).

Page 66, Paul Tillich: *The Shaking of the Foundations* (New York: Charles Scribner's Sons, 1948), quoting from page 36.

Page 66, Tillich developed these thoughts further: *The Eternal Now* (New York: Charles Scribner's Sons, 1963). See also *The Essential Tillich*, edited by F. Forrester Church (New York: Macmillan, 1987), Chapter 13.

Page 66, acrostic: In fact, I had learned as a child that the same property coincidentally held true also in the King James Version, "God so loved . . . Only Son, . . . not Perish, . . . Everlasting Life."

Page 67, made also by experts: Indeed, the dean of all Johannine scholars, Raymond E. Brown, began his translation in the same way: "Yes, God loved the world so much . . . "; see *The Anchor Bible* **29** (Garden City, New York: Doubleday, 1966), page 129.

Page 67, All other translations: To my astonishment, this statement turns out to be false. Immediately after hearing my lecture, Timothy Chow wrote to refer me to *The Complete Gospels: Annotated Scholars Version* (Sonoma, California: Polebridge Press, 1992), where Mark 3:16 is translated thus: "And to Simon he gave the nickname Rock."

Page 68, Greek Bible: The Septuagint, translated by Jewish scholars in Egypt about 200 B.C., is still in use by the Orthodox churches today.

Page 68, stern letter: See St. Augustine's letters 71:5, 75:22, and 82:34–35, in Jacques-Paul Migne, *Patrologiæ Cursus Completus, Series Latina* **33** (Paris: 1841), 242–243, 263, 290–291; English translation by J. G. Cunningham, *The Works of Aurelius Augustine* **6** = *Letters of Saint Augustine* **1** (Edinburgh: T. & T. Clark, 1872), 262–263, 299–300, 344–345; English translation by Wilfrid Parsons, *The Fathers of the Church* **12** (Washington, D.C.: Catholic University of America Press, 1951), 327, 366–367, 418–419. The actual situation was more complex than I have implied: Although the Septuagint called the plant a gourd, Jerome decided to call the plant ivy, following a *different* Greek translation, because he decided not to refer to the actual castor-oil plant (which was unknown in Rome). The original correspondence between Augustine and Jerome took place in 403–405 A.D.

Page 70, *Concrete Mathematics*: a textbook by Ronald L. Graham, Donald E. Knuth, and Oren Patashnik (Reading, Massachusetts: Addison–Wesley, 1989).

Page 70, several mystery novels: See, for example, Ronald Knox, *The Viaduct Murder* (London: Methuen, 1925); Evelyn Waugh, *The Life of the Right Reverend Ronald Knox* (London: Chapman & Hall, 1959).

Page 70, highly original translation: Ronald A. Knox, *The New Testament of Our Lord and Saviour Jesus Christ* (London: Burns, Oates and Washbourne, 1944); *The Old Testament* (London: Burns, Oates and Washbourne, 1949), two volumes.

Page 71, charming little book: Ronald Knox, *On Englishing the Bible* (London: Burns, Oates, 1949). The "cat's cradle" quote appears on pages 5 and 6.

Page 71, Georges Perec: *La Disparition* (Paris: Denoël, 1969). English translation by Gilbert Adair, *A Void* (London: Harvill, 1994). Perec went on to write *Les Revenentes* (Paris: Julliard, 1972), which used no vowels *except* 'e' . . . ; and *this* in turn was translated by Ian Monk as "The Exeter Text: Jewels, Secrets & Sex" in *Three by Perec* (London: Harvill, 1996). "Perec, here, never respects the sterner tenets, never keeps them secret. . . . Wherever we peer, we see decent men felled helter-skelter, wretchedness, demented schemers. . . . E-lessness, *en effet*, never lets her strength be felt. Nevertheless, even here, Perec's glee perseveres. . . . The fetters, then, were never senseless, never mere perverted pretence. These fetters were seeds."

Page 72, my TEX manual: Donald E. Knuth, *The TEXbook* (Reading, Massachusetts: Addison–Wesley, 1984), especially pages 340–341. Russian translation by M. V. Lisina, edited by S. V.

The Servant

words: Dave Luenberger

tune: Doug Owen; setting: Don Knuth

A ser-vant toils with spade and plow, re-turns at dusk to mas-ter's home.

The mas-ter, with no praise, com-mands that din-ner be pre-pared and served.

So you, as well, when toil is done, ask not, nor seek re-ward;

But lis-ten to your mas-ter's word, and re-af-firm your ser-vi-tude.

Luke 17:7–10
Mount Cross, California
17 October 1992

Klimenko and S. N. Sokolov, *Vse pro TEX* (Moscow: AO RDTEX, 1993), especially pages 404–405.

Page 76, Saint Paul was pretty much writing in English: The best translation of this verse might, however, be a phrase that I learned from Rev. Dave Buehler of Providence: "Shalom vobiscum."

Page 78, hymn: I believe that this hymn, "The Servant," is not only singable, it carries a profound message that I did not appreciate before the day of our retreat. (The message is not a popular one nowadays, but popularity does not correlate well with profundity.)

Page 78, a book by Peter Gomes: *The Good Book: Reading the Bible With Mind and Heart* (New York: William Morrow, 1996), especially page 12.

Page 79, Professor Hofstadter's most recent book: *Le Ton Beau de [Clément] Marot: In Praise of the Music of Language* by Douglas R. Hofstadter (New York: Basic Books, 1997).

Page 81, scholars have debunked: I have found no evidence that any Bible scholars were influenced by Newton's paper published in 1733, but they came to similar conclusions. The word in question was θεός (*theós*) in all Greek manuscripts that were known to John Calvin. But Newton showed that this reading was almost certainly not original, and scholars like J. J. Wettstein and K. von Tischendorf independently confirmed that key manuscripts had indeed been altered (in different handwriting from the original). Although Newton thought that the original was ὅ, a relative pronoun of neuter gender, the current consensus based on the best available manuscripts is that the original word was ὅς, which is like ὅ but has masculine gender. See Werner Stenger, "Textkritik als Schicksal," *Biblische Zeitschrift* **19** (1975), 240–247; I. Howard Marshall, *The Pastoral Epistles*, The International Critical Commentary (Edinburgh: T. & T. Clark, 1999), page 505. In my own translation of the word in question I used the word "Christ" to identify the relative pronoun, based on the assumption that Paul was quoting from a familiar hymn in which Christ's name was implicitly understood.

Page 82, cut and dried: See the remarks by Buttrick, quoted in the notes to the panel discussion below.

Page 82, his masterwork: Georges Perec, *La Vie mode d'emploi* (Paris: Hachette, 1978); translation by David Bellos, *Life A User's Manual* (London: Harvill, 1987). The English translation is brilliant, yet it is best appreciated with the French original also in hand, even when one knows only a little French.

Page 82, Oulipo: See *Oulipo Compendium*, edited by Harry Mathews and Alastair Brotchie (London: Atlas Press, 1998). The meeting that I attended on 16 March 1996 was the 425th of the group, which was founded in 1960 by François Le Lionnais and Raymond Queneau.

LECTURE 4: AESTHETICS (3 NOVEMBER 1999)

Today's topic, aesthetics, is a huge subject, very important, and I'm hoping that some of my experiences will help to deepen your own understanding of it. I guess I should start out by saying that aesthetics was the first of what C. S. Peirce, about a hundred years ago, called the *normative sciences*. According to Peirce, the three normative sciences are aesthetics, ethics, and logic. Aesthetics deals with things that are admirable; ethics deals with things that are right or wrong; logic deals with things that are true or false.

It's kind of interesting to look at the history of the word "aesthetics," because up until about 250 years ago it was used in a very general sense, where it referred to anything that had to do with a person's emotions or feelings, the senses. Only in the eighteenth century and later did it become associated with notions of beauty and fine art exclusively. In fact, it's very similar to the word "art" itself, which originally was used to designate anything that was not present in nature, anything that was made by people. For example, the word "artificial" comes from art in its old sense. As time went on, people began to think of art primarily in the sense of fine arts, although we do also have liberal arts and martial arts. Aesthetics went through a similar, even more dramatic evolution in its meaning.

Somehow the whole idea of art and aesthetics and beauty underlies all of the scientific work I do. Whatever I do, I try to do it in a way that has some elegance; I try to create something that I think is beautiful. Instead of just getting a job done, I prefer to do my work in a way that pleases me in as many senses as possible. So I'm really happy that Stanford allowed me to choose my own title when I retired from university teaching: My official title now is "Professor Emeritus of The Art of Computer Programming." I like especially to be associated with art, in the sense of making things of beauty.

Twenty-five years ago I gave a lecture about "Computer programming as an art," and I tried to explain how a person is actually able to write computer programs that are *noble*, truly magnificent. Somebody came up to me afterward and gave me what he thought was a counterexample. "Okay, Don," he said, "what would happen if you were working for a bank, and you had to write a lot

91

of programs in COBOL for this bank." It took me about half of an hour before I could think of a decent answer to that one, but in general I believe that there is a way to find beauty even in COBOL programming.

Back in the 70s, I needed to create the system called TEX because of the books that I was writing. I just couldn't be happy writing *The Art of Computer Programming* if those books wouldn't look good in print. A revolution was taking place in the printing industry, where the tried-and-true machines for typesetting with hot metal type were becoming like dinosaurs. People who knew how to use the old techniques properly were dying out; and the new machines, unfortunately controlled by computers, had lost the fundamental principles of good spacing—especially with respect to technical books that had anything to do with mathematics.

The printing industry was eventually able to resolve the problems for simple books and for magazines, but mathematics got short shrift, so I was beginning to despair. How could I stand to write a book that would look atrocious? Fortunately I happened to notice that the new technology was digital, therefore it was something that I could understand, something that I could control by myself. With digital printing equipment, the only hurdle was a small matter of programming, after which I could produce any page that I wanted. So I changed my whole life plan and spent the next ten years working on the aesthetics of publishing.

Conversely, now that I have TEX, I'm sure that I'm motivated to write better books than I would have written before. Also I have a lot of books now in my library that probably would never have existed without TEX, because their authors shared my feeling that you don't want to write a book unless you will be able to enjoy looking at it and holding it in your hands.

While I was working on typography, I read a story about Herbert Hoover, who apparently discovered that he could work more efficiently if his drafts were set in type rather than typewritten. Whenever possible, he would have galley proofs prepared before proofreading what he had written; then, of course, he would say, "Oh no, I've got to change this word, and delete this phrase." The point was that he could perceive defects or the lack of defects in his writing much better when his drafts appeared in an attractive font. I believe he operated in this way from the time he was President in 1929 until his death at age 90 in 1964.

Thus I know that there are other people besides me who don't like to spend time doing things unless they can also take pride and pleasure in seeing those things turn out to be beautiful.

Soon after I came to MIT this fall I learned about the "aesthetics and computing" project that John Maeda is running at the Media Lab. So I went over there a couple of weeks ago and I talked to several of his students. Boy, there certainly are lots of fantastic new possibilities for engaging your left and right brain simultaneously, now that computers are so fast and we have so many cool ways to make graphics! People have never before had so many exciting ways to combine beauty with technology.

Still, I want to emphasize that I don't foresee a convergence between art and science. Somehow I really think that questions of aesthetics are beyond logic. The way that I know something is beautiful, deep inside of me, seems to be completely different from the way that I know a mathematical theorem is true. And I don't see that this is ever going to change, although of course I can't prove that it will never happen. I certainly recommend that people try to understand emotional, nonrational things using rational means, but I'm not betting that they'll ever succeed. I'm just betting that people will find it interesting to continue getting better and better approximations to an objective understanding of aesthetics.

I do want to mention what may have been one of the earliest major efforts in that direction, because it took place here in Cambridge. George Birkhoff of Harvard published a book in 1933 called *Aesthetic Measure*. How many of you have ever heard of that book? (Okay, we have a few here, good.) At that time, a lot of people regarded Birkhoff as America's number one mathematician, and certainly he would have been placed in the top five by anybody's ranking. His book on aesthetics contains mathematical formulas by which you can supposedly compute how beautiful things are. On page after page you'll find different designs — for example, a hexagon, or an arrangement of squares, or more complex shapes — and underneath each design is a number, like .789. The higher the number, the more beautiful the shape. After dealing with the beauty of lines and curves, he went on to consider pots, I mean vases: With his formula, you could calculate the aesthetic measure of a vase. He also went into music and had numerical formulas for that.

Well, I must say that I've looked at his book and my numerical rankings don't correlate very well with his. Of course he has a right to work on whatever he wants, and he has a right to make big mistakes, just like I do. If I want to try out some ideas, I don't have to succeed.

But I am afraid that Birkhoff actually regarded this as one of his greatest successes. I looked up *Aesthetic Measure* last week in local online library catalogs and learned that there are copies in seven Harvard libraries; in fact, one copy at Widener was actually checked out. So people are still reading it. There's also a copy in MIT's "retrospective collection" (which is, you know, remote storage). His book was translated into Spanish and I also found excerpts published in French and German. In spite of this, I think it's kind of flaky.

I do have to admit that I myself did a similar thing with T_EX. If you try to break a paragraph up into lines and you want to evaluate the quality of a particular way to typeset the lines of a paragraph, I can supply you with a formula that will rate the appearance of any sequence of line breaks; and T_EX actually tries to find the breaks that have the least badness, according to my formula. Thus, I too have tried to measure beauty numerically.

The difference between Birkhoff and me is that I don't *believe* in my measure. I freely admit that it is just a crude approximation, that it tends to correlate positively with good layout but it shouldn't be taken seriously. I developed the formula only because I needed to compute something quickly that would usually not be too bad.

Now I'm planning an exercise for Volume 4 of *The Art of Computer Programming* that will ask readers to compose a piece of music that is optimum by Birkhoff's criteria. We'll see how it sounds.

I just happened to see an interview with John Polkinghorne in the current issue of *Science and Spirit*, where he said, "The mystery of music and the reality of music eludes science." I think it's great to learn more about music and art in quantitative ways, but it seems to me there's a huge gap between what will probably ever be achievable by a rational understanding as opposed to an intuitive, emotional understanding. Even in formal scientific and mathematical work, the elegance of a theorem and the "ah ha!" insights defy explanation. In general, I don't see why there should only be one way to understand things.

I plan to say more about such matters in later lectures, and we could debate these points, but what I want to do today is give concrete examples based on my experiences with the 3:16 project.

That project taught me a few lessons about how some beautiful images can make a real difference in the meaning that I associate with texts.

Those of you who have heard any of my previous lectures know that I prepared a book called *3:16*, based on some informal class sessions at my church where a few friends joined me to look at chapter 3, verse 16 of each book in the Bible. Since we were focusing on these verses, several of the women in the class who were good at calligraphy decided early on that our discussions would be enhanced if they would first write the verses out in nice big letters on a nice big piece of paper. Then we could hold the words in front of us as we were "shining a light" on those verses, trying to figure out what we could about them.

After a few years went by, I began to work on typography and I met a lot of people who were really the best in the world at creating beautiful letters. In particular, it was my great good fortune to become friends with Hermann Zapf, who has designed about twenty of the best typefaces that have ever been invented. Not only is he a great designer, he also is very sympathetic to computers, so I could invite him to Stanford and we could work together.

Therefore when I was struck by the idea that I should write a book about the 3:16 verses, I wrote to Hermann immediately, saying, "Hermann, I've got this idea for a very strange book. I wonder if you would be able to help me design the cover. I would like you to draw for me the most beautiful '3' in the history of the world, and the most beautiful '1' and most beautiful '6' that have ever been seen, and also the most beautiful colon to go between them." Then I tried to explain to him the concept of my book. Fortunately he liked the idea; he wrote back enthusiastically and said, "Don, I'll be glad to do the entire cover for you. And not only that, why don't we ask the top calligraphers of the world to illustrate the individual verses inside the book?"

At the time of the 500th anniversary of Gutenberg's press, in 1955, Hermann and his wife Gudrun had been among the main organizers of a project called *Liber Librorum*, which invited the best typographers from all over the world to print four or more pages of the Book of Genesis in the way they then considered state-of-the-art, 500 years after Gutenberg's invention. This project assembled a wonderful collection of more than 40 examples of fine printing, and it's now very highly prized by book collectors. When I first saw a portfolio of the *Liber Librorum* it almost made me cry, because it was so beautiful — so much more beautiful than I could ever imagine being achieved in any of my own books. It was a really great project.

When I wrote to Hermann in 1985, he envisioned my 3:16 book as sort of an analogous "Scriptor scriptorum" project, involving calligraphers from all over the world, each one doing one verse of the Bible. He knew essentially everybody, and I could drop his name; so we could write a letter of invitation to the people who were the leading calligraphers in each country and say, "Here's a verse. Would you please render this in your favorite way, for a book that will be coming out?" Hermann himself did John 3:16; we printed it as a four-page sample of what would be in the book, so that each artist could get some idea of what we had in mind. We sent out the letters of invitation in July 1986, when I was living in Boston, and 34 of the calligraphers accepted their commission within a month. Soon the artwork began to flow in; it was like receiving Christmas presents every day.

My wife and I soon realized that the artwork we received was so inspiring that we couldn't just keep it to ourselves. A printed book simply cannot capture the true vibrancy of an original piece of art. So we eventually decided to mount the works in frames and to put them into a show that traveled around the world (see Slide 1). It went to Europe several times; it went to Canada several times. The climax came when the exhibition appeared for six weeks at the National Cathedral in Washington, D.C. The works traveled to about 25 different places, and they reside now in the permanent collection of the San Francisco Public Library.

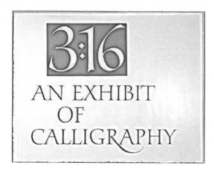

SLIDE 1.

I want to show you some of the items from the exhibit. Unfortunately, you won't be able to see the details as well as if you could see the originals. But I did bring with me the original of my new translation of John 3:16, and I hope you can take a look at it as you walk out afterwards so that you can see an example of true calligraphy. Then you can compare it with the computer printout that is downloadable from the Web. The computer version is okay, but there's really no comparison.

The artists had been asked only to prepare illustrations for book publication, so they didn't actually make their artwork with the idea that it would ever be exhibited. In most cases we obtained their permission afterwards. Here's one of the examples (Numbers 3:16):

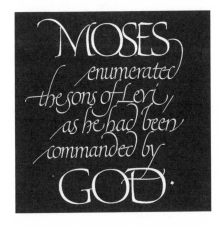

SLIDE 2.

The artist here is Erkki Ruuhinen, who I think is almost certainly the leading calligrapher/designer in Finland. He sent me this particular presentation, a photostat with instructions for printing; for example, if you ever have a chance to compare Slide 2 with the actual illustration printed in my book, you'll see that he asked me to use a different color for the word "God" at the bottom.

You have to remember as you look at all of these examples that I just presented each artist with a sentence or two, a bunch of words that didn't look like much. The calligrapher's job was to find a way to make those words somehow impressive, or rather expressive, to bring out their meaning.

In fact, what eventually happened is that I would keep the artwork in front of me as I was writing the accompanying text. The calligraphy had a great effect on the way I approached several of the verses. You'd have to experience it, I guess, to understand what I mean.

SLIDE 3.

Here's me at the Macintosh (Slide 3). I was working at this time to edit everything into digital form. When I did this, very few book illustrations were actually being printed with the digital technology I was using, although almost all of them are done that way now. Computers were very slow; the process of transmitting four megabytes of data from a computer in one room to a Linotronic machine in the next room could be quite an adventure, taking maybe 15 minutes. The way I prepared the illustrations for this book was certainly much worse than all the commercial methods for printing at that time, as far as expense and time were concerned, except with one big difference: My time was cheap compared to the time of a professional. For me, it was no sweat to spend four or five hours on each illustration, because I had already put a lot more time into writing the chapters; the extra work involved was only a small percentage of the total. But if I had gone to a studio and paid somebody by the hour for time on a big graphic-arts machine, it would have been quite a different proposition in those days. Digital printing technology definitely tends to favor people who want to produce a book just for the love of it.

I did this work at Adobe Systems. In fact, that was one of the great instances of serendipity associated with the 3:16 project: I called up John Warnock, the president; I found the phone number for Adobe Systems, called it and asked for John Warnock, and surprise! He actually answered the phone. I said, "John, I'm thinking about printing a book and I need to have the best software for doing some very beautiful illustrations." He said, "Sure, we've got just the stuff for you," and he gave me permission to come and use their equipment to my heart's content. (I've tried phoning him several times afterwards, and it has never worked again. But for some reason he was on the line that day.)

So for about three months I was the night watchman at Adobe. I worked in a room full of about 50 Macintosh computers, after most people had gone home for the night. The computers weren't very fast, but if I could get several of them going at once I could make good progress. It was something like playing a simultaneous chess exhibition, where a master player makes a move on one board and then goes to the next one and the next. That's what I would do: I'd start a program at one desk, saying "Fill this region," knowing that it was going to take maybe 20 minutes; then I'd go to the next machine.

At this time there was a brand new piece of software in pre-beta-test called Adobe Photoshop, and I was one of the first guinea pigs to use it. I interacted with its chief developer, Tom Knoll, who was in Ann Arbor but he came out to California a couple of times for discussions. My job in general was to take the calligraphy and convert it to digital format so that a printing machine could render it as well as possible; often this meant that I needed to do "fat-bits editing" as in Slide 3.

Yes, God JOHN 3:16
loved the world
so much that he
GAVE HIS
ONLY CHILD,
SO THAT ALL
PEOPLE WITH FAITH IN HIM CAN
ESCAPE DESTRUCTION,
AND LIVE FOREVER.

SLIDE 4.

Slide 4 shows the original John 3:16 that Hermann did. As I mentioned last week, I have a better translation now, so he's given me new artwork that you can look at after today's lecture. (See Example 14 of Lecture 3.)

Gudrun Zapf–von Hesse, Hermann's wife, has designed some very beautiful type fonts of her own. In fact, Hermann told me that he prefers to use her typefaces; her Diotima Antiqua font was widely considered to be the best in the entire *Liber Librorum* project. I knew that she loves the idea of peace, so I asked her to do this verse from 2 Thessalonians (Slide 5), which we talked about last week. (My plan for today is to show you first the verses we were discussing last week, while those verses are still fresh in your minds.)

SLIDE 5.

Consider now Genesis 3:16, as calligraphed by Robert Williams (Slide 6). He's a black man in Chicago, born in 1936, who spent many years working for the University of Chicago Press after

Turning to the woman,
GOD SAID:
"Great will be your troubles
during pregnancy, and your
LABORS during childbirth;
yet you will be filled with desire
for your husband, and he will
DOMINATE you."

SLIDE 6.

studying calligraphy in Great Britain. He had the tough job of dealing here with questions of women's liberation; he decided it would
be best to lighten things up a bit by decorating words like "troubles."

Here's Habakkuk 3:16 (Slide 7), one of the examples of poetry
that I discussed last time. The artist is Karlgeorg Hoefer from Germany, another one of the great masters who has a very unique style.
Any calligrapher looking at this will know immediately that it is his
work; his books on calligraphy give many examples. A few weeks
ago I met his son in Boston, and he told me that his father, born in
1914, is still in good health.

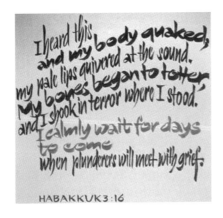

SLIDE 7.

Slide 8 shows the verse about Jonah. Lily Wronker from New
York went to the Bronx Arboretum to make an authentic drawing of
the *qîyqâyôwn* plant featured in this story.

SLIDE 8.

Another verse that we saw in Lecture 3 was this one — remember? — about the fat cows of Bashan (Slide 9). The artist is Peter Fraterdeus of Chicago. He has designed a lot of typefaces recently, and I saw him at the international type designers' conference in Boston a month ago.

SLIDE 9.

The verse from 2 Timothy — "All scripture, inspired by God, is beneficial" — was prepared by David Kindersley (Slide 10). Kindersley is best known for stone cutting and for developing some advanced theories about spacing of letters. I think it's fair to say that most of the top 20 stone cutters in England have been apprenticed to him at some time in the past. The letters here are quite typical of forms that he would have used when carving in stone.

SLIDE 10.

David unfortunately died a few years ago at the age of 80. Many of the artists were in their late seventies or early eighties at the time we asked them to contribute, having devoted much of their lives to working with letterforms. About ten of the other people whose work we'll be seeing have passed away since they did this work.

The verse from Nahum (Slide 11) was rendered by Gunnlauger Briem, a hale and hearty man from Iceland. When the show was reviewed by calligraphers for calligraphic magazines, they cited his work as perhaps most interesting with respect to novelty of the letterforms. They found new ideas here for putting energy into letters.

Nahum 3:16

Your merchants outnumbered the stars in the sky. Grubworms strip, then off they fly.

SLIDE 11.

Last week I spoke about the difficulty of translating the Greek word for conscience or consciousness in 1 Peter 3:16. The corresponding illustration (Slide 12) turned out to be one of my favorites. The artist is José Mendoza y Almeida, a Spaniard who lives in Paris. I was so glad to see that my choice of translation, saying "maintain good will" instead of "keep your conscience clear," helped make this a really nice piece of work.

1 PETER 3:16

maintain
maintain good will.
maintain good will.
Then, if people denounce you as criminals,
they will be ashamed
of themselves
for slandering your Christian conduct.
maintain good will

SLIDE 12.

The next example is by Adolf Bernd of Germany, another man who has passed away. Born in 1909 as the son of a well-known sculptor, he was the oldest of all the calligraphers in the 3:16 project. Throughout his life he had done a lot of artwork of all kinds, including many Bible texts. Notice that in this one, about Peter/Rock, he has placed the traditional symbol for Mark at the top. His way of forming the letters, in watercolors, was quite different from everyone else's approach. I had a great time with Photoshop, filling the colors in with different "alpha-channel masks" as I worked out a custom-made color separation scheme for my book.

SLIDE 13.

Now here's a verse that we didn't see last week (Slide 14). Before going further, I need to point out that when you deal with texts it's not difficult at all to make typographic errors. In this case the calligrapher was Allen Wong from the University of Oregon. I had always liked his work, and I chose him for 2 Chronicles 3:16 because I knew that he liked to put pictures in with his letters. This verse mentions pillars decorated with pomegranates, and I knew that he would make nice-looking pomegranates for my book.

He decorated the tops of the pillars with the chains, as in the inner shrine. One hundred specially crafted pomegranates were attached to each chain.

SLIDE 14.

But he didn't know two things. First of all, he didn't know that the pillars in Solomon's temple weren't marble pillars; they were made of bronze. He put nice marble veining in there, but I couldn't use it because it wouldn't have been true to the text. The other thing is, he added a word. Where he has "with the chains" it really should have said simply "with chains." I tried to talk myself into changing the translation so that "with the chains" would be okay, but it just wasn't right.

SLIDE 15.

Fortunately it's easy to edit a picture with Photoshop, so if you look at what came out in the book (Slide 15) you can see that I simply removed the veining and the extra word. (Well, it wasn't quite so simple; I had to change the 'p' a little bit so that it wouldn't interfere with the word "with.") Then, of course, I checked with the artist and asked if my corrections were okay, and he said fine. I had to do this in seven or eight of the cases, where a difference arose between the translation that I sent to an artist and what actually came back.

Let me show you the hardest such case (Slide 16). The artist here is Donald Jackson from England and the story is kind of interesting, because he's the calligrapher to the Queen and he had done a series of shows about calligraphy on BBC television. He has recently been commissioned by Saint John's Abbey to supervise the first handwritten, illuminated Bible in the modern era, and already in 1986 he was quite a prominent person. Several of the other artists had previously studied with him. I had asked him originally to do the Genesis verse and he said, "No, I'm not into domination; can you give me

SLIDE 16.

another one?" So I gave him the Isaiah verse, which he might have rejected too but in this case he went along. The verse says, "The women of this city are so haughty! They strut around with heads held high, flirting with their eyes;" — and then here he inserted a typo. My translation said, "They mince along with dainty steps, jingling with their feet": not *on* dainty steps, but *with*.

At this point in time Jackson was inventing a new style of calligraphy, done with special brushes; I learned later about shows of his work in which he had done large posters with quotations from Tolkien using this particular style of lettering. I thought it was great as I was digitizing it. In his letter to me, he described it as follows:

> Visceral and primitive and inky was the aim. A feeling within rather than an image as first priority. I loved the translation of the verse and got all the mixed emotions of contradicting kinds — the indignation mixed with fascination for these haughty ladies!

Well, I was sitting happily at Adobe doing fat-bits editing, just about ready to wrap this up as the next-to-last illustration in the whole book, because it was one of the last pieces of artwork to come in. Then all of a sudden it struck me that the words on my screen said "on dainty steps." What? Didn't I ask for "with dainty steps"? I wanted to have a parallel construction: strutting around with heads held high, mincing along with dainty steps. And I didn't think it was possible to mince along *on* dainty steps.

So here was a typo that I just couldn't fix with Photoshop. I certainly couldn't sneak the correct letters into place without doing violence to his whole composition. Oh my! This was the last obstacle to finishing my book, but how was I ever going to get past it?

Already I had had to pull teeth to get this illustration, because we had gone through two rounds of correspondence about it.

Just as I was about to tear my hair out over this problem, I happened to be sitting at a desk in the art department of Adobe, and there next to the Macintosh I was using I spotted a local graphics magazine with a special cover feature: "Interview with Donald Jackson." Lo and behold, there it was and it said, "Donald Jackson is leading a workshop in Santa Clara this weekend" — yes, he was in California, right nearby! So I jumped in the car and before long I was able to talk to him for the first time in person. I explained the problem and he promised to fix it. I had to remind him again later, but I did eventually receive artwork that says "with dainty steps" as required (Slide 17).

SLIDE 17.

When Jackson learned that there was going to be an exhibit, he suggested that we include some of the artists' rejects and rough drafts. He said, "I have quite a pile of them. This will provide a much different perspective than the 'dropped from heaven' impression gained from a first glance at the chosen art work."

SLIDE 18.

Here, then, is sort of a collage that we made (Slide 18) from some of the papers that he would ordinarily throw away as he was warming up. He began getting up to speed by writing "the women, the women of this, the women of this city," and so on. We put a few of these things in the show, so that people could study what goes on behind the scenes when artwork is being created (Slide 19).

SLIDE 19.

The next story I want to tell you was complicated by the communication problems that I faced when dealing with contributors from around the world. Two of the artists in the 3:16 project were from what was then the Soviet Union: one from Estonia, and one from the city of Krasnodar in southern Russia near the Black Sea. Remember that I wrote to the artists in 1986, when Gorbachev was just getting started in Russia and communication was still very difficult. Things sent to that part of the world might mysteriously disappear in the mail; everything was censored.

```
AЖGЖST,14, 1986

ДEAR PROF. ДONAЛД KNЖTH,
ЖANJ THANKS FOR JOЖR KiNД iNviTATiON TO
TAKE PART iN JOЖR BOOK. ЯAM HAPPJ THAT GREAT
SCRiBE ANД ЖETTERiNG ARTiST HEPЖANN ZAPP
HAS PECOЖЖENДiД ЖJ NAЖE TO JOЖ. iT iS VERJ
PЖEASANT FOR ЖE TO ЖAKE THE CAЖЖiGRAPHiC PAGE
FOR JOЖR STAДJ.
ONЖJ TOДAJ 1 CAЖE BACK TO KPAS NOДAR ANД
READ JOЖR THE ЖETTER OF 1ЖЖJ,4 ЖiCH ARRivEД
iN THiS TOЖN ON THE 1ЖЖJ,22. BE SO KiNД
AS TO iNFORЖ ЖE iF 1 ЖAJ STiЖЖ ЖAKE THAT ЖORK
FOR JOЖR BOOK.
ANД ЖHAT ДATE 1 ЖЖST SENД iT TO JOЖ?
ЖEANЖАiЖE ,1 STARTEД TO ЖORK AT THE QЖOTATiON
JOЖ GAVE ЖE AT ONCE FOR ЖJ PЖEASЖRE.
          CORДiAЖЖJ, ЖEONiД.
P.S. THE ЖABЖE OF THE AДДRESSES JOЖ PASTEД ON
THE ENVEЖOPE iS BEAНTiFЖЖ .

Леонид Проненко, 350065 Краснодар,
ул. Невкипелова,15-67  СССР
```

SLIDE 20.

Here (Slide 20) is the first letter I received from the artist Leonid Ivanovich Pronenko. It was fun because he had invented a unique way to type English using a Cyrillic typewriter. For example, in order to make an 'N' he did two 1's and drew in a bar by hand. To do a 'U' he typed the Russian 'I', which is like a backwards 'N'. To get an 'R' he took a 'P' and added a diagonal line. And so forth. He found as many usable Russian letters as he could. It turned out that mail from me needed only two weeks to get from Boston to Krasnodar, but more than six weeks went by before I received his cordial reply.

I had asked him to do 1 Timothy 3:16, and here (Slide 21) was his solution, received some months later. This is the passage I talked about in Lecture 3, the wonderful Greek poem that says "Christ was revealed in body, justified in spirit, witnessed by angels, proclaimed to pagans, trusted on earth, glorified in heaven."

SLIDE 21.

Several years went by before I was ready to prepare the artwork for final publication. And at the last minute, I discovered that my translation wasn't optimum. After further study of the original Greek in this verse I realized that the word "acknowledge" in the top line of Slide 21 is not really best. Instead of saying "We *acknowledge* that true religion is a great mystery," I should rather have said "We *know* that true religion is a great mystery," because of the context of those words. But I couldn't ask Pronenko to redo his artwork, because of the difficulty of communication and the long time delay involved.

Well, fortunately the word "know" is a subset of the word "acknowledge"; and Adobe Photoshop has a wonderful feature called the cloning tool. Since I couldn't ask the artist to change the words,

I did it myself with Photoshop. Here is the result that appears in the book (Slide 22). Pronenko had written the words on parchment, which he tore into little fragments and pasted to a base. By using the cloning tool, I could preserve the torn edges of parchment, while shortening the word just as if he had done it himself. I don't think you can detect my splicing even with a magnifying glass.

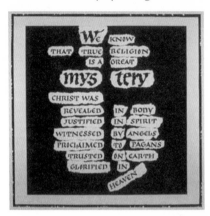

SLIDE 22.

   I also changed his art in another respect, because I felt it was important to illustrate the parallelism in the Greek poem. (I told you last week about the trouble I had taken to render this parallelism in English, using the words "revealed," "justified," "witnessed," "proclaimed," "trusted," "glorified" for the six lines of the poem.) Thus I had to move the word "revealed" down from Pronenko's original position in Slide 21 to its new position in Slide 22.

   Now comes the part of the story where I have to make a terrible confession. The exhibit of original artwork traveled to many parts of the world, as I said, and at one point it was in Canada where a TV show was made — a documentary of the exhibition. The commentator proceeded for half an hour to visit the different works in the collection, and afterwards I received a video of the show. When they got to Pronenko's work (Slide 21), the commentator said, "Look how this man in Russia has cleverly concealed an Orthodox cross between the lines of his pattern." (An Orthodox cross always includes a bar that's sort of at an angle near the bottom; I've been told that this symbolizes where Christ stepped off the cross.) Sure enough, here in the background between the letters he had definitely introduced a cross shape, and the diagonal placement at the bottom clinches the argument. I was completely unaware of this aspect of Pronenko's design, and alas! I had destroyed it. If only I had been able to check with him beforehand, this dreadful error would not have appeared in my book.

Well, I went back to Photoshop and made a further correction, so that 1 Timothy 3:16 finally has the artwork it deserves (Slide 23). The new image is available for downloading on the Web, and if enough copies of the book are sold we will be able to use this correction in the third printing. It's a sad story, but I have to admit that I blew it.

SLIDE 23.

Another illustration that I like very much came from another country behind the Iron Curtain. Edit Zigány of Hungary did 2 Corinthians (Slide 24). I think the way she has emphasized the word "LORD" is just great.

SLIDE 24.

Kerstin Anckers from Sweden is the person who for many years did the calligraphy for Nobel Laureates. If you got a Nobel Prize, she would be the one who made your certificate. When she sent me this artwork for Ephesians 3:16 (Slide 25), she wrote, "It was marvelous, the day that I received my verse, I really *needed* those words. God is so nice, He always knows! I hope you like what I have done, and that you can see it as a prayer moving upwards."

May GOD,
who is
SO RICH IN GLORY,
grant you
additional strength
through HIS SPIRIT,
so that
your inner selves
will be
powerful.   SLIDE 25.

Five years later my wife and I were visiting a mathematics institute in Sweden, so we called her up and asked if we might meet her in person. She invited us to her studio on one of the islands east of Stockholm, and to my surprise she had made two copies of this illustration. One was for me and one was for herself, and she had kept her own copy in the studio right over the desk where she works. I marvel at the wonderful way in which she was uplifted by the words in the assignment I had given her.

The next example (Slide 26) came from Czechoslovakia, in the part now called Slovakia. The artist, Lubomír Krátky, did a very clever thing here, because in this verse St. Paul is essentially "writing between the lines." Paul is being very rabbinical when he discusses a passage from Genesis in his Galatians 3:16. He says, "Notice that the promises were addressed to Abraham and to his offspring"; and then, sort of in parentheses, Paul adds that "the passage does not say 'and to off-springs' in the plural; it uses the singular, 'and to your offspring' — meaning Christ." Krátky decided there-fore to actually write between the lines, using red letters (which

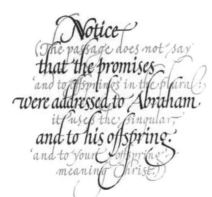

SLIDE 26.

look gray in this reproduction of Slide 26). I had a lot of fun reconstructing the portions of his strokes where red and black lines cross each other, because the scanner did not pick this up very well. Even if the overlapping colors had gotten through the scanner, I doubt if the necessary color separation could have been done automatically, because that is a very hard thing to do in software.

Judges 3:16 is an interesting passage that is strongly related to left-handedness, so I asked a left-handed calligrapher to do this one (Slide 27). His name is Robert Borja, a teacher of calligraphy and former president of the Calligraphic Society in Chicago. He emphasized the "handedness" by writing the text in mirror image: "Ehud made himself a short double-edged sword and strapped it to his right thigh underneath his clothes." The fact that the sword was on Ehud's right thigh where he could reach it with his left hand is an important element of this ancient Bible story. The left part of this illustration was not obtained photographically from the text on the

SLIDE 27.

right; it was written in mirror image just as it appears here. Borja told me that he often writes in mirror image when he's teaching a class, because he is left-handed.

Tim Girvin did this verse from Micah (Slide 28). Tim is a designer in Seattle who is quite famous for creating such things as the Banana Republic logo. When I communicated with him, I would generally have to do so indirectly through one of his associates. This is a well-known verse that Martin Luther King, Jr., used in his Nobel Prize speech: "People will dwell in the shade of their own grape vines and their own fig trees; nobody will make them afraid. For God Almighty has made this decree." Girvin created a nice tendrilly rendition of those words, and it was a challenge for me to capture his artwork in digital form without allowing the strokes to become too dark at the points where they join together.

SLIDE 28.

Another favorite (Slide 29) is from Revelation 3:16. The designer here, Rick Cusick, has long been head of the lettering department for Hallmark Cards, and he's also the main editor of *Letter Arts Review*, the leading calligraphy magazine in America. Here the verse says, "Since you are merely lukewarm — neither cold nor hot — I'm going to spit you out of my mouth!" And you can see all the dark spots.

When we mounted the exhibit, we asked each artist to comment on the approaches they had taken, and Cusick sent back a very interesting reply. We had told each artist that the book would be printed with a nonstandard palette of colors, using lines of solid ink for crispness instead of using the normal CMYK ("cyan-magenta-yellow-black") process colors with halftoning. The solid colors available to the artists, besides black, were a nice "Chinese" red, a

SLIDE 29.

rich blue-green, and a sort of parchment color. Cusick said that he started out trying to use all four of those colors, but then finally the solution hit him just to do everything in one solid color, but with this idea of spit coming through. Less is more.

I love it. This is kind of a climactic verse in the 3:16 project, actually; it talks about the idea that apathy and lukewarmness are worse than being cold or hot, worse than the extremes.

One of the strangest episodes occurred with the man from Poland, Andrzej Kot. It was quite mysterious. We wrote him the letter of invitation from Boston, and after I had returned to California a few months later a package arrived from Poland. It was a big package, full of all kinds of bookplates — about ten copies of each of about 30 bookplates. My wife and I looked at them and they were very interesting, but what kind of package was this? No letter, nothing else. At this time there was a lot of censorship in Poland, as in Russia, and Solidarity was getting organized; people's letters were all being read if they came from abroad. Anyway, Kot sent us this big package full of all kind of bookplates.

Two weeks later another package of bookplates arrived at our house, but this time we also received some examples of wedding invitations and other graphics that Kot had done in his unique style. My wife made a nice little booklet out of these. Another big package arrived a few weeks after that, and this time what do you know, here were five solutions to the verse that I had asked him for! "Elisha declared, 'Here is what God says: Pools of water will fill this dry riverbed.'" (This is 2 Kings 3:16; see Slide 30.) Maybe Kot was trying to get the censors warmed up to the idea that he often sends artwork to California, before sending me the real thing? I found out later that Alan Blackman, a calligrapher in San Francisco, had

SLIDE 30.

also received mysterious packages of bookplates from Kot at about the same time. For whatever reason, Kot's submission to the 3:16 project came in this peculiar fashion. We received five illustrations to choose from, using different styles of letters inside a fanciful fish.

SLIDE 31.

Slide 31 is the one I liked best of the five, but unfortunately it had a typo; he left out the word "fill," and there was no way I could stick that word in by computer editing. So I couldn't use this version, and I went to my second favorite for reproduction in the book (Slide 32). These drawings are huge actually, about three feet wide.

SLIDE 32.

There's something special about Kot's style . . . when the magazine *U.S. News & World Report* reviewed the 3:16 book, this was the illustration that they chose to use as a sample. Also *Die Zeit* in Germany chose the same one, from among all 59 verses illustrated. When I visited the Gutenberg Museum in Mainz in 1987, I noticed some of Kot's work on display there; it is instantly recognizable.

We still didn't have any letter from him, but we knew that he'd received payment for his contribution because he endorsed the check that we had sent. (His signature is interesting because it includes a little picture of a cat. I suppose "kot" is Polish for "cat.")

Several years went by and we started to make preparations for the art exhibit. As I was rummaging again through all of the illustrations that we had decided not to use in the book, I came across a piece of paper that looked like it contained a lot of funny markings, where maybe Kot had been sharpening his pencil or getting warmed up — strange letterforms going in all directions. But as I looked at it once again, the thought occurred to me that maybe those markings were words in Polish. That month we had a Polish visitor in Stanford's computer science department, and I showed it to him; sure enough, this was a letter that Kot had sent me three or four years previously. His letter had said, "I need pens. I need chocolate." Immediately we sent out a Care package to his address in Poland. But we never heard from him again, and several Polish people I know have been unsuccessful in learning whether or not he is still alive.

We have learned the meaning of *love,* because the Holy One laid down his *life.*

Just as he did this for us, we too should lay down our lives for each other.

SLIDE 33.

The calligrapher of 1 John 3:16 (Slide 33) was Jeanyee Wong, who lives in New York City. Like many of the other artists, she too is in her late seventies now. I have enjoyed her elegant style in many other works. For example, do any of you own the ten-volume set of history books by Will and Ariel Durant? Jeanyee Wong is responsible for the beautiful calligraphy on the covers of those books.

The next example I want to show you (Slide 34) is by Michael Harvey of England. He is a prominent type designer and book designer as well as calligrapher, another man who I was able to greet at the recent conference on typefaces. The style here is uniquely his and I like it very much.

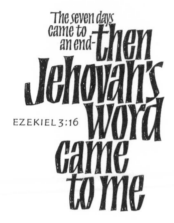

SLIDE 34.

Now it's time to look at the artwork that proved to be hardest of all to edit into electronic form for publication. Derick Pao in Hong Kong had developed a special way to take calligraphy and emboss it somehow on handmade paper. After doing that he would shine a "raking light" from the side, so that you could see the image. It's a very beautiful 3-dimensional effect, but I couldn't digitize it satisfactorily from the slide he sent me. So I asked him to send me the original artwork, which you see here (Slide 35).

Meanwhile I had noticed, while working on the other illustrations, that the digital scanner I was using would occasionally pick up things that I couldn't easily see on the artwork—things like Snopake (also called "whiteout"). Artists weren't forbidden from using whiteout on this assignment, because I had only asked them for calligraphy of publication quality, not necessarily for exhibition. But when I looked at a scanned image, after the artist had painted it with whiteout, I could see shadows that looked something like mountain ranges seen from above.

SLIDE 35.

Therefore it dawned on me that I could digitize Derick Pao's artwork by simply putting it in the scanner. The scanner had its own sideways light, which picked up the 3-dimensional aspect perfectly, even though the paper had a uniform color and no ink had been used. Thus, the side effect I had been fighting in some of the other illustrations turned out to be just what I needed in this case.

I had another problem as well, however, because his illustration was too big for the format of my book. The handmade paper had an interesting texture, and I wanted to retain the "organic" effects at the edges; but those edges were much too far away from the calligraphy. So once again I used Photoshop's wonderful cloning tool. I broke the original image into nine parts and reassembled them, after cutting the excess paper away. (The cuts were of course "virtual," not actual. I dare you to find the seams where I stitched the nine pieces together again electronically; I don't think they are detectable.)

SLIDE 36.

I had to switch to dark red for the background color, although Pao's original artwork was done on light yellow-brown paper, because the words weren't sufficiently visible otherwise. And I had to work painstakingly by hand, removing pixel by pixel with the mouse, in order to do the necessary color separation (Slide 36). So as I said, this illustration was the most difficult to prepare for publication. But I'm happy with the way it turned out.

Steven Skaggs sent me a great design that you can't see too well here (Slide 37) because I had to make some overlays with a lighter color. To illustrate the text from Hosea, "Orgies with old wine and new wine are making my people lose their wits," he took the letters for "orgies" and made them look like smoke wafting into the air, with the letters repeated and partly shown in rotation. When I first prepared this image, my combination of the individual layers and color separations was slightly off; the letters didn't fit together quite as well as on his original. Fortunately my wife caught this error just before the book went to the printer.

SLIDE 37.

The artist for Joel 3:16 was Friedrich Peter, who teaches art in Vancouver, B.C. He felt that this particular verse was so powerful that he couldn't do justice to it, and he kept sending me more and more solutions after I had already digitized the excellent one he had sent me in the first place. The verse says, "On that day God will roar from Mount Zion," and I kept getting packages from him with new approaches in which he said he couldn't resist trying again to capture the force of those words. Slides 38, 39, and 40 are three of his pieces that we put into the exhibit after I had already finalized the artwork in the book.

I show you these primarily because we noticed strong differences in the ways that people reacted to the show. I mentioned, for

SLIDE 38.

example, that *U.S. News* and a lot of other people loved Kot's work the best, while others would much prefer the style of Hermann Zapf, and still others gravitated to other artists. A lot of my German friends were especially fascinated by the Sturm und Drang in Friedrich Peter's style; they looked at it and said, "Wunderbar." I was reminded again that there are many different standards for beauty.

SLIDE 39.   SLIDE 40.

The refined style in Slide 41 is more suited to my own taste. The artist here, Guillermo Rodríguez-Benítez, was a prominent banker in Puerto Rico. He loved calligraphy and decided in his fifties to become apprenticed to master calligraphers, after which he became a master himself. He died a few years after doing this absolutely gorgeous interpretation of Philippians 3:16, in miniature on very delicate red paper.

SLIDE 41.

Claude Dieterich is a Frenchman with a German surname who was living in Peru when I requested him to do the verse from Jeremiah (Slide 42); now he lives in San Francisco and I've been able to get to know him. (In general I find that calligraphers are just about the nicest people I've ever met.) This work, in which he focuses attention on "The Ark of the Covenant of the Lord," is one of my absolute favorites in the book. But I have to keep moving fast through these slides because I have an abundance of riches to show you today.

SLIDE 42.

If anyone is more famous as a calligrapher than Hermann Zapf, it is Friedrich Neugebauer of Austria. This contribution (Slide 43) is an example of his absolute mastery. There's no such thing as whiteout on this; in every way its form is incredibly good. His unique and easily recognizable style is featured in his books on the subject.

After my book was published, Neugebauer asked for a copy of unbound signatures. He took them apart and mounted all the artwork in frames, setting up a show that was exhibited in several

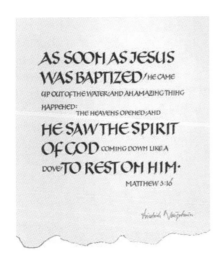

AS SOON AS JESUS
WAS BAPTIZED/HE CAME
UP OUT OF THE WATER/AND AN AMAZING THING
HAPPENED:
        THE HEAVENS OPENED/AND
HE SAW THE SPIRIT
OF GOD COMING DOWN LIKE A
DOVE TO REST ON HIM·
MATTHEW 3:16

SLIDE 43.

Austrian museums. The fact that a master like Neugebauer would not think I had ruined the art with my computer editing was great news for me.

Jean Evans of Cambridge, who lives near Harvard Square, did 2 Peter 3:16, which is an interesting passage (Slide 44): "Paul says this in all of his letters, whenever he refers to these things. Some of his writing is hard to understand; ignorant and insecure people distort his words, just as they twist the rest of the Scriptures, and they destroy themselves in the process." Since the words speak of Saint Paul's hard-to-understand writing, Jean used sort of a code in which you have to decipher the letters as you go.

SLIDE 44.

Tim Botts is one of the great calligraphers of Bible verses, and he has illustrated several books that feature his favorite texts. I asked him to do Luke 3:16 (Slide 45): "John told everybody, I am baptizing you with water. But someone more powerful is coming; I'm not even fit to untie His shoes! He will baptize you with a holy Spirit, and with fire." I want to point out especially the part of the translation where it says "a holy Spirit"; most translations say "the Holy Spirit." I went with the minority view in this case, because it reflected the original Greek text of Luke's gospel. Tim phoned me to check whether I had done this intentionally; I assured him that leading Bible scholars, such as Joseph Fitzmyer, had translated it in the same way.

SLIDE 45.

This led to an interesting little story. A magazine called *The Lutheran* chose this illustration for the cover of one of its issues a few years ago. Afterward somebody wrote a letter to the editor, saying that the Devil had gotten into *The Lutheran* because their cover denied the doctrine of the Trinity. He was shocked that this magazine would say "a holy Spirit," instead of "the Holy Spirit" as his own Bible did. One day I was walking in the hallway at Stanford and my secretary called out the door to me and said, "Don, what translation did you use in your book?" I replied, "It was my own translation"; so she told the person on the phone, "He did his own translation." It turned out that this was the editor of *The Lutheran*, and I didn't have any chance to discuss the situation with him. But everything turned out great. The editor responded quite properly that the reader should look at the original Greek, and should realize that the people who first heard the words of Luke 3:16 wouldn't have understood who "the Holy Spirit" was.

Ismar David did Leviticus 3:16 in his inimitable style (Slide 46). He had been part of the *Liber Librorum* project that I mentioned earlier, and when he died three years ago at age 86 he had spent much of his lifetime making beautiful editions of Biblical texts in Hebrew and English. Several of his books on Hebrew calligraphy are also available. In this example he has combined the English translation with an old style of Hebrew letters.

SLIDE 46.

I'm getting near the end, but I have to tell you a wonderful story about a man in Bombay, a calligrapher named Satyanarayan Mallayya Wadisherla who is an absolutely brilliant artist. He works for the *Bombay Times* and lives in some kind of a commune near the city, and I asked him to do 2 Samuel 3:16. He had never seen Bible verses before, but he was enthusiastic about this project because he was a great admirer of Hermann Zapf. He sent me back ten solutions to the problem of interpreting these words visually, and I had to choose only one for my book. I could very happily have chosen at least three of his contributions.

The verse in question, 2 Samuel 3:16, is part of a very touching Bible story that's not well known at all; at least, I had not known about it before I looked at the 3:16s. "Michal's husband walked behind her, sobbing, as far as Bahurim; then Abner ordered him to go back. So he went back." In this story King David had stolen Michal away from her husband. One of Wadisherla's approaches to this text, shown in Slide 47, was actually done with grains of sand, real sand. He applied paste to heavy paper and embedded the letters in grains of sand.

SLIDE 47.

Slide 48 shows another variation, in beautiful brush lettering.

SLIDE 48.

And in Slide 49 he used actual tears. He did the lettering with water-colors, then he used his own tears to enhance the effect of sobbing.

SLIDE 49.

Yet another version, with colored letters, featuring a big teardrop coming out of the eye, appears in Slide 50. Faced with so many beautiful and poignant illustrations, which one would you choose?

SLIDE 50.

The one that I actually chose, Slide 51, captivated me even more than the others. The main reason I settled on this one for the book was that the letterforms in this version are distinctively Indian. Besides their inherent gracefulness, they are imbued with a certain feeling that you cannot find anywhere else in the world. And as I said, Wadisherla sent me five more illustrations in addition to the five that I have just shown you.

SLIDE 51.

The last example I want you to see, however, is my absolute favorite of favorites (Slide 52). Julian Waters, who has been art director for *National Geographic* magazine among many other activities, did 1 Samuel 3:16: "Eli called him, saying, 'Samuel, my son.' And he answered [in a tiny voice], 'Here I am.' " You have to know the story to realize how great this is, because Samuel is sort of saying "Here I am" very timidly; this aspect has been captured perfectly with the weights of the strokes. As I was sitting at the computer screen digitizing these letters, they looked wonderful even at 100 times their true size. It was a treat to work with Julian's strong letterforms.

SLIDE 52.

The full title of my book, *3:16 Bible Texts Illuminated*, was suggested by my editor because the word "illumination" has a double meaning: Medieval manuscripts are said to have been illuminated by the monks who calligraphed them, and my book tries to shine a bright light on those verses as it explores how people have understood them. To me, there's actually a third meaning as well, where illumination stands for something like extrasensory perception coming through.

Walt Whitman, speaking to artists in 1851, said, "to the artist has been given the command to go forth into all the world and preach the gospel of beauty." In these slides I've shown you many examples of calligraphers working with Bible texts, and I think most of you know that other religions have even stronger connections with calligraphy. For example, calligraphy is intimately connected with the religious traditions of China and Japan. And right now at Harvard, a great exhibit of Islamic calligraphy has been mounted at the Sackler Gallery. I have the catalog here and it mentions an Islamic maxim: "Calligraphy gives greater clarity to truth." And the title of the catalog, which they chose from another Arabic metaphor, says that calligraphy is "Music for the eyes."

Let me summarize by saying that many people's most deeply felt religious experiences are connected with music and/or fine art. I think that in the future, mystical experiences will no doubt be associated also with new media such as computer generated videos. And fine art will enhance not only religious, mystical things, it will also enhance expositions of science and technology. I believe that our aesthetic experiences somehow transcend science, and I hope that the examples I showed you today illustrate why I think that rationality covers only a relatively small part of life.

I spoke even longer today than before, but there still is time for questions.

Q: Did you start by scanning in the actual artwork?

A: Yes, except in the case of Daniel 3:16. In that case the artist was head of type design at Adobe, and he presented me with a PostScript file that I could use directly.

The scanners weren't very good in those days, and the best one available to me (made by Microtek) had some bugs if you tried to get high resolution on a wide image. I had to edit those bugs out. Large pieces of art had to be scanned in two or more narrow sections, then spliced together electronically with Photoshop.

I tried most of the time to convert the calligraphy to line art, usually at a resolution of 600 dots per inch, instead of using a halftone screen. The conversion to line art was very delicate, and it was different for each piece because of the different colors and textures of paper that the artists had used. I had to do a lot of editing on individual pixels where strokes come together, to open the joints up so that ink would not fill in when my book was printed. Very small changes in the threshold for bitmap conversion would make large changes in the character of the letterforms. The tendrils on the grapevines in Slide 28 were particularly challenging. And when white letters were drawn on a dark background, as in Slides 5, 24, and 41, the problems were reversed. I can't imagine automating much of what I did.

Q: It seems to me that the purpose of art is to communicate emotion. The artist is trying to make someone experience something they've never felt before. I can also see crafts as being beautiful; arts and crafts both have beauty in them. But I can only see a computer program as a craft. I can't see how a program can communicate an emotion.

A: I guess you're right; I can't write a computer program . . . well, I might be able to animate something. But when I talk about beauty in programming, I'm thinking of it more in the way that you might think of beauty in literature, where you encounter something that really clicks because it's so elegantly stated or so obviously right.

Long ago when I was a college student, I was learning about compilers and assemblers by reading code, and I got hold of a program from IBM called SOAP, written by Stan Poley. That program was absolutely beautiful. Reading it was just like hearing a symphony, because every instruction was sort of doing two things and everything came together gracefully. I also read the code of a compiler that was written by Alan Perlis and some of his colleagues; that code was plodding and excruciating to read, because it just didn't possess any wit whatsoever. It got the job done, but its use of the computer was very disappointing. So I was encouraged to rewrite that program in a way that would approach the style of Stan Poley. In fact, that's how I got into software.

Such things are obviously very subjective, but I do think issues of style do come through and make certain programs a genuine pleasure to read. Probably not, however, to the extent that they would give me any transcendental emotions.

Q: What did you mean when you said that the compiler program was "plodding" along?

A: It would put something in one register and then move it into another. It operated by brute force. It would do in twelve instructions what you should have done in three.

Q: What was it like using a computer program to design a typeface?

A: Designing a typeface is an interesting case. People like to talk about proving programs correct, and with a lot of programs you can use formal methods to verify their correctness. But when I was writing programs to draw letterforms, there was no way that I could prove that the output was going to be, for example, a beautiful letter A. I would just have to try it and look at the results, and hope that when I'd invoke the same program with another set of parameters on another day, the new results wouldn't turn out to be ugly. I had no rational way to say formally what 'A'-ness was. (Doug Hofstadter once remarked that the most important question in the study of artificial intelligence is, "What is the letter A?" My response was that the second-most important question in the study of AI must then be, "What is the letter I?")

When I first began to use a computer to produce letterforms, I thought the task would be easy. But actually I had to work on the task for five years before I got anything that satisfied me. And the first book that came out was a great disappointment to me after I saw it in print. I *burned* with disappointment—I actually felt a hot flash when I first saw it. I opened the covers, expecting to be really happy, but "Oh, no!" It was back to the drawing boards; still more work was needed.

When you design something yourself you are overly sensitive to it. You can't view it dispassionately. If I'm watching a lecture in which my fonts appear in the slides, I can't concentrate on that lecture; I keep wondering whether I shouldn't have changed the letter S a little bit. I'm sure all artists go through this trauma. The more subjective a task is, the harder it is for you to know that you have produced anything of quality.

Professors see the same phenomenon with respect to doctoral dissertations. Students who write a theoretical thesis, in which some statement is proved to be correct, tend to finish a year earlier than students who do a purely practical thesis in which the main challenge is to do a good piece of design. In the latter case, the students almost always need another year to build up their confidence, before they are ready to believe that they have achieved something nontrivial.

Q: I came a little late and maybe you discussed this earlier, but why do you use the word "solution" when speaking of these works of art?

A: It's a solution in the sense that I presented the artists with a problem. If you had seen just the raw, unformatted texts of these words, they would just look like blah, blah, blah. The artists took those lifeless words and made them into something spectacular, something that moves you. I have this poster in my office and I've been looking at it for almost ten years now since it was printed, and I'm not tired of it yet.

Q: I guess it's just not the word that I think I would have thought of first. Maybe "rendition" or "expression"; I don't think of artwork as a "solution" to a problem.

A: That's true, but it was a commission that they were given. For example, in Tim Botts's other books, like *Doorposts*, he chose his own favorite Bible verses and decided to illustrate exactly how those verses made him feel. But in this case, I gave him a prescribed text. I was his client; the concept wasn't his own idea.

It's like taking a required course in college. I prefer not to teach such courses, because students have a different attitude when they don't elect a class for themselves. The verses I presented to the artists were not famous or extra special, except in a very few cases. Yet when the artists finished their assignments, they made it appear as if each 3:16 was a favorite verse. I was trying to shine a light on the words and illuminate them; the artists made them great. Thus they each solved a really tough problem.

Q: Do you think that beauty is just a subjective notion, or does it have some basis in objective reality?

A: I don't know how to write a computer program that will tell me if an image is beautiful or not. But I know when something affects me and when it doesn't. There's a famous saying, "It's pretty, but is it Art?" Sometimes I'm quite sure that, to me, I'm looking at an object of art. But don't ask me to quantify it, like Birkhoff tried to do, and don't ask me to give you an algorithm to test it. As far as I know, art belongs to the spirit realm.

Thank you all again for your questions and responses. Now I'd like to give you some homework for next time: I put on the Web a wonderful short story by Raymond Smullyan. Go to my home page and change the location from `index.html` to `smullyan.html`; then you can look at this story called "Planet Without Laughter." It's a marvelous parable on many levels, about the limits of rationality. You can read it to get insight about all religions, and about the question of form over substance in religion. You could even read it as a metaphor about the drug culture, or in a variety of other ways; in any case, I think you'll find it thought-provoking. And if you read it, you'll be better able to understand a few of the points that I plan to make in the remaining lectures.

Notes on Lecture 4

Page 91, normative sciences: See, for example, Peirce's Harvard Lectures on Pragmatism in *The Essential Peirce*, edited by Nathan Houser and Christian Kloesel, volume 2 (Bloomington, Indiana: Indiana University Press, 1998), Chapters 10–16. Incidentally, Peirce received authorization to deliver these lectures on March 16, 1903.

Page 91, Twenty-five years ago: "Computer programming as an art," *Communications of the ACM* **17** (December 1974), 667–673. French translation, with three supplementary paragraphs, in *L'Informatique Nouvelle*, No. 64 (June 1975), 20–27. Japanese translation by Makoto Arisawa in *bit* **7** (1975), 434–444; reprinted in *Kunusu Sensei no Program-Ron* (Tokyo: Kyoritsu-Shuppan, 1991), 2–19. English version reprinted with the supplementary paragraphs in *ACM Turing Award Lectures: The First Twenty Years* (New York: ACM Press, 1987), 33–46; reprinted with corrections as Chapter 1 of *Literate Programming* (Stanford, California: Center for the Study of Language and Information, 1992), 1–16. Russian translation by V. V. Martyniuk in *Lektsii laureatov premii T'iuringa* (Moscow: Mir, 1993), 48–64.

Page 92, system called T_EX: See Donald E. Knuth, *Computers & Typesetting* (Reading, Massachusetts: Addison–Wesley, 1986), five volumes.

Page 92, Herbert Hoover: "It was a habit apparently which had its beginning when he was President and he had a Government Printing Office and he could finish up a speech in the evening and send it up there and over night they'd set it in type for him. Then he'd make corrections in proof form." [Franklyn Waltman, as interviewed by Raymond Henle on 27 November 1967 for the Herbert Hoover Library Oral History Collection, page 4. I thank George H. Nash for this reference.]

Page 93, *Aesthetic Measure*: George D. Birkhoff, *Aesthetic Measure* (Cambridge, Massachusetts: Harvard University Press, 1933). See also *Quelques Elements Mathematiques de l'Art* (Bologna: N. Zanichelli, 1928); *Medida Estatica* (Santa Fe, Argentina: Universidad Nacional del Litoral, 1945); *Einige mathematische Elemente der Kunst* (Stuttgart: Edition Rot, 1968).

Page 94, a formula that will rate the appearance: Donald E. Knuth, *The TEXbook* (Reading, Mass.: Addison–Wesley,1984), page 98.

Page 94, John Polkinghorne: Chris Floyd, "The Spirit-Wrestler: An interview with John Polkinghorne," *Science and Spirit* **10**, 4 (Fall 1999), pages 17–19 and 38.

Page 95, Hermann Zapf: See, for example, the following books: Hermann Zapf, *Über Alphabete* (Frankfurt am Main: Georg Kurt Schauer, 1960); English translation by Paul Standard, *About Alphabets* (New York: The Typophiles, 1960); reissued in paperback (Cambridge, Massachusetts: MIT Press, 1970). *Hermann Zapf and His Design Philosophy* (Chicago: Society of Typographic Arts, 1987). *ABC–XYZapf: Fifty Years in Alphabet Design*, edited by John Dreyfus and Knut Erichson (London: Wynkyn de Worde Society, 1989). See also his CDrom, *The world of alphabets* (Rochester, New York: Cary Graphic Arts Press, 2001), ISBN 0-9713459-0-2. The present book has been typeset primarily in typefaces from Zapf's Optima family, with occasional uses of Palatino.

(In this lecture I will be mentioning the work of many outstanding artists, and I do not have space to give representative bibliographic information for them as I have just done for Hermann Zapf. In the notes below I will, however, try to cite a few of the key works known to me.)

Page 95, project called *Liber Librorum*: Paul A. Bennett, Francis Meynell, C. Volmer Nordlunde, Raul M. Rosarivo, Maximilien Vox, Bror Zachrisson, and Hermann Zapf, *Liber Librorum 1955* (Stockholm: Royal Library, 1955). See also Bror Zachrisson, "Liber librorum," *Stultifera Navis* **12** (Basel: Schweizerische Bibliophilen-Gesellschaft, 1955).

Page 96, put them into a show: See Carl Rohrs, "3:16 An Exhibit of Calligraphy," *Alphabet, The Journal of the Friends of Calligraphy* **16**, 1 (Fall 1990), 6–9.

Page 97, new translation: See Lecture 3, Example 14.

Page 102, David Kindersley: Many examples of David Kindersley's stonecutting appear in *Letters Slate Cut* by David Kindersley and Lida Lopes Cardozo (New York: Taplinger, 1981).

Page 104, Adolf Bernd: See Kurt Eitelbach, "Adolf Bernd," *Letter Arts Review* **7**, 2 (1990), 20–27.

Page 105, handwritten, illuminated Bible: This ongoing project is described at www.saintjohnsbible.org.

Page 109, Leonid Ivanovich Pronenko: Several years later he sent me a copy of his excellent book, *Kalligraphiíà dlíà Vsekh* (Moscow: Kniga, 1990). This book, incidentally, is of independent interest as one of the very last examples of fine printing to be subsidized by the policies of the former Soviet Union, having been received for publication in July, 1989. A total of 36,000 copies were printed in color on fine paper, and priced at only 5.20 rubles each.

Page 117, the illustration that they chose: "Scriptures at random," *U.S. News & World Report* **111**, 1 (1 July 1991), page 58.

Page 117, in Germany: Gero von Randow, "Der Vers 3,16: Ein Informatiker treibt fröhliche Theologie," *Die Zeit* (Hamburg) **47**, 41 (2 October 1992); this review appeared on page 43 of a special *Literatur* section for the Frankfurt Book Fair.

Page 118, ten-volume set: Will and Ariel Durant, *The Story of Civilization* (1935–1967). I am referring to the Simon and Schuster edition, which I once received as a premium for joining the Book of the Month Club. Jeanyee Wong did the calligraphy on the covers, and Lily Wronker did the calligraphy on the maps in the endpapers, although neither artist was explicitly credited for their work.

Page 122, Friedrich Neugebauer: See, for example, Friedrich Neugebauer, *Kalligraphie als Erlebnis, Baugesetze der Schrift—Schule des Schreibens* (Salzburg: Neugebauer Press, 1979); English translation by Bruce Kennett, *The Mystic Art of Written Forms* (Boston: Neugebauer Press, 1980). Many further examples of Neugebauer's work appear in the exhibition catalog *Neugebauer: Bibliophile Buchgraphik Schriftgraphik* (Salzburg: Neugebauer Press, 1983).

Page 123,   Austrian museums: See the review by Anton Durstmüller, "Internationale Schriftkunst in Österreich," *Graphische Revue Österreichs* **96** (January–February 1994), 19–20.

Page 123,   Tim Botts: See, for example, Timothy R. Botts, *Doorposts* (Wheaton, Illinois: Tyndale House, 1986), and the subsequent books *Windsongs* (1989), *Messiah* (1991), *Proverbs* (1994), *The Book of Psalms* (1997), all from the same publisher, where he is the senior art director.

Page 124,   Joseph Fitzmyer: *The Anchor Bible* **28** (Garden City, New York: Doubleday, 1981), page 463.

Page 124,   "a holy Spirit": See *The Lutheran* **5**, 2 (February 1992), page 64.

Page 125,   Ismar David: See, for example, *The Psalms* (New York: Union of American Hebrew Congregations, 1973); *Five Megilloth and Jonah* (Philadelphia: Jewish Publication Society, 1974); *Our Calligraphic Heritage: The Geyer Studios Writing Book* (New York: The Studio, 1979); *The Hebrew Letter: Calligraphic Variations* (Northvale, New Jersey: Jason Aronson, 1990); *The Book of Jonah* (Southwick, Connecticut: Chiswick Book Shop, 1991); and www.shunammite.com/aboutid.html.

Page 128,   Walt Whitman: "Art and artists," Remarks of Walt Whitman before the Brooklyn Art Union, 31 March 1851, in *The Uncollected Poetry and Prose of Walt Whitman* **1**, edited by Emory Holloway (Garden City, New York: Doubleday, Page, 1921), 241–247, especially page 243. (Whitman was, of course, paraphrasing Mark 16:15.)

Page 128,   exhibit of Islamic calligraphy: *Letters in Gold: Ottoman Calligraphy from the Sakıp Sabancı Collection, Istanbul*, an exhibition organized by the Los Angeles County Museum of Art and The Metropolitan Museum of Art. The exhibition catalog, *Music for the Eyes: An Introduction to Islamic and Ottoman Calligraphy* (Los Angeles, California: Museum Associates, 1998), was written by Mohamed Zakariya.

Page 129,   head of type design: Sumner Stone based his calligraphy of Daniel 3:16 on an early version of the typeface Lithos by Carol Twombly.

Page 130,   SOAP: More precisely, SOAP II. See my book *Selected Papers on Computer Science* (cited in Lecture 1), page 231.

Page 130, Doug Hofstadter: I know that he said this in a lecture, but I'm not sure that he ever did so in print. He comes very close in *Metamagical Themas* (New York: Basic Books, 1985), Chapters 12 and 13.

Page 131, a great disappointment: See my book *Digital Typography* (Stanford, California: Center for the Study of Language and Information, 1999), page 322.

Page 131, this poster: See the illustration in the second lecture.

Page 132, *Doorposts*: See the reference above.

Page 132, but is it Art?: Rudyard Kipling, "The Conundrum of the Workshops," first published in *Scots Observer* (13 September 1890).

Page 132, a wonderful short story: Raymond M. Smullyan, "Planet Without Laughter," Chapter 8 in *This Book Needs No Title: A Budget of Living Paradoxes* (Englewood Cliffs, New Jersey: Prentice–Hall, 1980).

LECTURE 5: GLIMPSES OF GOD   (1 December 1999)

In the first four lectures I explained the 3:16 project, where I studied chapter 3, verse 16 of every book in the Bible — sort of a day in the life of the Bible. Today I'm going to try to summarize the main lessons I learned from that experience.

A few years ago, my wife and I were in Sweden at this time of year. We were introduced to a fine piece of music called *Förklädd Gud*, a work by Lars-Erik Larsson, written for chorus and a small orchestra. A narrator also reads a poem by Hjalmar Gullberg. The word *förklädd* has something to do with putting clothes on, and the title "Förklädd Gud" means "God in Disguise." If I were at home in California now, I would play the CD of this music as I always do early in December. Actually, I would probably cry a little bit, partly in memory of the good times we had in Sweden and partly in memory of our friend who took us to the concert and gave us the CD, because she died earlier this year. But mostly I expect I'd cry (as I usually do) when I hear the narrator's touching words about God sometimes inhabiting the earth. If you ever have a chance to hear this piece, I can recommend it to you.

My title today is "Glimpses of God." We learn about God partly by observing the world, and partly by studying books like the Bible, because the Bible tells us about relations between people and God. My 3:16 project was an attempt to learn more about the Bible; what did I find out?

Overall, I found somewhat to my surprise that the Bible verses I studied closely were constantly interesting and full of stimulation, even for a supposedly educated person like myself. Either God contrived to put unusually excellent material into verse 16 of nearly every chapter 3, or else the Bible is extraordinarily rich. I was bowled over by the number of unfamiliar verses that turned out to be really inspiring.

Besides learning about the Bible, I also learned a lot about books *about* the Bible. And I learned a fair amount about theology, the academic subject that consists of intellectual reflections about religion. When I studied the 3:16s, I had an opportunity to use the libraries at many great theological institutions. For example, I was

139

able to consult books at the Andover–Harvard library when I was living in Boston. Then as my wife and I drove across the country on our way back to California, I spent three days at Yale Divinity School, another day at Westminster Seminary in Philadelphia, and another day in Pittsburgh. Eventually we returned back home and I was able to spend many days at the Graduate Theological Union in Berkeley.

One thing that struck me immediately when I compared these places to computer science departments was that theologians really know how to live — a lot better than computer scientists do. Their offices have a much nicer ambience. For example, I think the campus of Yale Divinity School is like heaven on earth. Maybe the new Stata Center at MIT is going to reverse this trend and give computer scientists some great office space; who knows? At the moment, however, the theologians are definitely way ahead.

More seriously, the 3:16 project gave me a chance to crack open thousands of books that I would never otherwise have had the motivation to look at. In this way, I could read parts of the works of theologians from many different centuries and from many different religious persuasions, because the indexes to those books would tell me where they had commented on one of the 3:16 verses that I was researching.

The random sampling methodology that I used could naturally be expected to give reasonable insights into *quantitative* things, involving numerical statistics. For example, the 59 verses I looked at contained a total of 1,567 words in the King James Version of the Bible. That's about 26.6 words per verse. The true average number of words per verse in the entire King James Bible, if you actually take the time to count it exactly, is about 25.4. In other words, from sampling, I can do numerical things well.

Moreover, when I looked at other translations I found that the Revised Standard Version of the Bible consistently has about 95% as many words per verse as King James Version does. That was a quite robust statistic. Even though I only looked at a few of the verses, I can be fairly sure that this is true overall. Curiously, two of the most readable translations of the Bible, the Today's English Version and the Living Bible, both turn out to have only 85% as many words as the King James when you look at the Old Testament. But in the New Testament, they have 110% as many words. Those statistics, again, were quite robust in the sample and they clearly indicate a distinctive editorial policy.

Incidentally, there was a big convention here in Boston a week and a half ago, when about seven or eight thousand theologians came to town. I went to one of the public sessions and learned about a new book called *The Dead Sea Scrolls Bible*, a new translation of the Bible based on the Dead Sea Scrolls. Naturally, I took a look at the display copy and looked up a few of the 3:16 verses that I knew by heart. From that experience I decided to request it for Christmas. I think it is probably a very good book to have.

Speaking about Boston, my wife and I recently did some history-tour-oriented things at Thanksgiving time, and I was reminded of a pamphlet called *The Age of Reason* that Thomas Paine wrote shortly after the American Revolution. One of the themes in his pamphlet was a violent attack on the Bible, and many of his comments can be seen today as valid criticisms of 18th century Bible interpretation. But in general, he went way overboard in his argument. For example, here's one of the things Tom Paine said:

When we read the obscene stories, the voluptuous debaucheries, the cruel and torturous executions, the unrelenting vindictiveness, with which more than half the Bible is filled, it would be more consistent that we called it the word of a demon, than the word of God.

My sample of 3:16 verses shows that in this respect, at least, he was dead wrong. You have to work very hard to imagine that even 5% of those verses have anything at all to do with what he claimed occupies "more than half of the Bible."

I did some more calculations too and I have to report that they actually cast some doubt on the validity of my sampling method. When I was in the midst of the 3:16 project I found out that a new edition of Strong's exhaustive concordance of the Bible had recently been published. And at the end of that book was a list of 1,861 verses, representing what the editors called "key verses . . . selected for their doctrinal importance and for their familiarity to readers." Those verses had been selected by a panel of Bible scholars from different groups, with the idea that they should somehow represent the most important verses in the Bible.

Naturally, I checked immediately to see how many of the best verses had been in my sample. The answer was that the 3:16s included exactly 10 of the verses those scholars had selected. "Wait a minute," I said; "this is very improbable." In fact, I worked out some probabilities, and found that the chance of hitting 10 verses

Let $p(g, k)$ be the probability that a random choice of $59 - g$ verses from $31110 - g$ will hit k of a given set of $1861 - g$ verses. Then

$$p(g, k) = \frac{\dbinom{1861 - g}{k} \dbinom{31110 - 1861}{59 - g - k}}{\dbinom{31110 - g}{59 - g}}.$$

	$g = 1$	$g = 2$	$g = 3$	$g = 4$	$g = 5$
$\Pr(k + g = 1):$	.02790				
$\Pr(k + g = 2):$	.10310	.02973			
$\Pr(k + g = 3):$	.18711	.10791	.03168		
$\Pr(k + g = 4):$	.22229	.19230	.11291	.03376	
$\Pr(k + g = 5):$	.19441	.22425	.19750	.11809	.03597
$\Pr(k + g = 6):$	.13348	.19245	.22599	.20270	.12346
$\Pr(k + g = 7):$	.07491	.12961	.19025	.22751	.20787
$\Pr(k + g = 8):$	.03533	.07132	.12563	.18780	.22879
$\Pr(k + g = 9):$	.01430	.03298	.06777	.12157	.18512
$\Pr(k + g = 10):$	.00504	.01307	.03070	.06425	.11741
$\Pr(k + g = 11):$	.00156	.00451	.01192	.02851	.06078
$\Pr(k + g = 12):$	.00043	.00137	.00403	.01084	.02640
$\Pr(k + g = 13):$	.00011	.00037	.00120	.00358	.00982
$\Pr(k + g \geq 10):$	.00717	.01944	.04826	.10857	.21879

TABLE 1.

out of a set of 1,861 was very small if I knew only that John 3:16 was a winner, because the Bible contains 31,110 verses altogether. The probability of hitting 10 or more of the special ones was only 0.00717, roughly one chance in 140.

So I began to realize that I must have been fooling myself a little bit. When I started the project I was thinking that chapter 3, verse 16 would be a completely random verse, except in the Gospel of John; but in fact that hypothesis is inconsistent with the observed statistics. What probably happened was that, subconsciously, the catchy number 3:16 had stuck in my mind. I would see a reference to Colossians 3:16 and I would think, "Hmmm, 3:16, that's kind of interesting." Somehow, in the back of my head, I must have known when I started the project that the sample was going to be a little bit salted, a little enriched rather than being completely ordinary.

What would happen, for example, if I knew in advance that a certain number of the 59 verses in my sample were good? Suppose

g of them were known to be good, and the other $59 - g$ were essentially random. Then it's not difficult to compute the probability that 10 or more of the 59 will lie in a given set of 1,861 good verses (see Table 1). As I said, the probability is less than 1% if $g = 1$, that is, if I know only the merits of John 3:16. And if I had known two of the good verses, the probability would also have been too small; it would have been 0.01944, which is less than 2%.

Therefore, the best I can conclude is that I probably knew four or five of those key verses somehow from my previous reading, and the fact that 3:16 occurred rather often was probably planted subconsciously.

There is a little bit of a bias because good verses tend to occur more often in chapter 3 than in chapter 45, for example. I checked that out too. I looked at the 1,861 verses and asked, "How many of these are in the first half of the book where they appear"? This statistic revealed a small bias: 54% of the key verses tended to occur early on in their part of the Bible. I guess that happened because the people reading those verses tired after reading the first half, or else the people writing those verses tried to put their best ammunition up in front.

Even so, suppose I knew that 5 of the 3:16 verses were going to be hits. Then 54 out of 59 were still completely unknown. And the fact that those other 54 turned out to be remarkably interesting still makes my conclusions pretty much the same as if I had known only about John 3:16.

I have to apologize for being so numerical here, because it is quite obvious that quantitative questions about the Bible are inherently quite limited. It is just that I am a numerical kind of guy, so I had to address those things. But the most interesting results are the numerous *qualitative* things I learned from this study.

For example, I looked at hundreds of commentaries, maybe a dozen or more commentaries about each book of the Bible, and the 3:16 sampling method made it pretty easy to calibrate those commentaries—to find out the special talents and biases of each author, and to see how well they each had "done their homework" in various respects.

Early on I started to notice, for example, that I was consistently getting interesting material from a multivolume commentary that was published in England about 100 years ago, called *The Pulpit Commentary*. I found it in the Boston Public Library. In this series, there would usually be four authors writing independently about each group of verses in the Bible.

Some of the authors in *The Pulpit Commentary* would bring up really good points. Others were what we might, today, call "flamers"; these were people that could sit at their desks and fill up pages with hot air about just any topic whatsoever. Even so, the neat thing from my point of view was that all these people were good British writers. So even the flamers had a wonderful vocabulary. They knew words that I had forgotten, because I had no occasion to use them in my computer books. As I would read *The Pulpit Commentary*, I would say to myself, "Hey, I've gotta find a way to use these great words."

Of course, there tends to be a runt in every litter, and some of the commentaries I ran across were big disappointments to me. In some cases the authors did a superficial job, not looking closely into the material as a good scholar would. They ignored the challenging questions that other commentators wrestled with. In other words, they were writing for another audience, not for me.

In several other cases the comments seemed to me very lifeless and dry. They reeked of academic gamesmanship. Being a college professor myself, I think it is fairly easy to smell such pretensions from a long way off. Of course, I can't help but sympathize with people who work in academic departments of theology, because they have to deal with much harder questions than I ever need to face. It must be enormously more difficult to do innovative work in a field that has been in existence for thousands of years than it is to do computer science research today. I suppose the best way to get tenure, as a theologian, is to say the wildest new things while not disagreeing too strongly with the people at your institution who received tenure just before you did. In any academic field, people's egos are bound to intrude on the work they do, especially when their livelihood is at stake.

Fortunately, enough people are left who really love what they do and who aren't just acting out some supposed strategy for success. I did run across a number of commentaries that I thought were not only excellent but also truly great. They combined superb scholarship with a genuine love for the subject that came through in the writing.

For example, one of the authors that became a personal hero for me in this regard was Raymond Brown, a Sulpician priest formerly at Union Seminary in New York. After I finished the 3:16 book, I learned that he had retired to a small seminary in Menlo Park, California, which was near my home. I had the opportunity to meet him in person and to present him with a copy of the completed book. To my delight, he actually read it and claimed to like it. I was very sad to learn of his death a year ago, especially because I didn't hear about it in time to attend the funeral service.

One advantage of a project like this, in which I was reading various materials about the same topic that had been written over a period of many hundreds of years, is that it gave me a feeling for the dynamic nature of Biblical interpretation. As people's understanding of the world changed, so did their understanding of the Bible. Each generation of scholars would correct the misapprehensions of the previous generations. Sometimes they would come up with brand new ideas; sometimes they would realize that the ideas rejected in the previous generation weren't so foolish after all. But nobody seemed to point out that their own ideas would probably be largely discredited by future generations.

As I was writing the 3:16 book, I knew that it would be pointless to be politically correct with respect to the scholarship of the 1980s, so I tried to anticipate the swings of the pendulum and to imagine what a future consensus might be. Of course, I knew that this meant half of my book would seem hopelessly out of date to today's Biblical scholars, but in a few years maybe the *other* half of my book might be out of date. Anyway, I did my best to select points and ideas from what I read that seemed likely to have the most longevity.

In view of all these continually changing trends, I had to ask myself, "Is God happy with the ways the Bible has been interpreted and misinterpreted over the years?" And my studies of the 3:16s actually lead me to answer this question with a resounding "Yes." One of the messages that came through loudest and clearest is that God definitely wants people to be actively searching for better understanding of life's mysteries, even though those mysteries will never be fully understood. In the words of Joseph Sittler, the Bible is best described not as an "open book" but rather as an "ever-opening book."

For example, Revelation 3:16 (the last of the 3:16 verses) says in effect that God prefers an atheist to a person who is apathetic about religion. Based on the verses I read, I learned that the policy of continually asking and trying to answer the difficult and unanswerable questions is far better, from God's point of view, than the alternative of ignoring those questions. The situation is analogous to a software company that solicits continuous feedback from its users so that better manuals can be written.

Peter Gomes, who has been Harvard's preacher for more than 25 years, puts it this way:

> All our scholarship and research, our linguistic and philological skills, the tools of every form of criticism available to us, are merely means by which the living spirit of the text is taken from one context and appropriated totally into ours. The history of interpretation, perhaps the most useful field in which to study the dynamic dimension of scripture, bears witness to this in every age. In this sense, then, scripture is both transformed and transformative; that is to say, our understanding of what it says and means evolves, and so too do we as a result. ... The Buddhists say, "Seek not to follow in the footsteps of the men of old; rather, seek what they sought." To understand the dynamic aspect of scripture, we must appreciate the fact that "what they sought" seeks us, and in fact, "what they sought" is apprehendable to us in terms and times that we can best understand.

From the 3:16 project I learned that there often are no easy answers. I also learned to be glad about that. Thank God there is no way to prove or disprove the existence of God! Here is a similar sentiment that Eugene Wigner, a Princeton physicist, expressed in 1981; he was speaking about physics instead of about religion. Wigner said:

> It is good that the completion of our scientific work is an unattainable ideal. Striving toward it is attracting many of us, and gives much pleasure and satisfaction. ... If science were completed, the satisfaction which research, the furthering of human knowledge, had provided, would disappear. Also, even more men would strive for power and domination. ...
> We know that there are facts and insights which we cannot communicate to animals — no animal is familiar, for instance,

with the associative law of multiplication. [Incidentally, I think that is a pretty neat observation.] . . . Is it not possible that our understanding of nature also has limitations? . . . I hope that, even if this should be true, we will be able to continue the extension of our knowledge indefinitely, . . . even if the limit thereof will always remain widely separated from the complete knowledge and understanding of nature.

I also ran across a relevant quote from a sermon given by Harvard astronomer Owen Gingerich a few years ago in Washington's National Cathedral. (I see that he is actually present here today, so I hope I can quote it right.) He said:

The search for God is subtle, but perhaps it is this long journey, this search, more than anything else, that makes us human. We are the thinking part of this vast and sometimes very intimidating universe, and our quest could well be the purpose of it all.

Perhaps the most interesting thing that I learned from studying the 3:16s, which are largely a random selection of verses, was that the balance of topics they address is rather different from the things that are most often preached about in churches, or most often associated with the Christian religion.

For example, lots of people associate religion with prohibitions, like "Don't have sex." Sure enough, three of the 3:16s have something to say about sex — that's 3 out of 59. One of them glorifies sex; another one brings out the important point that childbearing is painful; and the third one is about morality and holiness. Another one of the 3:16s warns us that drunkenness has its down side.

On the other hand, at least five of the 3:16s talk about worship. Five of them talk about God's spirit, four about spiritual peace, and four about Bible study itself.

The curious thing is that only two of those verses deal with the supposedly central doctrine of salvation, about heaven; and one of them, John 3:16, was not found by randomization. Now, I certainly don't want to belittle the notion of Jesus Christ as Savior, and I am sure that the promise of heaven was very important to me when I was growing up. But I remember being happy to realize, maybe 20 years ago, that heaven was no longer a big deal for me. I am extremely glad that God has something in mind for me in the future, whatever it is, and I trust that it will be the right thing; maybe the computers in heaven will be really terrific, and maybe I'll be able to continue doing mathematical research and font design. But the prospect of heaven has basically nothing to do with why I go to church every Sunday.

The important thing to me, as Wigner and Gingerich said in different words, is not the destination, but the journey. Philippians 3:16 expresses it well: "Meanwhile, let us keep in step with the pace we have set." This concept is the main point of the Biblical book of Ecclesiastes, and I keep seeing it again and again being rediscovered by people who notice how different this concept is from the bottom-line mentality of the present era.

I think about such things often as I bike along the Charles River, every morning at sunrise on my way to MIT and every afternoon at sunset as I return home. How great it is to be alive and going somewhere! I could take the "T" and get to my apartment a lot faster, but I wouldn't see the beautiful Charles River and all the other things that make life worthwhile.

In a similar vein, I realized many years ago that the real purpose of playing golf is not to put the ball in the hole. It is to have a good excuse to be outdoors in a beautiful place. The same goes for other sports.

At this time of year, a month before Christmas, the main theme of sermons in Christian churches is *waiting* — waiting for God. This concept is not the same as what computer scientists call "busy waiting," in which we are just spinning our wheels, nor is it the same as going to sleep until receiving a wake-up call or some kind of interrupt signal. It's an *active* waiting that I plan to say a little more about next week.

I recently ran across a 150-year-old quotation by Oliver Wendell Holmes, the Harvard professor of medicine whose son was a famous Supreme Court Justice. Here is what he said:

> I find the great thing in this world is not so much where we stand, as in what direction we are moving: To reach the port of heaven, we must sail sometimes with the wind and sometimes against it, — but we must sail, and not drift, nor lie at anchor.

In a way, Holmes didn't quite get it, because he talked about "reaching the port of heaven." People can probably only understand the worth of doing something if it has a purpose. My present attitude is that the purpose of having a purpose is so that we can have a fulfilling journey.

Holmes went on, a few pages later, to compare the process of living to various phases in a horse race. He said:

[The final winning post is] a slab of white or gray stone where there is no more jockeying or straining for victory! [The final place in the race] matters very little, if [the horses] have run as well as they know how!

So I hope you understand this point about the journey being more important than the destination.

Ever since I started to work on TEX, about 20 years ago, people have been accusing me of being afraid to finish Volume 4 of *The Art of Computer Programming*. They don't want me to be always in the state of writing it. Well, I have to report that my main purpose in studying the 3:16s was to get insight into what God wants me to do. The most repeated theme in all those verses is that *people are encouraged to do their best to be in harmony with God's wishes*. And I'm happy to report that I do think God wants me to finish Volume 4. That book won't be the crowning achievement of God's creation, but I am certainly trying to make it a step in the right direction. Meanwhile, I also do continue part-time to explore the mysteries of God, even while knowing that I won't get to the bottom of them.

I put Raymond Smullyan's short story "Planet Without Laughter" on the Web because I think it is a great thought-provoking parable that can be understood on many different levels. I am hoping that it might help a few of you to understand some things, as it helped me to understand some of the mysteries about the concept of faith and about the limits of rationality.

One of the things that the 3:16 project did for me was to prepare me to appreciate the insightful sermons of Paul Tillich, which I have just begun to read since coming to MIT (thanks to Anne Foerst). In one of Tillich's sermons from the 1940s, he gave an excellent description of the way I sometimes feel, deep down. He spoke of

... a victory not attained by ourselves, but present beyond expectation and struggle. He said, "Suddenly, we are grasped by a peace which is above reason, that is, above our theoretical seeking for the true, and above our practical striving for the good. ... We know that now, in this moment, we are in the good, in spite of all our weakness and evil.

Just like the people in Smullyan's story, who tried unsuccessfully to acquire a sense of humor by practicing how to laugh, Tillich spoke in another sermon about how a new thing mysteriously happens inside of us. He said, "We cannot force it, we cannot calculate it." But the people in "Planet Without Laughter" did eventually get it. Therefore, I think the bottom line is: *Seek and you shall find, and keep seeking.*

Thanks for today; now I'm ready for questions. In fact, we have plenty of time for questions.

Q: You spoke about various theologians who picked their favorite passages, and how it seemed that the correlation of their choices with the 3:16 verses was out of whack with the assumption that your 3:16 rule was random. Is it possible that the choices the theologians made were influenced by that magic number 3:16?

A: No. I looked at the verses and I can't believe that. In fact, two of the key verses are Micah 4:4 and Zechariah 4:6, from chapter 4. There is nothing magical about it. I am sure that if I had done 7:7, I would have come up with similar impressions, while hitting fewer of the key verses. I absolutely reject the idea that there is something mystical about the numbers 3 and 16.

FIGURE 1.

I still keep running into those numbers in unexpected contexts, however. Last week I put a puzzle on the door of my office that I had just noticed when looking at a Sam Loyd puzzle book from a hundred years ago. It is called the "Dunce Puzzle," and Loyd drew pictures of three boys wearing shirts that contain the numbers 3, 1, and 6. (See Figure 1.) And I also found the number 316 on the sidewalk, a block from Harvard Square (Figure 2). But I can't believe that it has any relevance whatsoever.

The most famous 3:16 verse other than John 3:16 is 2 Timothy 3:16, about scripture by inspiration of God. Also, 1 Timothy 3:16, the poem that I talked about in previous lectures. Colossians 3:16

FIGURE 2.

is a favorite verse for musicians; it is about worshiping with joy. Those verses are referred to sufficiently often that their numbers probably jumped out somehow into my head, but they would not have influenced the theologians' choices.

Q: In the opposite direction, it would seem like those 1800 verses might be clustered somehow in just a few Biblical books.

A: They actually span all books of the Bible. Of course, there are clusters, like the 10 Commandments. Each commandment gets in there.

But please, don't worry about saving my sample. I still have 54 or 55 random points.

Q: What makes you feel that God wants you to complete Volume 4?

A: It is similar to what Guy Steele said the other day. Why did God make me good at it, if that wasn't a way to glorify him somehow in the sense of fulfilling his plan of creation? If you were programming a robot, wouldn't you love to have it come up with Volume 4, or something like that? Joseph Sittler often remarked that creative arts represent "the theaters of the Divine activity."

I also know that Volume 4 is my destiny because the lectures I'm giving now are a once-in-a-lifetime thing. I'll never do anything like this again, although I'm glad that I am doing it once in order to encourage some of you to add to the discussion in a similar way. What I do well is write books.

Q: One of the 3:16 verses, 2 Timothy 3:16, wound up having very controversial and opposing interpretations. I suspect that you, as a fellow Lutheran, are very aware of how conservative Lutherans have used it to beat the drum over modern Lutherans by saying, "See, you guys don't accept all of the truth of the Bible and we do!"

A: This is a battle found in all denominations, of course, not just an unfortunate bone of contention among Lutherans. After I started the 3:16 project I noticed that 2 Timothy 3:16 is cited by its number on the book flap of Phillips's translation of the New Testament. The number 3:16 grabbed me immediately at that point, and I'm pretty sure that I would have seen it before. The more prominent a verse is, the more likely that it would have come somehow into my head; clearly this verse was famous enough to have influenced my sample. Thus the fact that it turned up in my book does not imply to me that one out of every sixty Bible verses is controversial.

I was actually glad to be able to write about 2 Timothy 3:16, even though I normally shy away from controversy, because I could perhaps help people see how dangerous it is to try to prove something from one single verse. I found many other books with helpful comments about 2 Timothy 3:16; one that I particularly remember liking was called *Beyond Fundamentalism,* which I ran across while browsing in the library of Trinity Church on Copley Square. When Saint Paul wrote 2 Timothy 3:16, he wasn't intending to argue about verbal inspiration of Scripture; indeed, most of the New Testament hadn't been written yet, so his reference to Scripture must have been to the Old Testament. Paul's point was rather that Scripture is *useful.*

Most of the verses treated in my book are, of course, far less controversial. Except for the unusual cases, the random sampling meant that I was looking at the Bible mostly in a way that was not biased by somebody saying, "Look at this particular verse." The randomly chosen verses are the ones from which I got a feeling for the overall balance of ideas in the Bible.

I have to say again that my experiment worked too well. That is, the fact that I had looked at these verses so thoroughly gave me more confidence than I should have had. It gave me a feeling of hubris because I had grasped a few things firmly. I still have to remind myself that I've carefully studied only 59 verses out of more than 31,000.

So don't take what I say as being absolutely definitive. But I think it was significant that the sense of balance that I wound up with pointed strongly toward this idea of being in tune with what God wants, and the notion that I should keep searching. That idea kept asserting itself throughout the 3:16 project.

Q: You use the phrase, "God's point of view." When I hear that, I infer that you are implying that the Bible represents God's point of view and that, perhaps, you take 2 Timothy 3:16 literally — that it is inspired by God. Did anything in your research make you conclude that?

A: I mentioned the other day that 2nd Timothy 3:16, by itself, is ambiguous and people have endlessly argued about it. Does it mean that all scripture is inspired by God and useful, or does it mean that all scripture is useful when it happens to have been inspired by God? That's why I said it was a battleground between people who are promoting the idea of verbal inspiration — the dictation hypothesis — as opposed to the opinion that the Bible was more or less strongly influenced by God yet subject to human error.

In the book *3:16*, I try to summarize what many people from many different persuasions have said about these things, and I try to waffle as far as taking my own stand on exactly which way I come down on these tough questions, because there is no definite proof. I think it is an important issue for everybody to work out for themselves.

My own feeling is that the Bible was inspired in a way that I can't explain, but I don't think it was dictated verbatim. I don't, however, press my opinion in the book. My personal opinion isn't especially important to anybody besides myself.

I spoke at the panel discussion about my experiences when I was writing *Surreal Numbers*, when I felt that some kind of a muse was dictating the words to a certain extent. During the week when I wrote that little book, I certainly seemed to be getting some kind of inspiration. But also, I myself was heavily involved; I wasn't merely copying down what some voice told me to write.

It is quite clear, from the study of the 3:16s, that many things have happened to the text of the Bible over the thousands of years since it was written. People with good intentions would copy a manuscript and say, "Does it really mean that? I think I'd better improve it, so that other people don't get confused." That's just what people tried to do with TeX, until I had to lay down the law.

In fact, the study of the Bible shows that we have to appreciate its long history. I mentioned briefly the other day how Isaac Newton had found where somebody had gratuitously changed 1 Timothy 3:16 in order to make the doctrine of the Trinity a little clearer. When I studied Romans 3:16 I learned of another interesting case where part of the New Testament got into the Old Testament because of copyists.

Therefore you have to be careful about what exactly you mean by the text of the Bible. Although I personally believe that the inspiration was there, I also believe that we have to look closely as we interpret it, knowing full well the dangers of circular reasoning when we try to impose our own ideas. Furthermore, I suspect that God has also inspired the canonical books of other religions.

Q: What would you say to the average person who wanted to figure out what God wants him or her to do, but maybe doesn't have the resources to undertake such a big project?

A: I'd say, don't be apathetic about God. Try to search, try to keep asking questions. And don't be discouraged if you don't ever get the answer, because asking the questions is really a good way to live.

Q: Do you think that the ambiguity of a passage is just the passion of the writing, is it by design, or is it introduced through translation and copying?

A: I really haven't got a good clue. I tried, in my translation, to keep the words ambiguous if they were ambiguous in the original language. So in that case I was being ambiguous by design. But when I give out exam questions in class, my questions have often been very ambiguous and I didn't intend that at all. All college professors are amazed at how creative the students can be when they are interpreting the words of an assignment. I suspect that most ambiguity arises unintentionally.

It could well be that God wanted the Bible to be ambiguous. I mean, suppose God had sent Jesus at the time of videotape, and we had a digital record of Jesus, with no ambiguity whatsoever. Then what would there be left for people to do, to think about and to wrestle with? I think God was very smart to finalize the Bible before modern technology came along.

Q: How did the project affect you? Did it change your faith, your beliefs, your spirituality?

A: Well, as I said, one unintended effect of the 3:16 project was that I acquired a feeling of hubris, an unwarranted self-confidence; knowing a piece of the truth made me think that I knew the whole truth. The project also affected me in other ways because it led people to call upon me to be a guru about things where I really didn't have much of a talent. For example, here I am giving these lectures.

But I guess I'm dodging your question. There certainly were more profound effects. The 3:16 project helped me to understand the complexity of religious studies, that things are not simply black or white. I became much less dogmatic about such issues. I began to learn about other religions and to see that God need not exclusively be identified with Christian dogma. At the same time, many aspects of Christianity became more precious to me, more deeply a source of inner peace, although I no longer considered them to be the necessary and sufficient way to approach God.

Of course the mere fact that I made such a study at all would mean that I naturally allocated a lot more of my brain cycles to such thoughts. But if the Bible hadn't been so stimulating, I wouldn't have pursued the project. I began to spend spare time looking at the Bible just as a kind of hobby, just as I've begun to spend spare time on other things. Then I got hooked on it and I could see that the issues were important.

Q: How did you become so interested in God and religion in the first place?

A: It was because of the family I was born into. If I had been born in other circumstances, my religious life would no doubt have been quite different.

One of the things that surprised me most as I was working on this project was the variety of attitudes that other people had developed toward religion. About 30 or 40 people volunteered to read the manuscript of my book before publication, and they sent detailed comments — often in single-spaced letters running to many pages. In two or three cases I was amazed to discover how angry these people were at God, because of something that had happened long ago in their family. This was a revelation to me; I hadn't known about such bitter feelings. In that respect I grew up in a totally sheltered world, in a loving community. Still, these people were sufficiently bothered by their relationship to God that they volunteered to look closely at my book and to help me improve it. I realized how fortunate I was to have been nourished in an atmosphere where I didn't have to feel threatened by God, and where I didn't have to deal with blatant hypocrisy.

Of course I don't mean to imply that my childhood was 100% idyllic, only that it was sufficiently good that I was blind to the existence of such tragedies in other communities.

Q: I have two questions. My first is kind of related to the last two. I was wondering how you would characterize your relationship with God before the project? You touched on it somewhat.

My second question is: Do you have any more of those shirts?

A: I got this shirt at a Stanford Craft Faire, probably at Christmas time many years ago. My wife made this nice patch for the armband after I had used PostScript to make a photographic plate for the cover of my book; it's unique.

Before starting the 3:16 project, I was essentially going to church on Sundays and oblivious to God the rest of the week. In fact, I was oblivious to religion most of Sundays too, since I always had lots of work to do. I had grown up in a close-knit family, undergirded by religious ties. My father was a church organist; both parents sang in the choir and were active in church activities. At home we always prayed before meals and celebrated religious holidays, things like that. I was educated in Lutheran schools until I went to college. But I was pretty much like a machine with respect to most aspects of my life, outside of mathematics and computer science. Not only with respect to religion but also with respect to reading great literature and appreciating great works of art.

Q (Manuela Veloso): I had never met you before hearing these lectures, but I had read your books thoroughly, as a faculty member in computer science. Given the precision of the first three volumes of *The Art of Computer Programming*, and the way you write—so eager to prove everything—I would have sworn that you were not a religious person. Because, in some sense, it seemed to me that mathematics, and your love for precision, was what drove your life. Do you think that the writing of Volume 4, after your 3:16 project, will now be different? When I read it, will I have a bit different feeling about what kind of person Don Knuth is?

A: I really doubt it. This is compartmentalization. Just like President Clinton . . .

Q: The title of today's lecture is "Glimpses of God." You have talked mostly about how you've wanted to understand God better. Are there aspects of your study of computer science and your study of the 3:16s that made you see God more? Like pieces of evidence in your life, not necessarily proofs?

A: I began by speaking about a piece of music, *Förklädd Gud.* The poem that accompanies this music is not based on a Christian text. It's based on Greek mythology, a story about Apollo. Yet this music is performed every year in Swedish churches at Christmas time. I looked it up on the Web yesterday in order to recall the name of the person who wrote the poem. And I found, right away, a web page that asks, "Should we perform this piece in a church, considering that it was based on pagan mythology?" And the conclusion was, "Yes, absolutely."

The English translation of "Förklädd Gud" is "God in disguise"; the poem is about how God somehow seems to be present on earth. Don't ask me to explain the mathematics of how it happens, or why it happens, or to prove anything about it. But just as the people in "Planet Without Laughter" seem to know instinctively what a joke is, I seem to know instinctively when some aspect of the divine is present. Now this might be my delusion, of course.

Q: Should you have started the 3:16 project sooner?

A: Well, you know . . . the timing . . . I felt called to do it at a particular time. It wouldn't have worked sooner, because part of what was driving this project was the beautiful artwork that went with it. And I didn't know any type designers until I started working on typography. So if I had done the work sooner, it wouldn't have turned out anywhere near the same. Somehow the timing was very serendipitous.

Q: I think that we are talking about something that Guy Steele hinted at in the panel discussion that we had the other day: One intellectual lever that we have, on the computational and mathematical side of the great cultural divide, is an understanding of Gödel's theorem. Early theologians didn't know Gödel's theorem; they didn't know the Heisenberg uncertainty principle; they didn't know these humility-producing things.

A: I am going to be talking about such things next week, although I can say a word or two now about Gödel's theorem. I know the proof of that theorem, and I don't believe that it is as relevant to theology as you apparently think it is. I'm more sanguine about Heisenberg's principle.

Q: What would you recommend for computer science students who have never read the Bible? Would you recommend a random sampling technique?

A: Well, the number one recommendation is that they should certainly read my book. You know, it makes a wonderful Christmas gift.

More seriously, I encourage people to think about all these things for themselves, not to listen to anything that I said particularly. In the book, I try to explain what impressed me about all the things that I found in the library.

As an introduction, I can recommend a book that I've just finished reading myself. It's by Peter Gomes, and it's called *The Good Book*. Gomes has talked to Harvard undergraduates for the last 25 years, so he knows what they need.

Q: One thing I notice about the scientific process, in general, is that scientists work in collaboration, in the sense that there is a scientific community and one tests one's work in what the community is up to. Theologians, and people in the church, certainly do very much the same thing, which is part of the theology of it all. This ties in with the question we just heard, I think. I would make the proposition that if someone is about to read the Bible from scratch, for the first time, it might be really helpful to become part of a community with other folks who are also attempting that exercise. Maybe you could tie in this project's work with the idea of community.

A: Yes. That's an excellent point. You don't have to do everything on your own. There are various groups of people that try to help each other in this way. That is what the people in Smullyan's story did too. (But I don't mean to push Smullyan's analogy too far, nor do I encourage people to subject their own ideas to the authority of a group.)

Q: The high hit rate of good verses you had in your random sampling makes me think that maybe, over time, the Bible's authors would deliberately do stuff to the 3:16 verses in the books, because it became like a marketing thing. "I know people are going to look at this verse and I'm going to make it really good." Maybe it was a bias by the authors.

A: That is not tenable because the verse numbers were added hundreds of years after the text was written.

I did find a commentary by Adam Clarke from the 1830s where he commented that, to his surprise, 1 John 3:16 was almost as good a verse as ordinary John 3:16. Other people have also been noticing 3:16 hits independently. But as I say, the nonrandom verses constitute only a very small part of the sample, and I don't think we should attach any significance to the numbers.

Q: Can you make any general statements or conclusions about the Hebrew Bible versus the New Testament?

A: In this respect my sampling procedure contains a source of bias that I didn't mention. Namely, a lot more books have been written about the New Testament than about the Old Testament, so I was given a lot more data about each New Testament verse, relatively speaking.

When I wrote the book, I decided to use exactly two pages for the commentary on each verse. In just about every case, my original draft had more material than would fit on two pages; so I marked some sentences as "discretionary," and I kept removing the least important material until the remainder would finally fit the format. With the New Testament, this task was a lot harder. It seemed to me that a lot more richness was present, that the ideas were harder to condense.

It might be that the New Testament verses are longer, or that the commentaries just brought up more ideas; but I did get a strong impression that the New Testament somehow had a higher density. The Hebrew Bible would cover similar topics but at a different pace.

Q: If you had to take a guess about all of your computer colleagues that you have worked with over the years, what percentage of them have faith in God?

A: From personal discussions, I would guess 5% to 10%. I remember one math professor at Caltech coming to me and saying he didn't have a faith but he was concerned about his children; he asked what I would recommend for them. Does that count?

It is very easy for people in the sciences to believe that once you have learned something, then you don't need much help for anything else. I've never been able to understand that point of view, although I guess the hubris I found in myself after the 3:16 project was similar. It seems to me that the more I discover in science, the more things I realize I *don't* know.

I always appreciate Saint Paul's comments about such things, at the beginning of his first letter to the Corinthians, whenever I come across his words again. First he quotes Isaiah, who said "the wisdom of wise men shall perish." Then he states a basic mathematical ordering principle, "the foolishness of God is wiser than men." And then he says, "God chose what is foolish in the world to shame the wise . . . so that no human being might boast in God's presence."

I guess that after I went to the "big leagues," to the world-class universities, I came across fewer and fewer people who have a strong faith; I came across more and more people who boasted that they didn't need it. And as I said in the first lecture, I was chiefly disappointed by the fact that all they knew about faith was what they had heard on the radio, from people who were pretty wild. My colleagues' conception of faith had largely been formed by "televangelists," who would do things like foretell the future based on the book of Daniel. Most of my university friends had no conception what God meant to me and to my friends at church.

Q: As opposed to the 10 of the 59 verses that were "good," what about the other end? Were there some that were, um, not duds but relatively mundane?

A: I could preach a sermon about any of the 59 and I think it would be uplifting (and, in some cases, too long). Even the one that was about genealogy turned out to be very interesting genealogy. That was just my gut feeling. I did have to stretch a couple of them a little bit, to look further into the context.

Q: Isn't that even more unusual than the statistics of 10 good ones?

A: Yes. That's the point: The richness that was there was definitely unexpected. Of course, if I hadn't encountered such surprising richness, I wouldn't have written the book, and nobody would have known about my experiment; there is a little bit of a bias in the fact that I found something. If you don't report something, it doesn't get into a database.

Q: In comparing the Bible with another text, there is an interesting phenomenon, namely that you have all the commentaries. If I had just written the same words, my writing might not seem like much, but after 2,000 years of interpretation it might become a lot richer. Maybe not for its inherent value but because of its interpreters, and because people look to it for inspiration.

A: That's right. I haven't done a controlled experiment with ordinary works or even with venerable works like those of Homer, Shakespeare, Chaucer, Dante, Goethe, Tolstoy, or whatever. I don't have the resources to do a similar experiment with the Koran. The secondary literature about the Bible is much larger. Still, I found the Bible extraordinarily rich.

I do believe that, with any complicated subject, you get more insight by taking some kind of a random probe into it. In this case, the commentaries helped me understand the depths of meaning, but I really got more payoff from the methodology I used. That is, I didn't just look at the verse and say, "ahhhh, how great" and close my eyes to everything else. I looked at other places where the same words or concepts had occurred. I could do that with any book that I was studying in this way. It was much easier with the Bible because of the other reference materials that have been compiled.

Q: Do you believe there is structure in these verses that, perhaps, the original authors had no concept of, where the authors would be surprised to see the modern interpretation? In some sense, is the modern interpretation false because of that, or does hindsight help us know more than the author did?

A: People often find extra meaning in a text hundreds of years after the original was written; a text written for one audience often turns out to be inspiring for another.

If you carry this to an extreme, you get to the idea of postmodern interpretations of literature, which is tearing up so many humanities departments now. For example, Stanford's German Department was up in arms about such things, split drastically into two camps. The people in one camp would say that in order to know about Goethe's work you should understand Goethe's life — where he lived, what vocabulary he used, and so on. The other half says they couldn't care less about Goethe as an individual; they'll say, "I loved his entrancing poem. Here is what it means to me, how it has led me to some new insights. Forget about the history of it, that's old stuff."

Certainly, some things are so rich that they can inspire people in a completely different way in another generation. As a writer myself, I know that I don't foresee what future readers will find in my book, and I'm sure that inspiration doesn't necessarily have to be confined to the original author of a piece. Take all the Hebrew scriptures, for example; the rabbis who have commented on them over the years have added important things to the text, in Aramaic Targums and in the writings of the Talmud.

I am glad you are asking such tough questions.

Q: Do you think there is a taboo in our culture towards glimpses of God?

A: It's natural for a society like ours to have a taboo about seeing glimpses of God, because we don't have reliable models of God and we are so much model-based now. We also know about the dangers that arise when people think that God wants them to kill somebody else, or whatever. There is a natural kind of hesitancy to accept any of this.

My own take on this notion is that I can't be sure that God is present, but somehow and at some times I think I am sure, in the sense expressed so well by Tillich.

Q: Can you look at the poster and recite for us a few of the verses?

A: Yes, I can read for you Revelation 3:16: "Since you are merely lukewarm — neither cold nor hot — I'm going to spit you out of my mouth!" And here is one that says, "We know that true religion is a great mystery: Christ was revealed in body, justified in spirit, witnessed by angels, proclaimed to pagans, trusted on earth, glorified in heaven." And I'll close with this one: "May the Lord of peace himself give you peace at all times and in all ways."

Notes on Lecture 5

Page 139, in memory of our friend: Roswitha Graham, 1935–1999; see *TUGboat* **20** (1999), 89.

Page 140, Stata Center: Final plans for a new Computer Science building, designed by Frank Gehry, were being drawn up at the time I gave this lecture.

Page 141, *The Dead Sea Scrolls Bible*: Martin Abegg, Jr., Peter Flint, and Eugene Ulrich, *The Dead Sea Scrolls Bible: The Oldest Known Bible Translated for the First Time into English* (New York[sic]: HarperSanFrancisco, 1999).

Page 141, Thomas Paine: *The Age of Reason* (1793); the quotation comes from approximately the 52nd paragraph of Book I.

Page 141, new edition of Strong's: *The New Strong's Exhaustive Concordance of the Bible* (Nashville, Tennessee: T. Nelson, 1984).

Page 144, *The Pulpit Commentary*: A 51-volume set of books edited by H. D. M. Spence[-Jones], Joseph S. Exell, and others. Published in many editions, originally I believe in London by Kegan Paul, Trench, and in New York by Anson D. F. Randolph, 1883–1895.

Page 145, Joseph Sittler: See the videotape cited in the notes to Lecture 1, at time 25:00.

Page 146, Peter Gomes: *The Good Book*, as cited in the notes to Lecture 3, page 21.

Page 146, Eugene Wigner: "The limitations of the validity of present-day physics," in *Mind in Nature*, Nobel Conference XVII, edited by Richard Q. Elvee (San Francisco, California: Harper and Row, 1982), 118–133, especially pages 125 and 128.

Page 147, Owen Gingerich: "The journey into darkness," *Platte Valley Review* **26** (Winter 1998), 11–16, especially page 16.

Page 148, Oliver Wendell Holmes: *The Autocrat of the Breakfast Table* (Boston: Phillips, Sampson, 1858), Chapter 4.

Page 149, Paul Tillich: *The Shaking of the Foundations,* as cited in the notes to Lecture 3, especially pages 100 and 182.

Page 149, the people in Smullyan's story: I recently learned from Doug Hofstadter about "Laughter Yoga," a technique of group laughter developed by Dr. Madan Kataria of Bombay. In an email to Hofstadter dated 10 April 2000, Kataria said, "Anyone can laugh for 15–20 minutes everyday without resorting to jokes. Each laughter session starts with deep breathing and the Ho-Ho, Ha-Ha exercises, followed by a variety of stimulated laughter like hearty laughter, silent laughter, medium laughter, lion laughter, swinging laughter, one meter laughter, cocktail laughter, gradient laughter and many other kinds." He has published a book, *Laugh For No Reason* (Delhi: Madhuri International, 1999).

Page 150, Sam Loyd: "A study in division," *Cyclopedia of Puzzles,* edited by Sam Loyd II (New York: Lamb, 1914), 19, 341.

> Those stupid boys, who were so dumb,
> They could not do a simple sum,
> Were marked with numbers three, one, six,
> And told these numbers they could mix,
> And find by many changes tried
> A sum which seven would divide!

The puzzle was reprinted in *Mathematical Puzzles of Sam Loyd,* selected and edited by Martin Gardner, volume 2 (New York: Dover, 1960), puzzle 96.

Page 150, a block from Harvard Square: Even more striking was the bold 3 and 16 that I encountered subsequently in Oxford, England — on the wall of St. John's College!

(It apparently identifies a fire hydrant in the street.)

Page 151, Guy Steele: See the panel discussion below.

Page 152, Joseph Sittler: See *Currents in Theology and Mission* **16** (1989), 5–28, especially page 21.

Page 152, Phillips's translation: *The New Testament in Modern English*, translated by J. B. Phillips (New York: Macmillan, 1962).

Page 152, *Beyond Fundamentalism*: James Barr, *Beyond Fundamentalism* (Philadelphia: Fortress Press, 1984).

Page 153, panel discussion: "Creativity, Spirituality, and Computer Science," a panel discussion by Guy L. Steele Jr., Manuela Veloso, Donald E. Knuth, and Mitch Kapor, moderated by Harry R. Lewis (17 November 1999), follows Lecture 6 below.

Page 154, New Testament got into the Old: Romans 3:12–18 was copied into many manuscripts of Psalm 14:3.

Page 156, this shirt: See the illustrations on pages 20 and 57.

Page 158, Gödel's theorem: Gödel's incompleteness theorem [Kurt Gödel, "Über formal unentscheidbare Sätze der Principia Mathematica und verwandter Systeme I," *Monatshefte für Mathematik und Physik* **38** (1931), 173–198] states that if a consistent logical system formalizes the theory of natural numbers, it contains a formula A such that neither A nor its negation $\neg A$ can be proved within the system.

Page 158, Heisenberg uncertainty principle: This principle [Werner Heisenberg, "Über den anschaulichen Inhalt der quantentheoritischen Kinematik und Mechanik," *Zeitschrift für Physik* **43** (1927), 172–198; English translation, "The physical content of quantum kinematics and mechanics," in *Quantum Theory and Measurement*, edited by John Archibald Wheeler and Wojciech Hubert Zurek (Princeton University Press, 1983), 66–84] states that the inaccuracy in any measurement of a particle's position times the inaccuracy in any simultaneous measurement of that particle's momentum is never less than $h/(4\pi) \approx 5.27 \times 10^{-28}$ erg seconds, where h is Planck's constant.

Page 158, *The Good Book*: See the notes following Lecture 3.

Page 160, beginning of his first letter: See 1 Corinthians 1:18–31.

Page 160, he quotes Isaiah: Isaiah 29:14.

LECTURE 6: GOD AND COMPUTER SCIENCE   (8 DECEMBER 1999)

Thanks to all of you for sticking with me until the end here. I have to confess that when I made up the table of contents for these lectures during the summer, I had almost no concept of what I might say in the last one. But I figured that I had two months' time at MIT to come up with something, and if I'd only keep my antennas open and tuned to the right frequencies, I might pick up some appropriate ideas. Well, sure enough, there's no shortage of stimulating ideas that relate God and computer science. I hope I'll be able to explain today some of the ones I think are most interesting and important. In fact, I thought of more than enough things to say in one lecture, and I've had to rank order them; so I might not have time to talk about everything that I promised you last week.

Lots of people have, of course, written about God and science in general. Shortly after my arrival here, I went to a dinner hosted by a thriving local organization called the Faith and Science Exchange, celebrating its tenth anniversary. Also, ever since the early 1980s, the University of California at Berkeley has had an active Center for Theology and the Natural Sciences.

But computer science is an *unnatural* science. Computer science deals with artificial things, not bound by the constraints of nature. When I chose the title of this lecture, I had a gut feeling that computer scientists could shed some new light on the subject — in addition to the fine contributions already made by biologists, physicists, and other scientists as well as theologians — because I think computer science gives us new analogies and theories that can help us to understand God.

For example, when Arthur Peacocke wrote twenty years ago about *Creation and the World of Science*, he compared God to the composer of a symphony, writing music that obeys fixed laws but contains random elements. Peacocke saw God as an "improvisor of unsurpassed ingenuity." Music is indeed a useful analogy, because it's a flexible form that moves through time. But certainly computer programs are much richer in this respect, because programs not only move through time, they also interact with people and they can even modify themselves.

167

When I talk about computer science as a possible basis for insights about God, of course I'm not thinking about God as a super-smart intellect surrounded by large clusters of ultrafast Linux workstations and great search engines. That's the user's point of view. I'm thinking about the *science* part of computer science, the abstract notions of processes, the theories that computer scientists have been developing about how to deal with large quantities of nonuniform data in dynamic ways. Such things are much better understood now than they ever have been before, and they clearly have intimate connections with God's role as creator and sustainer of the universe. Furthermore, computational models are better able to describe many aspects of the universe better than any other models we know. All scientific theories can, for example, be modeled by programs.

Years ago, I was pondering the difference between science and art. People had been asking me why my books were called *The Art of Computer Programming* instead of *The Science of Computer Programming*, and I realized that there's a simple explanation: Science is what we understand well enough to explain to a computer; art is everything else. Every time science advances, part of an art becomes a science, so art loses a little bit. Yet, mysteriously, art always seems to register a net gain, because as we understand more we invent more new things that we can't explain to computers.

During the panel discussion a few weeks ago, it developed that a lot of people in the audience — maybe a majority — thought that science would soon catch up with art and there wouldn't be any art left. According to that opinion, we'd know how to program a robot that would be able to do everything the people on the panel could do, and also the people in the audience I guess.

Now I personally see no signs that any such thing is on the horizon, but I do want to mention a point that Brian Hayes brought up earlier this year in *American Scientist*. Hayes observed that if we can create such robots, those robots would also be able to create such robots, and so on. And you see this would increase the likelihood that we ourselves were created by some designer.

In any case, I think people who write programs do have at least a glimmer of extra insight into the nature of God for that very reason, because creating a program often means that you have to create a small universe. For example, I spent most of this year writing programs to simulate a new computer called MMIX. One of those programs was probably the most difficult that I've ever written, and I thought hard about how it would be to live with such a machine and with the new tools that I was creating — sort of like living in a new subculture.

I think it's fair to say that many of today's large computer programs rank among the most complex intellectual achievements of all time. They're absolutely trivial by comparison with any of the works of God, but still they're somehow closer to those works than anything else we know.

My main point, though, is not to debate the merits of computer science. Rather, I want to discuss some of the things that our experiences with computers during the past fifty years have taught us.

First I want to mention the fact that computing gives us great appreciation for the size of finite numbers. I spoke about this topic in Boston many years ago, at a big meeting of the American Association for the Advancement of Science held in 1976. My paper was called "Coping with finiteness," and it was reprinted later in several books. I hate to repeat myself, but I suppose some of you here today were unable to hear my talk in 1976; and maybe you never read the paper either. And even if you did, you've probably forgotten about it. So I'm going to spend the next few minutes repeating some simple but eye-opening facts about finite numbers.

I want to start small and remind you that the product x times n means x plus x plus x plus x and so on, the sum of n copies of the number x:

$$\overbrace{x\,n = x + x + \cdots + x}^{n \text{ copies of } x}.$$

Similarly we can talk about $x \uparrow n$, or x to the nth power, which is the *product* of n copies of x:

$$x \uparrow n = \overbrace{x\,x \ldots x}^{n \text{ copies of } x}.$$

For example,

$$10 \uparrow 10 = 10 \cdot 10 \cdot 10 \cdot 10 \cdot 10 \cdot 10 \cdot 10 \cdot 10 \cdot 10 \cdot 10$$
$$= 10{,}000{,}000{,}000\,;$$

it's ten billion. People usually write that number as 10^{10}, but I like to write it with an arrow because of the next step up, which uses *two* arrows. I mean, if you have two arrows as in $x \uparrow\uparrow n$, you are computing x to the x to the x to the x and so on, n times:

$$x \uparrow\uparrow n = \overbrace{x \uparrow (x \uparrow (\cdots \uparrow x) \cdots)}^{n \text{ copies of } x} .$$

Now this arrow notation is my big claim to fame, because it's what got me into the *Guinness Book of World Records*. In particular,

$$10 \uparrow\uparrow 10 = 10^{10^{10^{10^{10^{10^{10^{10^{10^{10}}}}}}}}}$$

$$= 1 \text{ followed by } 10^{10^{10^{10^{10^{10^{10^{10^{10}}}}}}}} \text{ zeros.}$$

That's a fairly large number. If you put a monkey down at a typewriter and wait until he types out the entire text of Hamlet, with no errors, the expected number of trials is only 1 followed by about 40,000 zeros. Our number $10 \uparrow\uparrow 10$ is 1 followed by quite a few more zeros than that. Now you understand ten double-arrow ten.

The general rule, of course, is that if you have k arrows, you just define it as the operation with $k-1$ arrows, over and over again:

$$x \overbrace{\uparrow\uparrow \ldots \uparrow}^{k \text{ arrows}} n = \underbrace{x \overbrace{\uparrow \ldots \uparrow}^{k-1} (x \overbrace{\uparrow \ldots \uparrow}^{k-1} (\cdots \overbrace{\uparrow \ldots \uparrow}^{k-1} x) \cdots)}_{n \text{ occurrences of } x} .$$

I want to give you a small example of the arrow functions so that you can better understand these finite numbers. Let's look at ten quadruple-arrow three. By definition that means ten triple-arrow ten triple-arrow ten:

$$10 \uparrow\uparrow\uparrow\uparrow 3 = 10 \uparrow\uparrow\uparrow (10 \uparrow\uparrow\uparrow 10) ;$$

so we first have to evaluate ten triple-arrow ten. Well, of course, ten triple-arrow ten is

$$10 \uparrow\uparrow (10 \uparrow\uparrow (10 \uparrow\uparrow (10 \uparrow\uparrow (10 \uparrow\uparrow (10 \uparrow\uparrow (10 \uparrow\uparrow (10 \uparrow\uparrow 10)))))))$$

and that is

$$10 \uparrow\uparrow (10 \uparrow\uparrow (10 \uparrow\uparrow (10 \uparrow\uparrow (10 \uparrow\uparrow (10 \uparrow\uparrow (10 \uparrow\uparrow (10 \uparrow\uparrow 10^{10^{10^{10^{10^{10^{10^{10^{10^{10}}}}}}}}})))))))$$

$$= 10 \uparrow\uparrow (10 \uparrow\uparrow (10 \uparrow\uparrow (10 \uparrow\uparrow (10 \uparrow\uparrow (10 \uparrow\uparrow (10 \uparrow\uparrow 10^{10^{\cdot^{\cdot^{\cdot^{10}}}}}))))))$$

where the stack of tens is $10 \uparrow\uparrow 10$ levels tall. I can't even tell you how big that stack of tens is without using double-arrow notation.

It's such a huge number, I can't even write it down, but then we repeat the double-arrow operation again, getting an even huger number; and so on, until finally we get this thing evaluated. We can save space by calling the final result $\mathcal{K}$. (If you look with a magnifying glass you'll see that I have worked hard to make a very fancy K here; I couldn't just use an ordinary letter for such an immense quantity.)

Of course we're not done yet. $\mathcal{K}$ is just ten triple-arrow ten. In order to get the final number that I started with — ten quadruple-arrow three — I have to take ten triple-arrow to this fancy K, namely

$$10 \uparrow\uparrow\uparrow\uparrow 3 = 10 \uparrow\uparrow\uparrow \mathcal{K} = \underbrace{10 \uparrow\uparrow (10 \uparrow\uparrow (10 \uparrow\uparrow \cdots \uparrow\uparrow (10 \uparrow\uparrow 10) \cdots))}_{\mathcal{K} \text{ times}} .$$

If you stop to think about this, you'll have to admit that, if anything is mind boggling, this is; it's *incredibly* huge. In my paper I noted that the three dots " $\cdots$ " in this formula suppress a lot of detail — so much that I should probably have used four dots.

Now that we have evaluated $10 \uparrow\uparrow\uparrow\uparrow 3$, let's call it Super K. If you don't agree that Super K is so large as to be beyond human comprehension, I can at least prove conclusively that if you consider all the numbers less than or equal to Super K, almost all of them are impossible to describe in any way in the universe, because of a theorem by which computer scientists know that most number descriptions are incompressible. On the other hand, Super K is very small as finite numbers go; almost all finite numbers are a lot bigger than this. I don't care. Super K is big enough for me.

As soon as you begin to understand the immensity of Super K, you will realize that just being finite isn't much of a limitation, and you will see how pointless are the philosophers' discussions about finite versus infinite. Infinity is a red herring. I would be perfectly happy to give up immortality if I could only live Super K years before dying. In fact, Super K nanoseconds would be enough.

Many years ago, I learned about Cantor's famous theory about higher orders of infinity. I learned the beautifully simple fact that the set of all ways to label the elements of any given set with zeros and ones always has strictly more elements than the given set itself has. And I once thought, if I ever had to preach a sermon in church, I would try to explain Cantor's theorem to my non-mathematical friends so that they could understand something about the infinite.

But now I realize that infinity is not necessarily even one of God's attributes. I'm quite willing to grant that God might indeed be infinite, and that God might have the power to examine infinitely many possibilities in an instant. But even the ability to deal with finitely many numbers, on the order of Super K, is much more than enough to inspire awe.

Moreover, I don't think theologians can legitimately disagree with me on this. To say that God's abilities are not infinite, but limited by quantities like Super K, is not a realistic limitation at all. Such a limitation cannot contradict the Bible or any other sacred text, because natural language has no words to distinguish meaningfully between such unimaginably large magnitudes.

For example, the word "infinite" itself occurs only three times in the King James Bible. The first time is when one of Job's comrades says, "Job, your iniquities are infinite." In the second place, God's understanding is said to be infinite. And in the third place, the power of Egypt is said to be infinite. You see, only the second of these three applies this attribute to God; and the Hebrew words in that verse can be translated more accurately by the phrase "too big to count."

The amount of academic hair splitting about finite versus infinite in the literature is itself too much to count; but it misses the point. The real point, I think, is made rather well in Psalm 139:

(1) O Lord, you have searched me and known me . . .
(2) . . . You discern my thoughts from afar . . .
(4) . . . Even before a word is on my tongue,
        lo, O Lord, you know it altogether . . .
(17) . . . How vast is the sum of [your thoughts] —
(18) If I try to count them, they are more than the sand.

In other words, God knows incredibly more than we can understand.

"Lord, you discern my thoughts from afar." I grew up with the idea that God constantly reads my mind, and I've always been comfortable with that invasion of my privacy. As a result, I haven't been especially successful in cryptographic research about keeping secrets. Of course I don't understand how it's possible for God to read my mind or to penetrate anybody's consciousness, especially because every individual brain probably has its own code for information processing. But that doesn't make me disbelieve that God can do it, even if we limit God to having finite capacity of size Super K. Peter Gomes has wisely described the Bible as an effort "to cram into the human imagination the unimaginable immensity of God." But he doesn't mean to imply that the Bible makes technical distinctions about subtle mathematical details.

Let's look at another example, based on a rather deep result of computer science that came out of an MIT Ph.D. thesis — Larry Stockmeyer's thesis in 1974, working jointly with Albert Meyer. I don't want to talk too much about it but there's a theorem of Büchi according to which we know that certain statements about the positive numbers can always be proved or disproved in a finite amount of time. (Technical people in the audience will understand that I'm talking about "weak second-order arithmetic.") Any statement in weak second-order arithmetic can be expressed in terms of 64 symbols, including a blank space. The statements might involve so-called quantifiers: For example, the statement "For all x there exists y such that y is less than $x + 1$" is written $\forall x \exists y(y{<}x{+}1)$.

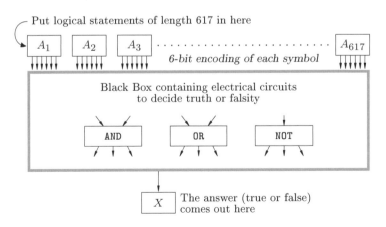

FIGURE 1.

According to Büchi's theorem, we can build an electrical circuit that will decide the truth or falsity of any statement in weak second-order arithmetic, if that statement has a bounded length, say 617 characters or less. We start out by adding blanks to make the statement exactly 617 characters long; then we use a 6-bit encoding for each of the 617 symbols, giving 6×617 inputs to the circuit shown in Figure 1. Then if appropriate combinations of "and," "or," and "not" have been put into the Black Box, out comes the answer: The statement is true, or false, as the case may be.

This circuit is finite. But Meyer and Stockmeyer proved that every such circuit must use at least 10^{125} components. And 10^{125}, which is of course really puny when compared to Super K, is still plenty big; it is larger than the number of protons and neutrons in the entire known universe. Furthermore, if we change 617 to 618, the problem gets harder yet. So you can see that there are absolute, fundamental limitations of complexity in certain computational problems.

I think it's fair to say that God may well be bound by the laws of computational complexity, even if we grant (as I do) that the Bible is God's inspired word. The Bible doesn't deal with Büchi's theorem or any other such fine points of detail, nor was it ever intended to.

Computer scientists today know many things about all kinds of levels of incredible difficulty that are inherent in the solution of different kinds of computational tasks, even when those tasks are solvable in finite time. These theoretical results could be used in academic discussions to restrict God's ability to be all-knowing and/or all-powerful in certain ways, if we assume that God has finite resources of a certain size. But I don't recommend that theologians undertake a deep study of computational complexity (unless, of course, they really enjoy it). Because the fact is, God can know much more than enough, and can be plenty powerful enough, to do *anything* relevant to the universe, *without* being strictly all-knowing or all-powerful. Finiteness is *not* a limitation in practice.

When I say that the question "finite or infinite?" is a red herring, I don't mean simply that philosophers and theologians have often been arguing about an unimportant issue. I also mean that physicists and other scientists fail to realize this. For example, take the literature of chaos theory: Hundreds of papers have been written about the behavior of solutions to unstable recurrences, by people who assume that *real* numbers are *real*.

(Let me explain, to non-mathematicians in the audience. When mathematicians talk about real numbers, they mean decimal numbers that have infinite accuracy — infinitely many decimal places.)

Well, the fact is, real numbers are an abstraction, an idealization. I grant you that they're an immensely useful abstraction: The concept of real numbers allows us to apply calculus and other tools of mathematics to solve all kinds of important problems.

But it's a tremendous leap of faith to assume that real numbers apply perfectly to the real world — to assume, for example, that two physically realizable objects could be in different places, even though their positions in space agree up to Super K decimal places. I can understand why people unconsciously make this assumption: All textbooks of mathematics start with real numbers. The concept is familiar and easy to work with.

In a similar way, I thought I "knew" what parallel lines were after I learned geometry in high school. Given any line and a point off the line, that line and that point determine a plane, and in the plane there's exactly one line through the point that's parallel to the line you started with. Parallel means that it never intersects that line. This statement is called Euclid's fifth postulate, Euclid's parallel postulate, and it seems obviously true.

Years later I learned about non-Euclidean geometries, which satisfy the other axioms stated by Euclid but not this parallel postulate. In some geometries there can be two or more lines parallel to the given one; in other geometries there aren't any at all.

I thought this was an amusing curiosity, but I never believed for a moment that non-Euclidean geometries had anything to do with reality. The possibility didn't even cross my mind, since I *knew* that the universe was Euclidean. Maybe twenty years went by before I was shocked to realize that I had no grounds for that hypothesis at all. Euclid's law was convenient for the practical calculations I needed, but it wasn't good enough for astronomers who were faced with the actual properties of the real world. And most scientists today believe that the geometry of the universe is *not* Euclidean.

Some years ago I wrote a book about so-called *surreal numbers*, which are much richer than real numbers because they include not only the real numbers but also infinitesimally small quantities, as well as numbers like $\omega^{\sqrt{\omega}}$ (infinity raised to the power of square root of infinity). You can add and subtract, multiply and divide surreal numbers, and they're algebraically closed.

In a sense, surreal numbers are actually simpler than real numbers, although they weren't discovered until fairly recently. For example, you can define surreal numbers with only two very simple axioms. I suspect that if physicists had been trained since childhood to work with surreal numbers they would implicitly imagine that surreal numbers describe the actual universe we live in. Certainly surreal numbers are no less likely than real numbers are for this purpose.

It seems to me that a new branch of physics is needed, called maybe "discrete physics" or something like that, to study the effects of the assumption that parameters can be infinitely precise and to consider instead that the universe probably has only a finite-but-extremely-large number of states. I've heard of a few people who are working on this; it seems to me that such ideas deserve to get into the mainstream.

Plato once said, "I have never known a mathematician who was able to reason." I think he was referring to the fact that mathematicians tend to believe that their abstractions apply perfectly to a world that is more complex than they can imagine. On the other hand, according to James Jeans, "Nature abhors accuracy and precision above all things."

Well, I can't dwell any longer on this subject, because I also want to cover several other ideas today. The next topic I want to discuss is John Conway's "Game of Life," as an example of an artificially created universe. It's an idea that John came up with about the same time that he invented surreal numbers in the late 1960s, and it's probably the simplest example of a cellular automaton that has really interesting properties.

We can imagine a grid that consists of square cells extending arbitrarily far in any direction. At every instant of time each cell is either off or on. In Figure 2, for example, the black ones are on and everything else is off. Exactly 197 cells are on.

There's a simple rule for determining the state of each cell at the next instant of time, based on the current state of that cell and its eight neighbors. Suppose k of the neighbors are on at a given time instant t. Then at time $t + 1$ (the next instant):

- the cell becomes off, if k is less than 2.
  (If you don't have enough neighbors, you go off.)
- the cell becomes off, if k is greater than 3.
  (If you have too many neighbors, you go off.)

FIGURE 2.

- the cell becomes on, if k is exactly 3.
  (Three neighbors will turn you on.)
- the cell remains in the same state, if k is exactly 2.
  (Two neighbors do not affect you.)

The configuration in Figure 2 is an interesting one that Bill Gosper came up with on November 19, 1997; it's called a "totally aperiodic glider wave." Let's look, for example, at what happens after one unit of time. Several black cells have no neighbors, so they're going to go away. Some of them have too many neighbors; they're going to go away too. But the ones that have exactly two neighbors are going to stay as they were. The cells that have three neighbors are going to go on if they were off, and after one step you get the pattern in Figure 3. Now 202 cells are on.

The Web has wonderful resources for exploring this Game of Life. Just go to your favorite search engine and say "Conway Life," and you'll find an abundance of material, including some terrific Java applets. You can watch the cell patterns to your heart's content. I've heard people say that during the 70s more computer time was spent simulating this game than anything else; many companies banned it from their computers because it was chewing up so many machine cycles. It's quite fascinating to watch what happens.

FIGURE 3.

After 100 steps in this particular case, the cells have begun to send out so-called gliders, and the gliders interact in a really interesting pattern. (See Figure 4, which shows only 176 of the 394 cells that now are on.) The reason Gosper's construction is called "totally aperiodic" is that if you look at any cell whatsoever, its sequence of states is not periodic. No cell by itself could be described by a finite automaton.

I could give several lectures concerning lessons about real life that can be learned by studying examples of artificial life like this. But I have time to mention only a few of the main points. First, it's abundantly clear that a programmer can create something and be totally aware of the laws that are obeyed by the program, and yet be almost totally unaware of the consequences of those laws. Running the program with different starting configurations often leads to really surprising new behavior.

Secondly, the Game of Life illustrates the power of evolutionary mechanisms. Stable configurations arise out of random soup, usually very quickly; and many of those configurations have properties analogous to biological organisms. You can find a glossary of hundreds of names for such things on the Web: Besides the gliders in Figure 4, Lifenthusiasts are familiar with ants, beacons, bookends,

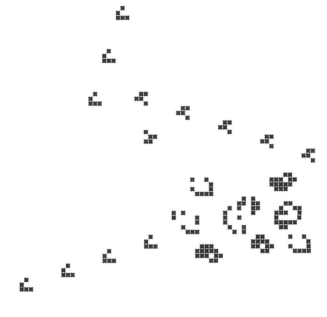

FIGURE 4.

bunnies, caterers, clocks, eaters, lightbulbs, and many other flora and fauna that tend to materialize almost spontaneously.

But the thing that strikes me most about this game is the fact that it is obviously *deterministic*, and I think it sheds light on the age-old question of free will versus a deterministic universe. At least it has helped me a bit with this issue. Somebody, I don't remember who it was (maybe Conway himself), told me in the 1970s that the computer-simulated behavior of patterns in this game tend to be so lifelike that it actually gave him pangs of conscience whenever he would shut the computer off or set it up to work on something else. He was killing off the poor creatures before those creatures had fulfilled their potential.

But Conway's Game of Life is completely deterministic; it needs only simple rules about having two and three neighbors. Thus all the future generations of every pattern must exist whether we simulate them or not. They can't die. Pulling the plug before a computer counts up to a million doesn't harm the number one million.

Now let's imagine that our universe — the real universe — is to-tally deterministic and finite, but of course extremely large. Conway and Gosper have proved that the Game of Life is *universal*, in the sense that this game can simulate anything that is computable by deterministic laws. Therefore, in principle, we could set up a gigantic on-off pattern that would perfectly describe the future of the entire universe, starting at any given state, if we simply followed Conway's rules. In fact, we could do this on a finite two-dimensional game board whose sides would not be much larger than the number of entities in the universe itself. The simulation wouldn't run in real time; it would in fact be mighty slow. But it wouldn't miss any detail.

That's what a deterministic universe is like. Such a universe exists without needing to be simulated, in the same sense as any number exists without needing to be named.

Raymond Smullyan's short story "Planet Without Laughter" ends with a discussion of free will. I actually like the early parts of that story better than the ending, but Smullyan is certainly entitled to his opinions, and here are some of the words that he put into the mouth of God in his story:

> Humans are like children. The only way you can get them to *do* anything is to make them think that it is *they* who are doing it. Their pride is so great that without having the illusion of free will they will never go forth and amount to anything.

In other words, Smullyan is saying that we don't have free will, but God wants us to think we do, because otherwise the world would get nowhere.

Apparently, then, the *illusion* of free will is good enough, because it's essentially indistinguishable from actually having free will. In a similar way, computer programmers have found that pseudo-random numbers turn out to be just as good as truly random numbers, for all practical purposes. Well, if that is true, the illusion of free will could even have *evolved*, by Darwinian principles.

Albert Einstein didn't believe in freedom of the will. He said, "This awareness ... preserves me from taking too seriously myself and my fellow men as acting and deciding individuals and from losing my temper." Here I cannot agree. Such thoughts are so totally different from my own, that when I first read them I thought they were self-contradictory. If lack of free will kept Einstein from losing his temper, he didn't have any temper to lose. You don't decide whether or not you have free will, if you don't have the power to make decisions.

But after thinking about it some more I had to admit that Einstein's viewpoint is indeed logically consistent, even though I don't subscribe to it myself. In my own view, people ought to take responsibility for the things they choose to do, and I think I can learn to control my temper about other people's choices without believing that they had no choice. Indeed I think it's impossible to be a parent and to observe one's own children *without* believing in free will.

The traditional argument against free will by some theologians is that God cannot know everything unless God knows what choices we're going to make. This debate goes on, but I think the evidence for that argument is fairly weak because of the inadequacies of natural language to deal with such technicalities in a precise way. It seems much more likely to me that God is interested in our decisions, and that he purposely held back from asserting total control. Why create something if you already know the outcome?

As a software designer I greatly enjoy watching surreptitiously what other people are doing with the programs I've written. (Well, sometimes I wince too.) It's similar to the feeling that parents have when their children are developing "attitude." Sometimes they're very happy about what their children come up with, and sometimes they're alarmed, but it's always interesting. Dorothy Sayers said that she enjoyed writing plays better than writing novels, because the actors and actresses would reveal deeper meanings that she hadn't specifically planned.

To carry this discussion further I need to talk a little bit about quantum mechanics. Several years ago, I chanced to open Paul Dirac's famous book on the subject and I was surprised to find out that Dirac was not only an extremely good writer but also that his book was not totally impossible to understand. The biggest surprise, however — actually a shock — was to learn that the things he talks about in that book were completely different from anything I had ever read in *Scientific American* or in any other popular account of the subject. Apparently when physicists talk to physicists, they talk about linear transformations of generalized Hilbert spaces over the complex numbers; observable quantities are eigenvalues and eigenfunctions of Hermitian linear operators. But when physicists talk to the general public they don't dare mention such esoteric things, so they speak instead about particles and spins and such, which are much less than half of the story. No wonder I could never really understand the popular articles.

The extra detail that gets suppressed when quantum physics gets popularized amounts to the fact that, according to quantum mechanics, the universe actually consists of much more data than could ever be observed. Dirac's preface states, for example, that

> [Nature's] fundamental laws do not govern the world as it appears in our mental picture in any direct way, but instead they control a substratum of which we cannot form a mental picture without introducing irrelevancies.

Quantum theories are almost exactly 100 years old now, and they seem to be holding up rather well even though Dirac's book first came out in 1930. James Jeans explained the need for quantum physics in this way:

> At the end of the nineteenth century it first became possible to study the behaviour of single molecules, atoms and electrons. The century had lasted just long enough for science to discover that certain phenomena, radiation and gravitation in particular, defied all attempts at a purely mechanical explanation. While philosophers were still debating whether a machine could be constructed to reproduce the thoughts of Newton, the emotions of Bach or the inspiration of Michelangelo, the average man of science was rapidly becoming convinced that no machine could be constructed to reproduce the light of a candle or the fall of an apple.

Well, I can't give you a tutorial about quantum mechanics today, but I do want to mention it because a lot of computer scientists have been working together with physicists for the past several years to develop something called quantum computing. These concepts have not yet been proved in practice, but steady progress is reported; and it's not impossible that quantum computing could turn out to be a truly revolutionary breakthrough, perhaps allowing us to deal with exponentially many possibilities in linear time. I'll try to describe the situation as simply as I can, without speaking of eigenvalues but still (I hope) conveying some of the essence of the ideas.

Every year at this time for the past six or seven years I've traditionally given a so-called Christmas tree lecture at Stanford, dealing with some aspects of tree structures. Tree structures such as the complete binary tree illustrated in Figure 5 rank among a computer scientist's most beloved concepts. Now please keep in mind that what I'm about to say is an idealization and oversimplification, but we have to start somewhere. Imagine starting at the top of the diagram in Figure 5, which represents a branching point where some choice has to be made. Also imagine that going to the left or going to the right will affect the entire future history of the universe. First the effect will be very small but eventually the effects will build up. After the first choice (say we go to the left), another decision has to be made—maybe go to the right and then right and then left. The number of possible destinies for the world goes from two to four to eight to sixteen to thirty-two and so on. All of the paths in this tree are consistent with the laws of quantum mechanics, regardless of which choices are taken.

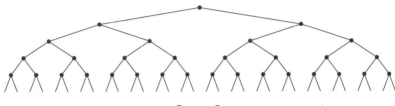

FIGURE 5.

If any of you saw the movie *Run Lola Run* that came from Berlin this year, you'll have a clearer idea of what I'm saying. There are three parts to that movie, and all three parts begin almost exactly the same except that Lola starts to run maybe one second later in the second part and two seconds later in the third. But then what happens in the three parts turns out to be quite different as the stories start to diverge, leading to three completely different endings. In one case the heroine dies; in one case her boyfriend dies; and in the other case they both live happily ever after. It's a fun movie, but it can also give you some idea about what I'm saying here about profound changes in the entire state of the universe, based on very small individual changes that each are consistent with quantum mechanical laws.

The most popular way to account for what we can see in physical experiments is to imagine flipping a coin at each branch point. Einstein made a famous comment that "God doesn't play dice with the universe," and he held to that position for the last thirty years of his life. But nowadays that's definitely a minority opinion. For example, Rustum Roy gave a major lecture in London twenty years ago called "Living with the dice-playing God." David Bartholomew's book *God of Chance*, published in 1984, said that God *uses* chance, because chance offers "many advantages which it is difficult to envisage being obtained in any other way," for example in genetic evolution.

Indeed, computer scientists have proved that certain important computational tasks can be done much more efficiently with random numbers than they could possibly ever be done by any deterministic procedure. Many of today's best computational algorithms, like methods for searching the Internet, are based on randomization. If Einstein's assertion were true, God would be prohibited from using the most powerful methods.

On the other hand, earlier this year Stephen Hawking said, "All the evidence points to [God] being an inveterate gambler who throws the dice on every possible occasion."

Some people, of course, are very suspicious of random choices. For example, Hugh Montefiore in 1985 said, "Chance and necessity may produce creativity but they cannot produce purpose." On this point I believe he was dead wrong: I use random numbers all the time with a very definite purpose, namely to help me discover something. Arthur Peacocke's opinion is that God has perfect knowledge of the *probabilities* of events like radioactive decay, but he doesn't have knowledge about the *outcome* of those events. And Peacocke also says that God created such a universe intentionally.

The picture isn't quite as simple as you might think, however, because quantum theory also implies that the probabilities aren't necessarily independent of each other. They're said to be *entangled*. In fact, quantum theory insists that certain observations have to agree, even though they are individually random, and even though they're being made simultaneously in two completely different parts of the universe. Mind boggling as it seems, quantum mechanics *requires* action at a distance, as if there were instantaneous communication much faster than the speed of light — in spite of what you may have been taught about the theory of relativity.

Yet quantum mechanics doesn't contradict the theory of relativity, because these widely separated events are individually random. Professor Abner Shimony of Boston University says that there is peaceful coexistence between those two theories, because he says there's not really "action at a distance" but rather "passion at a distance" — because of constraints on the way that entangled choices reveal themselves.

Exploiting the counterintuitive properties of entanglement is the basis for hopes about quantum computing, because entangled choices can perhaps be coerced to run through many, many possibilities almost simultaneously and to sort out the good ones based on some kind of resonance. I can't claim to understand much at all about entangled bits; but for me the significance of the probabilistic model for quantum theory is that it clearly makes room for free will, and it allows God to exert dynamic control over the world without violating any laws of physics.

In other words, using the simplified model of Figure 5, we can think of God as a tree pruner, occasionally influencing the outcome of various branches while simultaneously adjusting the nonobservable information behind the scenes so that all observations remain consistent with quantum mechanics. And we ourselves — even us, our spirits or souls or minds or whatever you want to call this part of our being — we might be little tree pruners too, with much more limited and local powers, of course, but still able to exercise free will in this way. Who knows, such a thing might even be *easy*, if God has set us up behind the scenes with some sort of useful hardware, off in the hidden dimensions. The word "spirit," meaning "breath of life," seems curiously appropriate in the context of tree pruning.

James Jeans said in 1930, "For ought we know, or for ought that the new science can say to the contrary, the gods which play the part of fate to the atoms of our brains may be our own minds." Last Sunday I heard another relevant quotation, this one from Martin Luther King, Jr.: "We through our deeds and words, our silence and speech, are constantly writing in the Book of Life."

Now in closing I want to say a few words about *consciousness*. Stuart Sutherland, in the 1996 edition of the *International Dictionary of Psychology*, gave a great "definition" of that word. Here's what he said.

Consciousness: The having of perceptions, thoughts and feelings; awareness. The term is impossible to define except in terms that are unintelligible without a grasp of what consciousness means. . . . Consciousness is a fascinating but elusive phenomenon: it is impossible to specify what it is, what it does, or why it evolved. Nothing worth reading has ever been written on it.

Well, during my visit here at MIT I did find one book about consciousness that was at least partly worth reading, namely *Mind and Matter* by the physicist Erwin Schrödinger. Schrödinger's main insight was to equate consciousness with learning; after you've learned something you do it unconsciously.

Yet consciousness remains the largest major question about which science has so far made little or no real progress. Computer scientists studying artificial intelligence may well have the best chance of unraveling this mystery, if it ever can be demystified. The most promising approach that I've heard of is the notion that consciousness might be a kind of genetic algorithm in which a large pool of ideas is constantly competing for attention in our brains. These ideas fertilize each other and the fittest survivors continue the process in Darwinian fashion; as I'm talking to you now, there's all kinds of survival going on inside our heads. Maybe some theory like that is going to work out. It seems to have many of the right properties.

But maybe the reins will still have to be controlled by free spirits acting outside of the observable portion of quantum mechanics. As Peter Gomes has said, we experience "close encounters of the transcendent kind that suggest relationships beyond the power of our experience to reckon, but which we know in some fundamental way to be true."

(Please excuse me for giving so many quotations. As I was preparing these lectures, I ran across lots of things that were said better than I could say them myself, and I couldn't resist giving you the benefit of these other people's wisdom.)

I would like to conclude by quoting one more thing from the end of a talk that James Jeans gave many years ago about a similar topic. He said,

> Every conclusion that has been tentatively put forward [in this lecture] is quite frankly speculative and uncertain. We have tried to discuss whether present-day science has anything to say on certain difficult questions, which are perhaps set for ever beyond the reach of human understanding. We cannot claim to have discovered more than a very faint glimmer of light at the best. ... [Thus] our main contention can hardly be that the science of to-day has a pronouncement to make, perhaps it ought rather to be that science should  leave off making pronouncements: the river of knowledge has too often turned back on itself.

I hasten to add that, yes, we should stop making dogmatic pronouncements, but we should certainly not stop trying to learn more. Thank you for listening. Once again I'm ready for questions.

Q (Guy Steele): I've got a comment. Twenty-two years ago I took a course here at MIT and the title of the course was "Digital Physics," taught by Ed Fredkin.

A: He was one of the people I had in mind when I mentioned that subject, but I didn't know he had actually taught such a course.

Steele: I distinctively remember a discussion in class about the possibility of modeling the universe as a cellular automaton. Fredkin spoke rapturously, I think, of electrons possibly being represented by billions of cells in some 3-D framework. One of the students in a very distressed voice said, "Wouldn't that take an awfully long time. Wouldn't it be awfully slow?" Fredkin said, "How fast do you want it to be?" And another student piped up and said, "One second per second."

A: The universe could very well be made out of discrete components — very, very tiny — and Fredkin has thought a lot about that. Besides this, a man named Poston in Warwick came up with some extremely interesting ideas that I read awhile ago.

When I study computer algorithms I have to keep track of the difference between continuous approximations and the discrete truth all the time. There's always the ideal thing, given by infinite calculus, to be compared to the reality of the computer program with its finite basis. So I have to say that X is equal to Y plus big-O of Z, and the big-O is what's missing in the books on theoretical physics that I consulted. In my own work *The Art of Computer Programming*, whenever I discuss an algorithm for which the original author has given only an asymptotic analysis in the style of a physicist, I always have to rework the argument to keep track of the errors being made. I think it would be extremely valuable to develop all the theories of physics with the big-O in there, to make rigorous estimates of the magnitudes of errors in your data and in your answer.

In some mathematical arguments, I have not been able to carry out the extra analysis of an appropriate big-O-type estimate. When things like the Borel–Cantelli lemma and other nonconstructive principles like subadditive functions are employed, I have no way to compute bounds on how fast a limiting value is approached. But I believe that the main theorems, the things that apply to reality, almost always allow you to understand the tremendous difference between the assumption that something is infinitely accurate and the assumption that its accuracy is finite but extremely precise (like good to one part in Super K).

Steele: Perhaps another answer to the student's question would be, "Yes, this simulation is slow, and it's slow down to Super K, but that's very small as finite numbers go."

A: Right. Or, my answer might have been, "Yes, it's slow, because it makes the universe operate at a student's speed."

Q: Suppose we make an assumption that at some point in the distant future, everything that our nervous system is capable of perceiving will be computable as a function of the observable state of the universe at that time, using some mechanism that we may not be able to conceive of right now. It's easy to say that computers are not capable of doing such things at the moment, but I find that argument very weak. But if we reach a state when deterministic computability is feasible, do you think that could then in some way negate the possible existence of God?

A: The question, if I understand you, is: If the world is deterministic, does that disprove the existence of God? No, it just disproves the existence of free will. Those are different questions.

But in fact, the idea of recording the entire state of everything in the world is quite incompatible with the theory of quantum mechanics, because modern physics uses complex numbers and all kind of unobservable things that can only be observable (converted from complex to real) if you destroy the information that's hidden.

The physicists have a nice theory about the way things work when they're undisturbed, and then they have this nice theory of what happens when you make a measurement. But I haven't seen any treatment about what happens when you close a loop, so that the physicist who takes a measurement and decides what to do next is also part of the picture, I mean part of the universe that obeys the laws of quantum mechanics. There should be a way to make the picture close on itself, the way it does when we write loops in computer languages. "While measurement X gives a result less than Y, perform measurement Z." The theory about what happens in such cases wasn't addressed in any of the books I looked at. And I didn't have time to look further or to explore it myself, so I decided to continue writing Volume 4 instead.

Q: What do all these issues of computational complexity, infinity, and the positing of God have to do with good, bad, and purpose?

A: That's a terrific question. I didn't focus on aspects of purpose in my lecture, except for saying that I use randomness for my own purposes, and for talking about some of the reasons why I like to write computer programs and why Dorothy Sayers liked to write plays. I guess I sort of assumed, mistakenly, that God would have certain purposes as if God were a human being.

I know that it's not valid to try to second-guess God with human concepts, but human analogies are the only way I have of trying to understand transcendental things. Certainly there are big questions about such things: Why did the firemen die last week? Shouldn't God have done something so that it didn't happen? We have no idea what would have happened if other branches of the tree had been taken, in my simplified model of choice points for destiny.

I'm afraid that I haven't got any good answers to add to what people have said over the years about such questions. Leibniz said that we live in the best of all possible worlds, with an emphasis on *possible*. In other words, Leibniz argued that God has looked ahead and seen all the worlds that are possible, and there aren't very many that are possible — meaning consistent with the laws of physics. But of the ones that are possible, God chose the best, even though God's choice doesn't necessarily agree with our own idea of best. We just don't know what's possible and what's impossible. That was Leibniz's answer, and there have been many other people thinking about such things over the years. I don't know if computer science has anything to add.

Well, wait a minute, maybe our experience with software design does shed a little more light on the subject. I can design a program that never crashes if I don't give the user any options. And if I allow the user to choose from only a small number of options, limited to things that appear on a menu, I can be sure that nothing anomalous will happen, because each option can be foreseen in advance and its effects can be checked. But if I give the user the ability to write *programs* that will combine with my own program, all hell might break loose. (In this sense the users of Emacs have much more free will than the users of Microsoft Word.)

For example, my T$_E$X system allows users to construct macros that can compute any computable function. This flexibility accounts for the fact that T$_E$X continues to be used in new ways by new groups of people on new generations of printing equipment, even though T$_E$X itself does not change. But the ability for users to add their own arbitrary programs to those of T$_E$X is also dangerous; experience has shown that it is best to restrict T$_E$X so that it cannot change the contents of system files under any circumstances. Otherwise viruses could be constructed to wreak great havoc.

From this standpoint we can see that the symmetry in Figure 5 is misleading, because it suggests that the choice points are fixed in advance and that the tree has a more-or-less uniform structure. I believe God has given us free will not only to choose between a given set of options in a menu, but also to change the options and to substitute new subtrees. My term "tree pruner" is inadequate to describe this vastly more significant aspect of our free will, unless we remember that the left branch of a tree might be totally different from the right branch. The second choice on the left and the second choice on the right might typically govern completely different aspects of the universe. One branch might trigger a nuclear holocaust.

·I suppose we could even regard Figure 5 as the Tree of the Knowledge of Good and Evil. As we learn more about science, we find that the fruits of this tree include not only the ability to choose between given options, to choose either "the lady or the tiger," but also the far more dangerous ability to change the basic ground rules of the environment that we live in.

Q: Can you comment on Martin Luther's view of free will?

A: Luther did not believe in a deterministic universe, but he said that the free will of human beings is inherently limited to relatively low-level decisions — what to eat, whether to have children, whether to be Democratic or Republican, whether to give lectures or write books. Above all, he stressed that we cannot will ourselves to have faith; our own reason and strength are insufficient for that, just as the people in Smullyan's story were unable to will themselves to have a sense of humor. Faith is a gift of God, not a product of human free will. We can't control our own thoughts. In my tree-pruning metaphor based on Figure 5, the human tree-pruners have limited scope compared to the tree-pruning ability of God.

Luther was particularly concerned that nobody should be able to boast of having earned their own salvation by means of a choice they had made with their own free will. I agree strongly with that view, but I also think people have an ability to choose to follow God's wishes. Luther was uncomfortable with the latter idea, because he thought people would then be entitled to claim merit for having made the right choice. On the contrary, I think the proper attitude is that people deserve blame for messing up, but they don't deserve praise for just doing their job. The parable of the servant in Luke 17:7–10 brings out this point nicely. My view is essentially that God has provided us with some kind of hardware by which we can exercise our limited free will. We are doing the job expected of us if we control it well, but we are forgiven if we don't.

Q: What makes you think that the Bible is the word of God? Or is that an axiom chosen at random?

A: The assumption that the Bible is God's word is an unprovable axiom that I tend to find confirmed as I look at it. I don't treat the words of the Bible literally as axioms though. I don't say, for example, that the Book of Revelation is a set of axioms from which I could deduce theorems as Euclid did in geometry.

I do think that the Bible reflects God's messages. As time goes by, we understand more and more about the way in which it was written and the historical process it has gone through, the difficulties of transmission over thousands of years. I think the Bible holds some of the best clues other than the universe itself as to what God wants us to do; I spoke about that last week. But I would never expect to be able to persuade anyone else about this hypothesis by using a mathematical argument.

I also have great respect for several other religions, and I believe God is speaking in their scriptures as well.

Q: It's hard to express this question because I'm not sure I can find the right terms. Let's take "material" to mean those things describable by physics or understandable by physics. If that's the case, do you see God as standing outside the material universe or coexistent with it?

A: I don't think of God as standing outside the universe letting it run, I see God as active all the way though.

In fact, the way I view God myself has a lot in common with pantheism, where God is everywhere. Some people think monotheism and pantheism are diametrically opposed concepts, but we can see from the standpoint of computer programming that they aren't essentially different. I mean, we can think of distributed computing, when there are lots of cooperating processes but really only one program — in the same way as an ant colony can be thought of as a single organism, or in the same way as the individual neurons of our brains are part of a single person.

Q: So God is "material" in that sense?

A: Well, I guess not; it's in another dimension, I think, orthogonal to physics. You do understand that if we lived in a two-dimensional universe there would be 3-D things that we couldn't perceive.

Q: Then it will never be describable by physicists?

A: That's true. But I don't think that's bad. If you could describe it, it would be kind of boring after a week.

Q: You have this discrete deterministic model, which is a kind of computer, and we know the speedup theorem that there's no way to know what's going to happen without its happening. So doesn't that mean that the determinism you have is really quite a bit different than the kind people think of where you can calculate, say, the next position of the planets any time in the future?

A: That's an interesting point. Since classical physics deals with infinite-precision real numbers, their deterministic models are not realizable on actual computers.

There's also a classical question, "If a tree falls in the forest and nobody can witness it (because maybe the forest is in a black hole), did the tree really fall?" In the setup I talked about, there's a similar but maybe more subtle question: "If nobody has ever named the numbers up to Super K, do they exist?"

I'm quite willing to believe that the number five exists, and six and seven and so on, and all the numbers I can count up to. But does that mean that all finite numbers have an independent existence? I implied as much when I said that the deterministic results of the Game of Life need not be simulated because they have always been present. It's something like if all the jokes in the world were numbered, and a person would come up to you and say "37!" and you would roar with laughter. Our universe would be number such-and-such in an appropriate encoding system, if it were finite, yet nobody could ever know that number.

I may therefore be guilty of the same sort of error that I've ascribed to physicists and philosophers. Why should I consider a sharp distinction between determinism and nondeterminism, or between existence and nonexistence, to be any more relevant than a distinction between finite and infinite? There might well be degrees of existence, when we consider the computational complexity of naming things.

Suppose, for example, there exists a million-digit number K_w that contains the key to wisdom. But suppose further that it will take at least 100 years to compute K_w, even if we use all of the world's fastest computers. Should the United States Patent Office grant a patent on the numerical value of that integer, once it has been computed, even though purely mathematical things are not patentable, and even though one surely cannot patent a simple number like 2009?

Your question also reminds me of a completely different thing, the so-called "many-worlds hypothesis." I tend to think that it's too wild to be true, but some people have used such an assumption to account for entanglement, where they say that all of the branches in Figure 5 actually are present. In other words, as we're talking right now the universe is cloning itself into many almost-identical copies of itself, and we all exist in all those branches. And all three of the things that happened to Lola happened. Because all branches of the trees are solutions to the equations of quantum mechanics. This is the way a computer scientist looks at nondeterministic computation, as if all of them are going on. And we think we have free will in each thread.

Now we have no way to test this hypothesis; in some of those worlds we just die earlier. And then perhaps you have to ask the question "What is consciousness?" in a new way, because each of our individual consciousnesses is different on each branch of the tree. Lots of speculation of this abstract kind has been going on, but as I say it does seem quite far out to me. I probably didn't answer your question, but those are some of the complexities that are associated with it.

Q (David Rosenberg): This is sort of a follow-on to the last two questions. Rather than state it in general form, I'm going to pose only one specific example. Are you part of God?

A: Am I part of God? I'm not sure exactly what you're getting at, but it's Christian dogma that God is in us and we're in God. That is why, for example, the Bible verse 1 Thessalonians 3:16 says, "Refrain from sexual immorality because you're part of God." In other words, that's part of my motivation. I'm not an antagonist of God, because we're part of the same team. But I'm not entirely a subset of God in the mathematical sense, because I do think I have a free will that's independent of God.

Q: Is there any sense to which it can be true then that each of us is all of God?

A: Do you mean each of us individually?

Q: Yes.

A: Well I suppose there exists the sense, but I certainly don't feel like God.

Q: In your mathematical understanding of things, do you find a demarcation between running an experiment, as the question was asked back there, and a Gedanken experiment which you merely think through what might happen as Einstein did?

A: The distinction between running an experiment and thinking about the experiment? Are you assuming that my thought processes are accurate? Mine aren't, but maybe a perfect computer or perfect creator would be able to go through and wouldn't have to run anything.

My personal view is that God is dynamically involved and actively interested in the choices that we make. But, as I say, there is no way to prove or disprove any of these things.

I see it though like ... it's a weak analogy, but still about as good as I can come up with from the standpoint of a software user ... like when Joel Moses created the MACSYMA system at MIT twenty years ago. I used to log in from California to use MACSYMA, and people at MIT were often watching me as I was using it. And I was glad to know that they were following what I was doing, because every once in awhile I'd get stuck, but then my terminal would magically type out a message like "Try the TELLRAT function." Now *that's* the kind of attitude I'm thinking God is using with me in life.

Q: My question was somewhat different, tied in with the paradox of Schrödinger's cat.

A: Oh. I've heard that paradox a couple of times, but there's something about a cat dying and I hate to think about such things.

Q: What are your thoughts on prayer? Is prayer an effective way to communicate?

A: My thoughts on prayer are complicated and hard to verbalize, but I'll try to explain them. I don't believe in prayer for selfish things, where I would pray in order to get an advantage of some kind. I think of prayer as a conversation with God. Even if I didn't know that prayer was effective I would do it anyway. It's just something that feels natural.

When I was a child I thought about prayer in a very selfish way. I remember quite vividly being told that, if you ask God for something, and if you truly believe in Him, then He will grant your wish. And I wanted a Ferris wheel. (Really, it's true: I was visiting relatives in Cleveland, and we had gone to an amusement park, and I fell in love with the Ferris wheel.) So that night when I went to sleep and said my prayers, I said, "Please God, put a Ferris wheel on the front lawn tomorrow morning." I'm serious. And the next morning I ran to the window, fully expecting to see it there. I was devastated to see that the lawn was still empty.

That, I say, is a completely wrong attitude to have about prayer. But now I understand that prayer is a conversation. Maybe I hope that God will do something, but I don't pray in order to get an extra bonus. It's just something I feel like doing. When I give a prayer of thanks, it's essentially like the way I feel when I'm hugging my wife. And when I pray, I might also express disappointment or anger, like when I'm arguing with my wife. Communication is much better than keeping your feelings bottled up.

Q: In a nondeterministic world, let's say there are two brothers who are twins. Their behavior cannot be predicted, but if you look at the correlation between them they have a perfect correlation. So if you observe one's behavior you kind of know what the other is doing at the same time. Or let's suppose they have 90% correlation in their behavior with each other. In such a case, do you consider that each of them have free will individually, or do you consider that together they have a free will?

A: Well, of course I've never known twins whose behaviors are correlated in this way. I know that when identical twins are separated at birth and raised in completely different environments, they still turn out to have mannerisms in common, probably because of their genetic makeup.

But I guess I'm interpreting your question too literally. What you are saying is really a metaphor for entanglement, but with respect to human beings rather than to abstract bits. Then I'd say it is certainly reasonable to imagine that either their souls are correlated, or that consciousness without a soul is governed by very similar mechanisms. I haven't thought about this enough to say more.

Q (Doug Ross): Sometimes our free will gets tangled up with the real world. And the simplest example I know of is the fact that you so often get documents that say, "This page intentionally left blank." Do you have a comment about how to solve that problem in a proper way?

A: What you have to say is, "The *previous* page was intentionally left blank."

Q: I want to sort of try to tie together a lot of the comments you've made today. On the one hand, the sense seemed to be along the lines of peeling away more or less logical objections that some people would have to the existence of God. On the other hand, you've spoken of resonant images or metaphors, or whatever, that help you conceive of God. The gap I'm experiencing a little bit is that at least my own way of coming to a religious sensibility was much more experiential; I had to get rid of some intellectual objections, while probably not as erudite as the kind of things you've been mentioning. So far, your comments don't seem to connect with the relationship aspect of religious belief experience. This is not so much a question as maybe a point of departure.

A: I focused my talk on things where computer science might contribute new notions to the mix of ideas that I had seen put forward by scientists in other disciplines. When I had read comments by physicists, biologists, and chemists, I would think of other points that I imagine a computer scientist would be more likely to bring up.

One of the things I explored while I was preparing these lectures might be closer to what you want to hear, although I had decided not to bring it up today because it didn't fit directly with the other topics. Earlier this year, I had been somewhat surprised to learn that Plato had once discussed something called "divine madness" — the Greek words are *theía manía*. He had Socrates speak about a God-given state of being beside oneself, which is manifested in four different ways: prophecy, catharsis, poesy, and eros. I learned a little bit about such things from the reading that I've been doing these past few weeks, and I think they add another significant dimension to the whole mystery of consciousness. But I didn't think computer science helped me understand *theía manía* in any special way.

Q: What was the thing you promised to talk about last week but didn't have time to discuss today?

A: That's a sneaky question, but I'm glad you asked. I had originally thought that I would discuss some experiences that I had when I was designing a computer chip. But this week I decided to leave that story out, because it relates more to economics than to God. I'll tell you anyway, because you asked for it, and because it does have possible connections to the organization of the universe.

So here's the story. As I was designing a chip for a very simple RISC computer, I was surprised to find that the easiest and somehow the best way to design this chip was to have it doing all kinds of things that would never be needed afterwards. I mean, two binary numbers were input to the chip at each clock cycle, and the adder would add them and the subtracter would simultaneously subtract them, and the multiplier would multiply them. These things were all going on at once inside the chip, but only one of those results would survive and actually be used in the computation in the next step. In this way the chips were operating quite differently from the computer programs I had been writing before.

The alternative would have been to design the chip so that every circuit inside the multiplier had extra inhibitors on it saying, "Don't multiply unless I tell you to." That would add an awful lot to the hardware.

I started thinking about this as an interesting metaphor for society and the world in general. It might help us to reformulate our notions of "purpose." There is good reason for a thousand people to work on a problem even though only one of them is going to solve it, and even though the people know in advance that only one of them is going to influence the final answer. Everybody can take pride in what they do even if it doesn't show up in the next generation, because otherwise less would get done and people would be idle.

You might find it interesting to muse about that a little bit.

Q: It's easier to let people make mistakes than to have such a tightly controlled environment that no one can make mistakes.

A: Yes. I remember something Dijkstra told me once. On his first visit to Stanford he saw the linear accelerator, and he just couldn't believe so many experiments were going on simultaneously. He thought you should run the accelerator for an hour and then sit and think for a year about what you learned; then it would be time to turn the machine on again. The other attitude was the American way instead of the Dutch way.

Q: Since there is time for only one more question, I want to ask you to mention one more thing that you had to cut from the main part of your lecture for reasons of time.

A: Well, I noticed debates in the faith and science community about "top-down causality" versus "bottom-up causality." I thought I might point out that my research on so-called *attribute grammars* shows that top-down and bottom-up causality can coexist quite nicely. But I never had time to explore that in depth.

In conclusion I want once again to thank the MIT administration in general and Anne Foerst in particular for inviting me to give these lectures. I thank you all for coming and asking such excellent questions. My fondest hope is that you continue to seek answers, even though the questions may be unanswerable.

Notes on Lecture 6

Page 167, improvisor of unsurpassed ingenuity: Arthur Peacocke, *Creation and the World of Science* (Oxford: Clarendon Press, 1979), Chapter 3. See also Arthur Peacocke, "Chance and law in irreversible thermodynamics, theoretical biology, and theology," in *Chaos and Complexity: Scientific Perspectives on Divine Action*, edited by Robert John Russell, Nancey Murphy, and Arthur R. Peacocke (Vatican City State: Vatican Observatory Publications, 1995), 123–143, especially page 140.

Page 168, art is everything else: See the reference to my paper "Computer programming as an art" in the notes to Lecture 4.

Page 168, panel discussion: See below.

Page 168, I personally see no signs: This in spite of recent books by people I respect, such as *Robot: Mere Machine to Transcendent Mind* by Hans P. Moravec (New York: Oxford University Press, 1998); *The Age of Spiritual Machines* by Ray Kurzweil (New York: Viking Press, 1999).

Page 168, Brian Hayes: "Computational creationism," *American Scientist* **87** (September–October 1999), 392–396.

Page 169, probably the most difficult: Donald E. Knuth, *MMIXware* (Heidelberg: Springer, 1999), especially pages 150–331.

Page 169, reprinted in several books: Donald E. Knuth, "Coping with finiteness," *Science* **194** (17 December 1976), 1235–1242. Reprinted with corrections in *Electronics, the Continuing Revolution*, edited by Philip H. Abelson and Allen L. Hammond, AAAS publication **77-4** (Washington, D.C.: American Association for the Advancement of Science, 1977), 189–196; and in *Mathematics: People, Problems, Results*, edited by Douglas M. Campbell and John C. Higgins, volume 2 (Belmont, California: Wadsworth, 1984), 209–222. Bulgarian translation by G. Chobanov and Z. Dokova in *Fiziko-Matematichesko*

Spisanie **21** (Sofia, 1978), 58–74. German translation by Arthur Engel in *Der Mathematik-Unterricht* **25**, 6 (1979), 5–26. Reprinted with corrections as Chapter 2 of *Selected Papers on Computer Science* (Stanford, California: Center for the Study of Language and Information, 1996), 31–57.

Page 171, because of a theorem: See, for example, Ming Li and Paul Vitányi, *An Introduction to Kolmogorov Complexity and Its Applications*, second edition (New York: Springer, 1997), Theorem 2.2.1.

Page 172, Cantor's famous theory: Georg Cantor, "Über eine Eigenschaft des Inbegriffes aller reellen algebraischen Zahlen," *Journal für die reine und angewandte Mathematik* **77** (1874), 258–262. See also Joseph W. Dauben, *Georg Cantor: His Mathematics and Philosophy of the Infinite* (Cambridge, Massachusetts: Harvard University Press, 1979).

Page 172, three times in the King James Bible: Job 22:5, Psalm 147:5, Nahum 3:9.

Page 173, Peter Gomes: *The Good Book* (see Lecture 3), page 313.

Page 173, a rather deep result: Larry Joseph Stockmeyer, *The Complexity of Decision Problems in Automata Theory and Logic*, report MAC TR-133 (Ph.D. thesis, Massachusetts Institute of Technology, 1974), Chapter 6. See also the exposition in my paper "Coping with finiteness" cited earlier.

Page 173, theorem of Büchi: J. R. Büchi, "Weak second-order arithmetic and finite automata," *Zeitschrift für Mathematische Logik und Grundlagen der Mathematik* **6** (1960), 66–92.

Page 175, tremendous leap of faith: Coincidentally, I happened to see a car with the bumper sticker

Question Reality

when I returned to California.

Page 175, *surreal numbers*: See Donald E. Knuth, *Surreal Numbers* (Reading, Massachusetts: Addison–Wesley, 1974).

Page 176, Plato: *The Republic*, vii:531e.

Page 176, James Jeans: *The Mysterious Universe* (Cambridge University Press, 1932), page 30.

Page 176,   Game of Life: Martin Gardner's original column "Mathematical Games: The fantastic combinations of John Conway's new solitaire game 'life,' " *Scientific American* **223**, 4 (October 1970), 120–123, in which Conway's game was introduced to the world, has been reprinted with extensive additions in Gardner's book *Wheels, Life and Other Mathematical Amusements* (New York: W. H. Freeman, 1983), Chapters 20–22. See also Conway's own description in *Winning Ways* by Elwyn R. Berlekamp, John H. Conway, and Richard K. Guy (London: Academic Press, 1982), Chapter 25.

Page 176,   probably the simplest example: An even simpler example of a universal cellular automaton was discovered by E. R. Banks in his Ph.D. thesis at MIT in 1971. The transition rules in his system involve only the four nearest neighbors of a cell: If three or four of those neighbors are on, the cell goes on; if exactly two are on and they are adjacent, the cell goes off; otherwise the cell's state doesn't change. However, this scheme apparently needs to have infinitely many cells in each of the two states, while Conway's scheme requires only finitely many cells to be on. See Edwin Roger Banks, "Universality in cellular automata," *Symposium on Switching and Automata Theory* **11** (1970), 194–215.

Page 177,   an abundance of material: For example, a good starting point is "Paul's Page of Conway's Life Miscellany," by Paul Callahan, www.radicaleye.com/lifepage/.

Page 178,   artificial life: For a stimulating introduction to this active area of research, see *Artificial Life* by Steven Levy (New York: Pantheon, 1992).

Page 180,   Planet Without Laughter: See the end of Lecture 4. This quotation begins on page 181 (slightly paraphrased).

Page 180,   Albert Einstein: The quotation is from a speech, "My credo," to the German League of Human Rights, Berlin, in 1932. See *Einstein: A Life in Science* by Michael White and John Gribbin (New York: Dutton, 1993), page 262.

Page 181,   she enjoyed writing plays better: Dorothy L. Sayers, *The Mind of the Maker* (London: Methuen, 1941), page 64.

Page 181,   Paul Dirac's famous book: P. A. M. Dirac, *The Principles of Quantum Mechanics* (Oxford: Clarendon Press, 1930).

Page 182, Jeans explained the need: James Jeans, *The Mysterious Universe* (Cambridge University Press, 1932), page 22.

Page 183, *Run Lola Run*: A movie written and directed by Tom Tykwer, 1999; see the webpage www.spe.sony.com/classics/runlolarun/runlolarun.html. Or, in the original German, *Lola Rennt*, www.lolarennt.de.

Page 183, God doesn't play dice: Albert Einstein, letter to Max Born, 4 December 1926: "Jedenfalls bin ich überzeugt, dass *der* nicht würfelt," in *Albert Einstein, Hedwig und Max Born, Briefwechsel* (Munich: Nymphenburger, 1969), page 130. English translation by Irene Born, *The Born–Einstein Letters* (New York: Walker, 1971).

Page 183, Rustum Roy: *Experimenting with Truth: The Fusion of Religion with Theology Needed for Humanity's Survival* (Oxford: Pergamon, 1981), page 188.

Page 183, David Bartholomew's book: David J. Bartholomew, *God of Chance* (London: SCM Press, 1984).

Page 184, more efficiently with random numbers: See the first note on Lecture 2. I must admit, however, that this statement is true only in the limit as our horizon becomes infinite. Deterministic rules of finite complexity Super K would be quite adequate for our universe.

Page 184, methods for searching the Internet: See Andrei Z. Broder, Moses Charikar, Alan M. Frieze, and Michael Mitzenmacher, "Min-wise independent permutations," *Journal of Computer and System Sciences* **60** (2000), 630–659.

Page 184, Stephen Hawking: "Does God play dice?" www.damtp.cam.ac.uk/user/hawking/dice.html, 12 July 1999.

Page 184, Hugh Montefiore: *The Probability of God* (London: SCM Press, 1985), page 98.

Page 184, Arthur Peacocke's opinion: See "God's interaction with the world: The implication of deterministic 'chaos' and of interconnected and interdependent complexity," in *Chaos and Complexity* (as cited above), 263–287, especially page 280.

Page 184, Abner Shimony: I found this in "Why God plays dice" by Mark Buchanan, *New Scientist* **159**, 2148 (22 August 1998), 26–30.

Page 185, James Jeans: *The Mysterious Universe* (as cited above), page 36.

Page 185, Martin Luther King, Jr.: I have not been able to trace the source of this quotation, which was part of last Sunday's sermon at the Methodist Church near Harvard Square. But King did say, "There is an invisible book of life that faithfully records our vigilance or our neglect," in an address given at Riverside Church in 1967; see *A Testament of Hope*, edited by James Melvin Washington (San Francisco: Harper & Row, 1986), pages 243 and 633.

Page 185, Stuart Sutherland: *The International Dictionary of Psychology* by N. S. Sutherland (New York: Crossroad, 1996).

Page 185, Erwin Schrödinger: *Mind and Matter* (Cambridge University Press, 1959).

Page 186, competing for attention: See, for example, William H. Calvin, *The Cerebral Code* (Cambridge, Massachusetts: MIT Press, 1996); William H. Calvin and Derek Bickerton, *Lingua ex Machina: Reconciling Darwin and Chomsky with the Human Brain* (Cambridge Massachusetts: MIT Press, 2000).

Page 186, Peter Gomes: *The Good Book* (as cited above), page 214. "There is in Celtic mythology the notion of 'thin places' in the universe, where the visible and the invisible world come into their closest proximity."

Page 186, James Jeans: *The Mysterious Universe* (as cited above), pages 187–188.

Page 187, Digital Physics: See Edward Fredkin, "Digital mechanics," *Physica* **D45** (1990), 254–270; "A physicist's model of computation," in *Massive Neutrinos — Tests of fundamental symmetries*, 26th Rencontre de Moriond (1991), 285–197; "Finite nature," in *Progress in Atomic Physics, Neutrinos and Gravitation*, 27th Rencontre de Moriond (1992), 345–354; "A new cosmogony," *PhysComp '92: Proceedings of the Workshop on Physics and Computation* (Los Alamitos, California: IEEE Computer Society Press, 1992), 116–121. A website for discussion of further developments related to Fredkin's cellular-automata-based approach has been set up by Joel C. Dobrzelewski at cvm.msu.edu/~dobrzele/dp.

Page 187, Fredkin has thought a lot about that: To my surprise I was greeted after this lecture by Fredkin himself, who I hadn't seen for more than 20 years; although he was in the audience, he chose to remain incognito and silent during the discussion.

Page 187, Poston: See Tim Poston, *Fuzzy Geometry* (Ph.D. thesis, Warwick University, 1971), 177 pages. An informal introduction to this work appeared in *Manifold* **10** (Autumn 1971), 25–33.

Page 189, the firemen: The big news story at the time of this lecture concerned the tragic deaths of six firemen in Worcester, Massachusetts on 3 December 1999.

Page 189, many other people: The best discussion I know on this question appears in Chapters 15 and 16 of Martin Gardner's book *The Whys of a Philosophical Scrivener* (New York: William Morrow, 1983); a second edition, published by St. Martin's [sic] Press in 1999, adds 32 pages of new notes.

Page 189, wait a minute: These comments did not arise during the public lecture but in a conversation with members of the audience immediately afterwards.

Page 190, Emacs versus Microsoft Word: Richard Stallman's editing program, Emacs, makes it easy for users to add new features of their own design. Microsoft Word, by contrast, allows only features that have been provided in advance, so that users who want more features must wait to purchase a new release of the program. (My analogy would therefore suggest that Microsoft Word should be considerably more reliable than Emacs. This, unfortunately, is not the case, but for entirely different reasons having to do with the concept of open source software.)

Page 190, the Tree of the Knowledge of Good and Evil: Genesis 2:17. This tree is "in the midst of the garden" (Genesis 3:3).

Page 190, Martin Luther's view: This question, likewise, came up after the lecture. I thank Anne Foerst and Jon Allen for presenting me with a copy of Luther's *The Bondage of the Will*, translated by J. I. Packer and O. R. Johnston (London: James Clarke, 1957); in the original Latin it was *De Servo Arbitrio* (Wittenberg: Johann Lufft, 1525).

Page 191, parable of the servant: See the hymn in the notes following Lecture 3.

Page 192, the speedup theorem: I'm not sure exactly which speed-up theorem the questioner had in mind. But it is easy to prove from the incompressibility theorem stated earlier that, for example, Fredkin's simulation of the universe by cellular automata operating in the universe could not run at a rate of 1.001 seconds per second.

Page 193, degrees of existence: For example, Shannon's information theory has proved to be hopelessly inadequate to express principles of cryptography; therefore that theory needed to be reformulated by taking computational models into account. See, for example, Andrew C. Yao, "Theory and applications of trapdoor functions," *IEEE Symposium on Foundations of Computer Science* **23** (1982), 80–91; M. Blum and S. Micali, "How to generate cryptographically strong sequences of pseudo-random bits," *IEEE Symposium on Foundations of Computer Science* **23** (1982), 112–117.

Page 194, Christian dogma: See, for example, Isaiah 7:14; John 6:56, 14:20; 1 Corinthians 6:15, 19.

Page 194, 1 Thessalonians 3:16: Actually 1 Thessalonians 4:3.

Page 194, Gedanken experiment: The questioner was probably referring to the famous paper by A. Einstein, B. Podolsky, and N. Rosen, "Can quantum-mechanical description of physical reality be considered complete?" *Physical Review* **47** (1935), 777–780. But I have a poor knowledge of physics and I didn't understand the question.

Page 194, MACSYMA: The Mathlab Group, *MACSYMA Reference Manual*, version six (Cambridge, Massachusetts: Massachusetts Institute of Technology, Project MAC, 1974).

Page 195, Schrödinger's cat: E. Schrödinger, "Die gegenwärtige Situation in der Quantenmechanik," *Die Naturwissenschaften* **23** (1935), 807–812, 823–828, 844–849; English translation, "The present situation in quantum mechanics," in *Quantum Theory and Measurement* (cited in Lecture 5), pages 152–167. This was Erwin Schrödinger's response to the paper of Einstein, Podolsky, and Rosen. According to Fredkin's paper of 1990 in *Physica*, cited above, cellular automata allow us to view such questions in a new way.

Page 197, Plato: See, for example, Josef Pieper, *Divine Madness* (San Francisco, California: Ignatius Press, 1995). "Divine madness" is sort of the opposite of what Governor Festus meant when he shouted, "Paul, you are out of your mind; all that learning of yours is driving you mad!" (Acts 26:24).

Page 197, very simple RISC computer: See Donald E. Knuth, *The Stanford GraphBase* (New York: ACM Press, 1994), 238–259.

Page 198, Dijkstra: Edsger W. Dijkstra. As far as I know he never has expressed such sentiments in print, but his general approaches to computer science problems have had an enormously beneficial effect as counterbalances to "conventional wisdom." See, for example, his *Selected Writings on Computing: A Personal Perspective* (New York: Springer-Verlag, 1982).

Page 198, *attribute grammars*: See, for example, D. E. Knuth, "The genesis of attribute grammars," *Lecture Notes in Computer Science* **461** (1990), 1–12, and the other papers in that volume.

PANEL DISCUSSION: CREATIVITY, SPIRITUALITY, AND
COMPUTER SCIENCE   (17 NOVEMBER 1999)

Anne Foerst: As part of this year's lecture series on God & Computers, we decided to use the time when Don Knuth happens to be visiting our campus to invite other accomplished computer scientists to contribute their opinions on the whole interaction of religion, God, and computer science. We now have in front of us five very famous, very good, and very *interesting* (which is most important for me), distinguished computer scientists.

But one of them is an exception, because Harry Lewis from Harvard University is actually the moderator. Even though Harry is a well-accomplished Harvard professor of computer theory, he also happens to be Dean of Harvard College, and therefore very much accustomed to interacting with people, forcing them to tolerance, making them shut up when they talk too long, and so on. At the same time he's also competent enough to know when something is important.

Therefore I welcome Harry very very much, and I welcome the other four panelists very very much, thanking you for having the courage to be here to talk about an area of your life that is not part of your professional work and not often openly discussed. I thank everyone for coming, and I hope that we all will have a wonderful interaction.

Lewis: Thank you and welcome to this panel on the subject of Creativity, Spirituality, and Computer Science. I am very grateful for the four distinguished guests who have taken the time to share their afternoon with all of us.

Let me tell you what I would like the format of this to be. First I am going to introduce the four panelists to you. Then I will ask each of them, in the order in which they are seated to my right, to make a few introductory remarks on the subject of the panel. Then we will probably have some cross talk among them, exchanging ideas and having some quick reactions. But I want to leave at least a half an hour for discussion with the audience, if not even more, depending on how long they take. There will be plenty of time for you all to jump in and ask questions and make statements.

Yes, my job is *tolerance enforcer*: That's my unofficial title for the day. Let me begin by introducing all four speakers.

Immediately to my right is Guy L. Steele Jr., who is a Distinguished Engineer at Sun Microsystems Laboratories. He received his A.B. in Applied Mathematics from Harvard College in 1975. He received his S.M. and Ph.D. in Computer Science and Artificial Intelligence from MIT in 1977 and 1980. He is the author or coauthor of four books on programming languages (Common Lisp, C, High Performance Fortran, and Java), as well as *The Hacker's Dictionary*, which many of us know and love. He is a recipient of the Grace Murray Hopper Award from the Association for Computing Machinery, as well as being an ACM Fellow and a Fellow of the American Association for Artificial Intelligence. Among his many achievements in the world of computer science, some that have had the most impact were his roles as designer of the original Emacs command set and as the first person to port TEX. At Sun Microsystems he is responsible for research and language design and implementation strategies, and architectural and software support for the specification of Java.

I will now depart from his formal biography to introduce a slightly autobiographical element. Guy Steele was a student in the first course I ever taught at Harvard, in the fall of 1974. I have no memory whatsoever of what the subject of that course was — I literally don't remember anything — but it was a great course; there were 17 people in it. I went back and looked at the grade sheet last night. It was really quite amazing. Two of them are now tenured professors at Stanford — Eric Roberts and Mike Genesereth. John Reif, who is a professor at Duke, was also in the  same class, as well as Guy and several other people who have also gone on to influential careers. The one thing I do remember about the course was Guy's final exam, because there, in the middle of some rambling, disconnected, and incorrect approach to a problem, all of a sudden there was a break. (I didn't write this down, I don't have the blue book, I just remember it 25 years later.) It broke, and he said, "Ahhhh. Now I see all too clearly the error of my ways." (Any of you who are students should remember that anything you write will survive.) I am sure neither one of us ever suspected that 25 years later I would be in a position to ask: Guy, what on earth were you talking about? And, can you relate that please to the subject of the panel discussion?

Steele: Well, actually I can't remember either and I can't remember what grade I got in the course, but I do have all my course notes. We should get together because I can go look those up.

Lewis: After Guy, we will have Manuela Veloso speak. Manuela is Associate Professor of Computer Science at Carnegie Mellon University. She received her Ph.D. in Computer Science from Carnegie Mellon in 1992, after having received a B.S. degree in Electrical Engineering in 1980 and an M.Sc. in Computer Engineering in 1984 from Instituto Superio Técnico in Lisbon.

Professor Veloso's long-term research goal is the effective construction of teams of intelligent agents where cognition, perception, and action are combined to address planning, execution, and learning tasks, particularly in uncertain, dynamic, and adversarial environments. She has been working on the concrete problem of soccer research — that is, robotic soccer research, not the NCAA championships. She has developed robotic soccer teams that have participated in the RoboCup international competitions in three different categories (simulated fully distributed agents, real small-wheeled robots, and Sony four-legged robots), and has had considerable success in those competitions. She is the author of over 70 technical papers and the editor of several volumes. She has been awarded the NSF Career Research Award in 1995 and the Allen Newell Medal for Excellence in Research in 1997.

To Manuela's right is Donald Knuth, who truly needs no introduction. I'm sure everybody in the audience has a Don Knuth autobiographical story in some way; at least, many of you I am sure do. My first job after I graduated from college (where I was a hacker) was to go to a national research laboratory in 1968. I remember, after I was there about six months, one recent arrival from the West Coast telling me that there was this guy at Stanford who had written this book about computer programming. He said it was different from the books about programming that you were used to seeing, which were mostly language reference manuals, although it had lots of code in it. It sounded quite fascinating. I remember going out and ordering a copy of this book and reading it. I came back to graduate school a number of years later, far more fascinated with the intellectual potential for the field than I had had from my experience as an undergraduate.

Don, of course, is Professor Emeritus of The Art of Computer Programming at Stanford. He has Bachelor's and Master's degrees from Case Western Reserve, and a Ph.D. from Caltech. He is the author of many, many highly influential books, not only *The Art of Computer Programming* series, but also the *Computers & Typesetting* series, and his nontechnical book *3:16 Bible Texts Illuminated*, about which he spoke here a few weeks ago. He has received many honors: the Turing Award, the National Medal of Science, the Steele Prize from the American Mathematical Society, the John von Neumann Medal, the Harvey Prize, and the Kyoto Prize, together with honorary degrees from many institutions.

Finally, Mitch Kapor is the fourth speaker. He is the founder of Lotus Development Corporation and designer of Lotus 1-2-3, the desktop productivity tool that led the way to the ubiquitous adoption of the personal computer as a business tool in the 1980s. For 20 years he has been at the forefront of the information technology revolution as an entrepreneur, investor, social activist, philanthropist, and most recently as venture capitalist. He is also a former teacher of transcendental meditation and a fervent admirer of the Dalai Lama.

Thank you all for being here and, Guy, I would like you to begin. Please do use the microphone.

Steele: I want to talk about spiritual inspiration in computer science both as a *means* of study and as an *object* of study.

The study of computer science, as we know it, is a human activity, so far; human activity is spiritual, at least in part; and therefore the study of computer science is spiritual, at least in part.

This may seem to beg the question. My point is that by "human activity" I mean to imply activity with a purpose. I want to talk here about purpose.

Why do computer science? Because it's fun? Because it is beautiful? To earn enough money to support a family? To earn enough money to buy mango ice cream at Toscanini's [an ice cream parlor near MIT]? To improve the lot of humankind? To serve God? (For me, it is all of the above.)

What we call "computer science" is actually an interesting mixture of science and mathematics. Now, there is often a confusion between the content of science and the methods of science, and between the content of mathematics and the methods of mathematics. The scientific method is not science, but an extremely successful cultural convention.

The *content* of science and mathematics has no purpose. It merely is. The content of mathematics is a logical description of relationships. The content of science is a set of mappings between the content of mathematics and the real world. A scientific theory may agree with or disagree with observations, but it has no intrinsic purpose. A mathematical theory may be consistent or inconsistent, but it has no intrinsic purpose. The *activity*, the human activity, that produces or discovers or uses such theories, however, *does* have purpose — multiple purposes, in fact, and those purposes guide our allocation of resources to the effort.

What is purpose?

I think purpose is related to consciousness. Purpose links our actions, or perhaps our mental states, from moment to moment. In many ways, purpose reminds me very strongly of the physical concept of momentum.

Zeno of Elea famously claimed in his Arrow Paradox that motion was impossible. Roughly speaking, he said that at any instant of time an arrow must be in a particular place, occupying a space just the size of the arrow, within which there is no extra space to move; and at another instant it is in another such space; then, he asks, where and when can the motion occur? Bertrand Russell put it this way: "The arrow is never moving, but in some miraculous way the change of position has to occur between the instants, that is to say, not at any time whatever."

Modern physics addresses Zeno's paradox, first, by using real numbers to model space and time and accepting the mathematics of limits as an explanation — though there are plenty of reasons to believe that this model is not realistic and breaks down at quantum scales; and second, by introducing the concept of momentum, which is a magic extra piece of state: At any given moment of time, the arrow has not only position but momentum, and momentum is exactly what distinguishes an arrow at rest from an arrow in motion. Momentum as such, like energy, is invisible and impalpable; you can't "see" it the way you see position. Momentum is the link through time; it describes how future positions of the arrow will be related to the present position. Of course, momentum can be altered by the action of outside forces.

In exactly the same way, I think purpose is the link through time that describes how future states of consciousness will be related to the present state, and purpose may be altered by outside influences.

Much of the content of religion has less to do with questions of fact than with questions of purpose. Where Genesis 1:1 says, "In the beginning God *created* the heavens and the earth," this is to me first and foremost a statement about purpose; where there is no purpose, we speak not of creation but of accident or happenstance. Where John 3:16 says, "Yes, this is how God loved the world: He gave His only Child *so that* . . . ," it is a statement about God's purpose.

Where does purpose come from?

Whatever we may regard as the source of the physical universe, I believe that it also is the source of purpose. It seems to me that purpose is exactly as likely to appear suddenly from nowhere as mass is, or momentum.

I believe, provisionally, as a scientist should with any theory, in most aspects of the Big Bang theory, though there are some problems with the details; and I believe that God was behind it and had a purpose. I believe, provisionally, in most aspects of the theory of evolution, though there are some problems with the details; and I believe that God is behind it and has a purpose.

I will madly conjecture that purpose may in some sense be conserved as rigorously as mass/energy or angular momentum, and that just as the universe appears to contain a preponderance of matter over antimatter, perhaps it contains a preponderance of good purpose over evil purpose. Then again, that may just be wishful thinking on my part.

The questions "Who?" and "What?" are answered by things. The questions "Where?" and "When?" are answered by states of things: positions in space and time. It makes me wonder why we don't have a question word whose answer is the momentum of a thing. The question "How?" is answered by a process, by some relationship between space and time; in fact, momentum is such a relationship, so maybe "How" is my missing question word. That leaves us with "Why?"; the answer to that question is a purpose.

What does this have to do with spiritual inspiration (the subject of today's panel discussion)? Let me point out that we can understand the word "inspiration" in two senses: (1) something that imparts a purpose, or (2) something that fulfills a purpose. Inspiration in the ongoing sense sustains the effort of a quest; inspiration in the instantaneous sense supplies the object of the quest. Such a quest may be intellectual, emotional, or spiritual — not that I think these three categories constitute sharp distinctions! On the contrary, when it comes to why we do what we do — whether it be computer science research, day trading, flipping burgers, or caring for lepers in Calcutta — all purposes are implicitly spiritual matters. Usually we associate the term "spiritual" with good, as opposed to evil, but I think it is fair to say that a selfish or thoughtless purpose is also spiritual in nature.

I don't have time in these preliminary remarks to explore the subject of good and evil or whether we have free will. I will remark briefly that I regard evil as exactly that which is opposed to *God's* purpose — this definition may be tautological — and that I think the most important aspect of the question of free will is not whether our choice of cake or pie for dessert is predictable, either by men or by God, or whether our study of computer science was predestined, but whether each of us has a free choice between good and evil.

Now let me turn to spiritual inspiration as an object of study.

To me, the core of computer science is the study of processes; of descriptions of processes (that is, programs); of descriptions of descriptions of processes (that is, programming languages); of descriptions of descriptions of descriptions of processes (that is, the theory of semantics); and so on.

And, oh yes, all their mathematical consequences.

And, as an afterthought, how well the descriptions predict the behavior of actual computing machines in the real world. That's the science part.

We find it very difficult to discuss processes of a certain complexity without using the terminology of purpose and a certain amount of anthropomorphism. I remember being struck by a comment I found in some source code, not long after I was hired as a systems programmer at Project MAC, which was the predecessor to MIT's Laboratory for Computer Science. The comment said something like, "This register is sacred to the garbage collector"! I had not expected to encounter the terminology of religion;

but "sacred" can mean "set aside for exclusive use, set aside for a purpose" and the meaning was instantly clear to me. It expressed not only a fact but a purpose in the code.

Analogies to human social structures such as committees and bus queues sometimes help us to design data structures and algorithms. Attempts to model human intellectual behavior on a computer have also led to important insights. So I suspect that the study of human purpose, inspiration, and spirituality may lead us in a similar way to important advances in computer science. And we will use metaphors rooted in these areas to help us deal with ever greater complexity.

I think we will be compelled ever more in the future to apply the vocabulary and concepts of purpose and perhaps even of religion in our study of computer science. A Turing machine can compute anything computable, *if* it makes state transitions in accordance with its rules. But whence comes the *impetus* to make those transitions? To compute *effectively*, a Turing machine needs, if not spiritual purpose, at least computational momentum; and the source of that momentum lies outside computer science.

As we study computational processes of ever greater complexity, we find ourselves drawn ever more to describe a process as having purpose: at first, the purpose inherited from its creator, but perhaps later a purpose of its own. And then we must face the question of whether this use of language is merely a metaphor or, in some deep sense, the truth.

At this point we get into such difficult questions as whether a computer program can have purpose, or consciousness, or free will, or even a soul. I do not propose to address those issues now, because I am still chewing on the same questions concerning myself.

Lewis: Before passing the microphone to Manuela, let me do what I should have done before Guy started speaking, which was to read you the question that I asked the four panelists to answer. (Of course if you're really good, you could have inferred it from Guy's answer.) Here was the question that I posed: "Computer science is an exact science if there ever was one, and arguably the ultimate man-made science. In what sense is spiritual inspiration a relevant concept in computer science?" It was a broad question, but an attempt to get people somewhere on the same subject. It would have been better if I had told you that before Guy started. Thank you. Manuela?

Veloso: I guess Harry didn't have to remind you of the question, because I actually would like to take these five or seven minutes to be more down to earth and talk about the problem that I face as a computer scientist.

Computer science, back in the 50s, was described by Alan Perlis, Allen Newell, and Herb Simon when they founded the computer science department at Carnegie Mellon in the following way: They defined it as, in their words, "the study of computers and the phenomena that surround them." Within these phenomena that surround them came artificial intelligence as one of the areas of computer science. I am engaged in research in this area of artificial intelligence — for short, AI.

AI has very, very ambitious goals that may seem to confront very deeply the concept of creativity, spirituality, and God. A core goal of artificial intelligence is to build fully intelligent artifacts with cognition, perception, action, learning, creativity, emotion, and all the characteristics, in some sense, of the creatures of God who, eventually, we are.

So there we go. I, eventually, believe in God. I do. But, I'm also an AI researcher.

Do I believe that such creatures can be invented by me, can be invented by my students, can be invented by my computer science algorithms? Are we going to be able to replicate, in the real world, these little creatures that we are?

To tell you frankly, I hope never to have to face this question. I just go on with my life. I do my research. I keep my beliefs in God. I just go on and I don't want to have to say, "Yes, there will be a little robot that will have its soul," or "No, that is an ultimately impossible goal." Now, because I actually don't want to face this question directly, let me tell you a little bit how I get my robots to, at least, show a little bit of intelligence.

Robotics has been seen as a science of precision. Last week I was in a robotics faculty retreat of Carnegie Mellon. (I am on sabbatical here at MIT.) Robots have been used in factories. I saw films, which many of you may have also seen, of production factories with hundreds of automated arms drilling precise holes, manufacturing parts, assembling products. These arms all move in synchronization, mechanically and automatically. Those are called robots. Then, we also could see precise robots that go into space and accurately operate in space. Such robots leave the earth and do their missions with precision. Other robots go down volcanos. Robotics can be seen as the science of precise automated control.

Instead in my research I really investigate robots that may be able to live with us, do the same things we do. And my little robots that play soccer, believe me, do not do precise things at all. They really do not kick into the goal all the time. They spin on the spot when the batteries go down. They try hard to do real passes. They push other robots, unintentionally, even if they know it is a foul. They do all sorts of wonderful things. And they actually get *me*, who coaches them (and all my students), shouting "Go", "Kick", "Do it", "Get out of the way", "Go around." This is very unscientific because you really act towards these little creatures as if they were alive.

I often see people who look at my soccer-playing Sony dog robots being literally moved by those little machines. When I am giving a big technical explanation, saying that the robot is a mechanical thing in which you can switch the legs, press a button, and put another leg on, I see this panic in the eyes of my audience like, "You are hurting the dog!" I say, "I'm sorry, this is a robot." Still I really have faced the problem of not being able to show how to switch a leg in the robot, because there seems to be always someone, especially in an audience of four-year-olds, who panics in front of me if I appear to be breaking the robot.

It is true that this concept of us having spirituality, in addition to flesh and bones, is not trivial. I would dare to say that one day we will mimic in robots everything humans have, but spirituality. And this may be because we may never know universally what is "spirituality."

You don't know what spirituality is for me. You don't know what my soul is. You don't know what I really am. And most probably no one will know about me as much as I do. So I find it impossible to mimic in robots what spirituality is. Robots will not be creatures of God. As cars and refrigerators are not.

One of the tricky things in creating robots, the way I aim at, is to be able to have them look at the real task to be executed as a probabilistic action selection problem rather than a precise deterministic algorithm. This will address the uncertainty of the world. My little robots are built as little machines that do probabilistic decision making. Their decisions surprise you because you cannot foresee

everything that will happen in the world and you did not prepro-
gram everything. Furthermore, we have a learning component that
adjusts online values that we know can be adjustable, but we don't
know how they are adjusted.

If you have a chance of one day watching these little robots,
or getting engaged in computer science research at the AI level, the
right approach that I defend is to create these probabilistic components. Such components will probably make the robots look
creative, capturing eventually some spirituality... That's my point.

Knuth: Before I start I want to mention that the general title of the
other lectures I've been giving in this series is, "Things a Computer
Scientist Rarely Talks About." But immediately after I gave the first
lecture a few weeks ago, the next morning I went to Morning Prayer
at Harvard Chapel, and the sermonette was given by none other than
Dean Harry Lewis. Thus not only is he an exception, as Anne said,
but he also is a counterexample to the title I chose for my lectures.

I was delighted to learn the title of today's panel discussion,
because it is about creativity and inspiration — so I figured that I
wouldn't have to prepare anything. I could just assume that the
spirit would move me to say something creative as time went on.

On the other hand, I couldn't help preparing something, because a couple of weeks ago when I was working on an unrelated
topic, I happened to be looking at *Scientific American* from 1958,
and there was an ad in the article I was reading that caught my
eye. The ad said, "This year in September we're having a whole
issue about creativity in science." So naturally, I turned to *Scientific
American* of September 1958 to see what they printed that month.
I found a really nice article by Paul Halmos, a leading mathematician who is also a great expositor. He addressed the question of
how mathematicians get their ideas. In brief, here is what he said:
"A mathematician is not a deduction machine, but a human being.
New mathematics comes not by pure thought and deduction, but by
sweat, experiment, induction, and, if lucky, inspiration." That sort
of describes the way it happens to me (a computer scientist) as well.

Now mathematics and computer science are the two *unnatural*
sciences — the study of things that are created by people instead
of being present in nature. That makes people like Halmos and
me somewhat different from other scientists. In mathematics and
computer science, we can actually prove theorems, solve problems

and know that we have an answer, because we get to make up the ground rules. In the natural sciences, researchers just accumulate more and more evidence for things without ever being able to reach closure. Yet even in the unnatural sciences our work rests largely on experiment, intuition, and (if lucky) inspiration.

I'd like to tell you about the most memorable experience that I've ever had, with respect to the subject of creativity. It happened a little more than 25 years ago. I woke up in the middle of the night, sort of knowing that I should write a little book called *Surreal Numbers*. I don't have time to tell you much about that booklet — it's a little novelette — but I got the idea of writing it because I figured that it would be the coolest way to describe a new mathematical theory that John Conway had told me about a few months before. My wife and I were on sabbatical that year and living in Norway. When she woke up the next morning, I told her I'd been awake thinking that, before I finish *The Art of Computer Programming*, I've got to write this other little book. I told her I could do it in a week. To my surprise, she said, "Hey, why not? It's a perfect time for you to do such a thing." We arranged our schedule so that I could rent a hotel room in downtown Oslo for a week in January. This hotel was very near to where Ibsen used to live; I figured that maybe some of his vibes might get through to me.

When I went there, it was a fantastic experience. Every morning I would start out eating a big
Norwegian breakfast. (Anyone who has ever been
to Norway will know that such food was enough to
keep me going; I didn't need lunch.) After breakfast
I would work on the book. Then, at about 2:00 in
the afternoon I would come to a stumbling block;
I couldn't advance it anymore. I would have to think
things over. So I'd go out and walk around the streets
of Oslo for an hour or so. All of a sudden the solu-
tion would present itself and I'd come back to my hotel room and
start writing furiously. Then I would have a leisurely supper, and go
back up to my room and write some more.

The amazing thing was that the book seemed to write itself. In
fact, after I would turn out the light, at the end of the day, the next
paragraph would come into my mind; I couldn't go to sleep without
turning the light back on again and jotting it down. The ideas were
coming so fast that I only had time to write down the first letter of

every word. I put them all down and then slept very soundly. The next morning after breakfast I would decipher what I had written, and I was ready to go until 2:00 again.

This went on for six days. I can understand now why people have conceived the idea of a Muse sitting over their shoulder. The text of the book seemed to be, not exactly dictated to me, yet . . . I dunno. The funny thing was, at the end of six days I finished the book, and then I rested.

On the seventh day, I tried to write a letter to my secretary telling her how to type it up. I would get to the middle of a sentence and I couldn't finish the sentence. All of a sudden, the muse had totally vanished. In the middle of a sentence I wouldn't know what I had intended to say; I'd have to scratch it out and start over again. Many other times in my life I've had a feeling that I was being inspired in some magical way, I have no idea how. But during the six days of *Surreal Numbers* that feeling was most intense.

The other topic I want to mention today is a book by Dorothy Sayers, *The Mind of the Maker*, first published in 1941 but recently republished in paperback. I brought it with me to Boston because I hadn't had time to read it before; it had been recommended to me. I think it's a wonderful discussion of creativity, spirituality, and such things, filled with lots of interesting material. For example, one of the first points Sayers made that impressed me was that ideas don't necessarily obey laws like the conservation of mass, energy, or momentum that Guy was talking about: You can get a new idea without having to destroy another idea.

I think Dorothy Sayers is probably the all-time best writer of detective fiction. Her novels are not only mystery stories, they are excellent on many different levels, with wonderful character development and other aspects all the way through. They're rich and they're wonderful. In *The Mind of the Maker* she talks about her experiences as a writer, with respect to that kind of creativity, and how those experiences have given her insight into the Christian doctrine of Trinity. She observes that her work has three aspects: (1) the creative idea; (2) the embodiment of that idea; (3) the understanding and communication of that idea. She sees that this actually is three things in one.

Let me mention just a few more things that can be found in her book. For example, she talks about the compulsion to write. She says, "Whenever the creature's desire for existence is dominant, everything else will have to give way to it. The creator will push all other calls aside and get down to the task in a spirit of mingled delight and exasperation." It's an almost perfect description of computer programming.

I like, especially, her last chapter, which is about problem solving. In mathematics and computer science, we state problems and then we solve them. I remember once Frances Yao telling me how she feels about research: She gets so interested in solving a computer science problem that she can hardly take time to eat or sleep. Then when she finally solves it, hurray! But two days later she has come up with another problem; one never gets to the end. Sayers observes that, in fact, this is the point. Once you solve a problem, it is dead; there is no more life and nothing more to do. You have to have another problem.

But Sayers also stresses that mathematical problem solving is quite different from most of the unresolvable issues that occur in real life. In the real world, there is tension between yin and yang, when one thing can only be improved at the expense of another, when tradeoffs are inevitable and problems are unsolvable. I remember reading a comment by Vaclav Havel about ten years ago, voicing similar thoughts — he said people are misled if they think that the problems arising in life are like puzzles that you can resolve just by finding the right trick. When I read Havel's remarks, I remember thinking, "Thank goodness for mathematics and computer science, in which we do have at least some problems that admit a solution." Sayers points out that mystery novels are appealing for that very reason.

A person like me might think, "Well, if the problems in real life are unsolvable, we can't do anything with them"; but Sayers doesn't stop there. She doesn't see life as a problem to be solved, but rather as *a medium for creation*. The irrelevance of math-type problem solving therefore actually proves to be an opportunity, not a curse. Her words express this thought better than I can, so I want to quote a few of them: "The concept of 'problem and solution' is as meaningless, applied to the act of creation, as when it is applied to the act of *procreation*. To add John to Mary in a procreative process does not produce a 'solution' of John and Mary's combined problem; it produces George or Susan, who (in addition to being a complicating factor in the life of his or her parents) possesses an independent personality with an entirely new set of problems."

In mathematics and computer science we use creativity to solve problems; but then, as Frances Yao taught me, we go on and create another problem. In the real world we use creativity to avoid having to choose between yin and yang; we take an apparently intractable problem and use it creatively to make a *new* thing. That's why creativity is so wonderful.

On the other hand I'm a little worried that creativity is dangerous. The world couldn't stand more than 10 people who are creative in just exactly the same way I am. If there were more than 10 Knuths in the world, we wouldn't have time to read each other's books! It would be terrible.

Fortunately, there are lots and lots of different kinds of creativity, and I'm glad to see creativity flourishing everywhere I look — for example, in the interactions between the security guards that I observed when I came to work in Tech Square this morning. As computer science matures, it is nice that our software is now becoming more interactive, so that users can be more creative as they use these tools.

Now I just have to think creatively about some punch line to end with. I did have one in mind . . . what was it? I guess the bottom line is that we needn't worry about living in a world where everybody is creative. In fact, having a good journey is more important than reaching a destination.

Lewis: Mitch?

Kapor: Well, this is a pretty difficult topic. I have very few firm answers, although I will take lots of firm positions, which may fool some of you into thinking that I actually know something. For that, I apologize in advance.

To provide some context here, I thought I would annotate the autobiography. I am not a computer scientist. I am more of a software designer. There are some significant differences between science, engineering, and design that really influence one's outlook on the issues at hand. Time doesn't permit going into that right now. What I would say, though, is that expecting me to be knowledgeable about computer science is sort of like asking a profound dyslexic to act as a scholar of literature. It can be done, but it is quite an art form.

A bit about myself: I am Jewish, by birth and cultural tradition. The particular branch of Judaism that I come from doesn't have spirituality. We have guilt.

For whatever reason, for about 30 years now, I have had a strong interest in spirituality, whatever that is; I will try to get into that. In particular, I've pursued forms of spiritual paths that come out of the East (India, China, and so on). I became a teacher of transcendental meditation in the 1970s. It was a very interesting experience. I can tell you that people really don't levitate. In fact, it is a cult, at least if you get highly involved with it. I have a lot of bruises acquired along the way from some of my involvement.

I am kind of a Buddhist fellow traveler, in the sense that I have a lot of affinity for a Buddhist's way of thinking; but I just can't seem to make it in any organized religion, including Buddhism. That is why I would say I am a fellow traveler rather than a practitioner.

On the "God" issue, I think it is a very interesting, and a particularly Western conceit, to link God and spirituality so closely — as if, without God there is no spirituality. There are some billions of people on the planet that just operate from a different point of view, being very comfortable saying that they operate in a spiritual context although the issue of God is one that is not front and center. I am kind of a devout agnostic on the "God" issue. I think I'll see what happens, but it is not a native thing inside my framework, whereas spirituality is.

One more thing, by way of context, just so you understand that I am perhaps a bit peculiar. I am really, genuinely, sincerely, *not* a materialist in the following sense. There are a lot of people who really genuinely believe that what there is comes down to molecules, and atoms, and subatomic particles; for them, that is it, period, in terms of the fundamental constituents of what there is. I am kind of on the other side in saying that this stuff ultimately, in some sense, feels to me to be an arising (a manifestation) of something that is a lot deeper, and a lot more mysterious — something that, in some way, I cannot articulate fundamentally. It also has to do with awareness or consciousness.

Given that, where does all this intersect with computer science? There is a remark that I have heard ascribed to Marvin Minsky, but I have no idea if Marvin actually said this, or not. In this context it doesn't matter. Allegedly, he said in effect that he vastly prefers a virtual sunset to a real one. I hear enough giggles from the audience to suggest that you have heard similar things. I have always been really puzzled by that, as I am a big aficionado of the virtual and of everything we can create with and through computers, whether in simulations, robotics, productivity tools, or name your favorite computer thing. But in the department of sunsets . . . ? I have always found virtual sunsets to be wanting in that they always sort of bottom out. If you meditate on a virtual sunset, sooner or later it dissolves into pixels or something like that. Whereas a real sunset, to me (of course I am speaking mainly metaphorically, but not entirely) is infinitely mysterious. There is always something new to discover, or some new experience of sunset, which is possible. It is kind of a guarantee about reality that we really haven't even come close to touching, despite our considerable progress in the creation of the virtual and artificial.

I don't seek to convert a single one of you to my own views, but personally it strikes me that some of the goals of hard AI, broadly speaking — goals that involve the creation of creatures or entities that are really like us — are idolatrous in a way. Even more important though, I think such goals are ill-fated. Because, I think, to believe *that* is to miss something about the sort of fundamental depth that people have and can have by themselves in their own awareness, with each other in relationships, and collectively. It's this enormous depth — again, I am speaking mostly metaphorically here — that I think distinguishes the human condition. It is what makes us capable of the worst evils and the highest good.

And I think the domain of the spiritual is the one, or one of the ones in this society, where we get to ask fundamental questions: Who are we? Where did we come from? How is it that, fundamentally, things are the way that they are? For me, those questions have always been very resonant. I have found that various spiritual traditions and teachings have a lot to offer as investigative tools along the way.

And so, coming back to computer science, and that which can be made from it and with it: To the extent that computer science too is seen and used as a tool to help us understand ourselves and reality better, to give us some insight, to extend ourselves — in the words of Doug Engelbart, one of my great heroes, to "augment our intellect" — I think it is a wonderful and terrific thing, and serves a spiritual purpose. Some of the artifacts and theories that we create, if they are a celebration of that deepest humanity, can also be viewed as spiritual work. Therefore, ultimately I do think that there is quite a lot of harmony, at least potentially, between spirituality and computer science.

Lewis: This was great. There were lots of interesting lines thrown out: anthropomorphizing ... spirituality ... the opportunity that some graduate student has here to create the first guilt-driven computer system .... . Now I would like to ask the panelists to comment on anything that any of the other panelists had to say. (No fair commenting on your own comments.)

Knuth: What Mitch said reminded me of a BC cartoon (you know, Johnny Hart's strip) that I saw about ten years ago, where there are two guys looking at a sunset. One of them says, "Oh, isn't this a wonderful sunset." The other one says, "Well, I dunno, I'd like a little more purple over on the left." It just struck me, when you know that something has been planned by a process you understand, how you have a different standard of beauty for it. Somehow, with a sunset, we don't expect it to be absolutely perfect by human criteria; we want to be surprised.

People sometimes ask why God didn't do things a little bit better. Why, for example, did God make the universe so sparse? He could have packed it with a lot more stuff and got a lot more done ...

Veloso: I would like to make a comment to Mitch about AI being ill-fated. As I said, I do also have a problem of accepting that we're going to really have robots that are like humans. But if we think it over, we are happy living with tons of other humans that are deficient in some ways. For example, my eyes probably don't work as well as yours. My lungs might not work as well, etc. We all have defects. What is the problem of thinking about robots that have the defect of not being spiritual? They are probably missing a soul. If we have a soul, O.K., robots don't — big deal. I don't think that this is much of a problem because we are also imperfect in some ways. What is the big deal of having AI with a goal of having humans that are not perfect just by this little aspect that they don't have a soul? Why do we think that this is a problem?

Kapor: I don't think it is a problem at all. You may have misconstrued my remarks. I think this stuff is really cool. These systems are very interesting because they show a lot of emergent behavior that you wouldn't predict from seeing any one of the parts. They are very bottom-up instead of top-down.

You know, this is a panel, we need to say something provocative; it's in the Panel Handbook. The only thing I have an objection to is this kind of golden calf vision of AI that, I suspect, finds something weak and flawed about the human condition. I find that this Pygmalion attempt to create something more perfect is a theme that undergirds some AI research. But I would, certainly, never make the case that any given researcher is driven by that. It is just kind of a pet peeve that I thought I would sound off on, since I'm on a panel.

Steele: I think it would be a great achievement to produce a robot that is as screwed up as I am. That's worth shooting for. One central puzzle of this is, how do we know when a robot has a soul, or not? I will ask, rhetorically, Mitch: How do you know whether I myself have a soul or intellect?

Kapor: For me "soul" is like this God thing. If you don't believe in God . . . I would be happy to find out that he or she exists. However, if it is not a belief, you are relieved of a lot of problems like "Why does God do X"? Similarly, I don't know about soul. The serious point is that this is kind of a concept that comes largely out of western paths of spirituality. If you go to Buddhism, for instance, you find endless tomes about all sorts of things, but the concept of soul doesn't arise. I hope that somebody will explain to me why we need that concept or what work it does. Then, it could be interesting to talk about whether robots could have them, or not.

Steele: We could back out of this a little bit, emotionally, and say that instead of discussing soul we are going to discuss purpose, or perhaps even just semantic meaning. Where does semantic meaning come from? How is it that a word or a person comes to convey meaning? There is this problem that if you start to get too rigorous and strict, and make your definitions too narrow, you find yourself backing into solipsism, which has problems of its own. However, if you don't back yourself into that corner, then you are bound to be a little bit too liberal and to make mistakes—as, for example, the four-year-olds who think that these robots are alive and, perhaps, that they feel pain. Well, maybe they do. I'm not sure.

Veloso: They don't.

Steele: I'll take your word for it. I would also like to make a couple of responses to some things that Don said. First of all, I wouldn't mind having two or three Knuths in the world. (On the other hand, I concluded long ago that I couldn't keep up with even one Asimov!) I think you are putting out just about the right amount of stuff and we are grateful for it.

I would like to push back on the notion that you can create a new idea without it destroying an old one. We like to program in Lisp, or Smalltalk, or Java, and pretend that we can "cons" new objects without destroying old ones. However, eventually you run out of memory and have to pay the piper. If your mind is finite, as I think mine is—I think that is a more useful model of it—then I think I agree with Sherlock Holmes that, after a certain point, for every new idea you take in, you have to get rid of something else in your mental attic.

Finally, I would like to allude to a theory that I actually heard from Gerry Sussman, that it is very important for you to sleep because that is when your brain is garbage collecting. A dream is when you get interrupted in the middle and there is junk left in the registers.

Knuth: I just want to say that I still can write a new book without having to remember what is in the old one. Dorothy Sayers says, "The poet is not obliged to destroy Hamlet in order to create Falstaff."

Lewis: If you don't want to talk to each other anymore, let's make a bigger conversation.

Question: I was taken by the idea of "process" in Guy Steele's talk. It reminded me of Whitehead; his process philosophy has led to process theology, the idea that God is subject to process, is changed by process. Another idea is that of Gordon Kaufman, professor emeritus of Harvard Divinity School, who defines God as "serendipitous creativity." Could you comment on some of these more modern ideas?

Steele: I am relatively ignorant of process theology. I don't have an opinion on it one way or another. I think it is possible that God is *at least* all those things. I generally find that, whenever I try to say God *is* something, and attempt to cut something specific off, I usually end up being wrong somehow. I think maybe a finite set of finite descriptions can't capture everything there is to know about God. I'll stop there.

Question: There is an area of thought that says that something does not truly exist without a purpose. For instance, if I have a hammer and I hang it on the wall, it is not really a hammer. It is only really a hammer when I am using it to drive nails. The next question is: What is the purpose of a man? From what you were saying, I got the impression that you feel that a purpose of a man is advancing God's will — just as we build systems (software, hardware) to advance our will, God created people to advance his or her will. If this is true, then a compiler doesn't understand or acknowledge its greater purpose. How, or why, should we acknowledge, or understand, any other greater purpose beyond what we can see and do? That is mostly directed to Guy Steele, but I would love to hear anyone's answers.

Steele: First of all, I note that you used the word "should"; this word has a free variable that needs to be bound to some purpose. To whose purpose should I bind that flapping free variable? My purpose? God's purpose? I think, however, that no matter how we bind it, there remains the problem of knowing what is God's purpose and trying to align ourselves with that. There is a question of whether you think that can be somehow derived or deduced by a rational method, a scientific method, or some other method; or, that it has to come by means of faith, divine revelation, the throwing of dice, or whatever your preferred method is. I happen to like the inspired revelation myself. You can try to cross-check in various ways. I admit that, ultimately, there is no way I can *prove* to you that we *should* do this or that. We muddle along on faith, I think.

Gerald Jay Sussman (for Mitch): I don't happen to have a religion, but I am going to quote, "God made man in his own image." That is a recursive definition.

Kapor: And therefore . . . ?

Sussman: I can create things that, themselves, can be creative.

Kapor: I don't have any problem with that. Under that interpretation of strong AI, I absolutely agree with you.

I wanted to just ask Guy to comment on this soul and/or purpose thing. Maybe you can shed some light on how you construct this. I gather that you see them in some sort of relationship, or continuum, which intuitively sounds very appealing. But for me, a purpose . . . What kind of an entity is it? Where does it fit into the concept ontology? A purpose is like . . . It's a kind of a behavior-descriptive entity. That is why you can talk about what a purpose is in terms of various behaviors and their relationship over time, and so on. Whereas — and I may have a very crude view of this — when you talk about soul, typically I experience that as a kind of physical or paraphysical entity.

It is a very different kind of entity than a mere description of purpose. I kind of feel a disconnect between those two. This is not word mincing. This is in search of illumination. If you make a connection, I would love to get let in on it.

Steele: In struggling for a metaphor, I'm led to ask the question of whether we think of soul as being more like a paraphysical entity, as you say, or whether it is, perhaps, more like a pattern — a pattern that may have an underlying physical substrate.

The best comparison I can make is to ask whether you think a computer virus is real, independent of the bits of magnetic oxide in which it is embedded or encoded in this or that instant?

Kapor: If you strip away all of the paraphysical stuff and you kind of talk about pattern, you describe patterns in terms of descriptions of behaviors and that's fine. With a virus, you can ultimately point back to the underlying substrate in a way that is pretty coherent. Can you do that with soul? It is the pointing back to the substrate, with soul, where things just seem to get really murky.

Steele: I'm not even sure that I mean to suggest that a soul is a pattern, quite literally, and to say that it is just a pattern in physical substance; or, whether I merely mean that as a metaphor. However, I think it is useful to think about computational objects such as viruses that seem to have some kind of minimal life of their own and some purpose of their own — at least, we talk about viruses as if they were good and evil. There are some "good" viruses that go around spreading vaccine against "nasty" viruses. Then again, I think that may have less to do with their inherent nature than with our projecting values onto their existence.

Question: With respect to artificial intelligence — the effort, the purpose, the desire to create computers that can have a soul or have human characteristics that make them indistinguishable from carbon based life forms — in all discussion here and previously, there is an incredible void: One thing that is always missing is the nervous system. There is good reason to think that it is just a matter of time before a reality can be created that is indistinguishable from real reality: indistinguishable, like any sensory modality. This entire conversation could be taking place in a black box. A perception of soul could be something definable in terms of neuroscience. Such notions are not politically correct because the soul seems so massively complicated, but it is not becoming that way. In 10, 20, 30, 50 years, we are going to be on a whole other wavelength from the point of view of the nervous system.

Kapor: Your evidence to this is what? Evidence to strong claims you just made about what is going to happen in 20 or 30 years? Just cite something so that I have a marker as to what your beliefs are based on.

Questioner: We have virtual reality now that seems to mimic the real world to a certain degree. I mean that each generation, in every 5 years or 10 years, is able to produce a virtual reality getting closer and closer. This work basically simulates aspects of the nervous system through artificial stimulation. It seems to be straightforward, and clear, that we are heading toward that future, and we are going to be able to examine the world from the point of view of the nervous system. You will not be able to distinguish a real thumb from an artificial one by touching or by any other means. That is going to happen.

Kapor: I am glad someone spoke up for that point of view. It was precisely such a viewpoint that I was intending to attack severely and undermine. If you just do a little bit of cultural history, just look back at the history of such claims that in 10, 20, or 30 years we will be able to do X. They are all variants of the harshly strong AI claim. None of them have come true.

In fact, what we see is that the goal is rather more distant than we ever thought it was, especially as we learn more about people. . . . You can go back to what people were saying in 1956 and 66, and 76, and see where we are now; it is a contrary body of evidence.

Lewis: I see a lot of people wanting to comment on this. But now I'm going to take a poll, O.K.? You heard the claim from the front row. How many people believe it? Can you please restate the claim?

Questioner: The claim is virtual reality and that in 200 years (or whatever time) that we are going to be able to replace what we sense now is reality. You will believe that you are here and that somebody is sitting next to you with a purple shirt ... but it will not be distinguishable from an artificial creation that simulates the nervous system.

Kapor: I just rented *The Matrix*.

Lewis: How many people believe that is going to happen? ... O.K., the claim is too vague to take a poll on, because everyone is going to interpret it differently. Charles, you're next.

Charles L. Perkins: I wanted to bring up the point that some people, including me, believe that within 50 years nanotechnology will happen. This is a technology that would, for example, allow us to map the brain theoretically from inside the neurons, bring that data out using radio frequency, and internally simulate the brain using neuron simulation. Let's just say that this happens in 50 years. The interesting aspect of it, for this panel, is — does it have any meaning? Not whether or not you believe it will happen in 50 years or that in 200 years we can produce this behavior. I happen to believe we can, but for the purpose of this question it doesn't matter whether or not such a thing has occurred. Philosophically, would it be of any interest to us?

Audience member: We don't need anything that complicated. We can observe what people are doing and what they do in their everyday behaviors. We can model those behaviors externally. We can start to predict what people are going to do. Then, people will really wonder what spirituality is.

Veloso: Being an AI researcher aiming to get to that day, I really don't think that that day is reachable, believe me. Probably we will have the sophisticated technology. But we will struggle and struggle to put the integrated intelligence there on the technology. I struggle to have robots do more than pushing balls, and Deep Blue probably struggles to do more than thinking about the next move for chess. By contrast, people are very "complete," meaning that we can do an enormous amount of things. This completeness that we have completely puzzles me.

I believe that we will eventually be able to have a thumb for which you won't know whether you are controlling your own thumb or whether some external neural stimulation is doing it. But are we ever going to have the ability to really encode into a computer program, into technology, our complete way of being, given the way that we do computer science now? Encoding a robust and broad decision-making procedure may require us to understand ourselves. That is a big question.

Yes, you can give me all the technology. But if you are claiming that, "Manuela, 100 years from now you could really know how you learn and you could reproduce on paper exactly how you go from not knowing anything at the beginning of your life until you are 40 years old," that could scare me. On the other hand if you actually make the claim that technology will give me an artifact that will have the ability to activate single neurons, this doesn't scare me at all, in the sense that it hasn't solved the big problem yet.

Question: Guy was talking about pattern and soul and what do you reduce it to and the substrate. I am pointing out that the substrate can be artificially created in a million different ways that are not the real world. The interesting question is: If you grow up in such a substrate that is not the real world, do you have a soul?

Steele: I can address the broader question as well. It seems to me that what you want to accomplish is: not being able to tell whether this is your thumb or someone else's thumb. You don't need fancy computers or nanotechnology. You can do that with a couple of bottles of alcohol. We have some experience with that—

well, humanity at large has some experience with that; I don't drink much myself.

There may be another obstacle to doing what the gentleman over here in the salmon sweater has suggested; there may be another possible technological obstruction. I will dredge up an old, slightly weird conjecture that I published in a paper back in 1981 in reply to something that Doug Hofstadter wrote (we were at a conference together). There is a possibility that the physical structure of the universe may be such that the only feasible embedding of intelligence—in a small enough space that you are not subject to speed of light considerations, and can interact with human beings in real time, at their natural speed—may be the biochemical one. In fact, we may run into problems trying to build electrical, silicon, or whatever computers out of other stuff than what our heads have been made out of, trying to get it into a small enough space that the pieces can interact quickly enough so that they can have conversations with us. That is a possible technological limitation that we shouldn't overlook in the debate.

Question: In religion, people tend to bury each other in incomprehensible complexity. The same sort of thing happens in computer science. I am working on trying to simplify software. When I tried to tell my employer that they were making billions of dollars burying their customers in needless complexity, they were not amused. I sort of felt like Martin Luther telling the Pope how to simplify Christianity. Is it going to go on like this forever?

Kapor: No.

Steele: I conjecture that 200 years from now we will have decided that computers aren't interesting, that they are really boring, and we will move on to something else. It will just be a technology in the background like refrigeration technology is now.

Question: I am having a little bit different view in that from Hinduism or Shintoism, your robots already have souls. If you look at it from a quantum-mechanical point of view there is no time. You have a sheet of the universe, which at the point of the observer, appears to create time by moving through that sheet. That is the soul. If the robot is interacting with the environment, or if a protozoan is appearing to move through a sheet of the universe as a point of observation, that is your soul, because your soul is an intelligence.

A protozoan has intelligence/soul. A flower has a soul under Hinduism. Therefore, your robot already has a soul. The problem is taken care of under quantum mechanics.

Veloso: I will let them know.

Knuth: Maybe we could take a poll as to how many years people think it will be before we will have the panelist, the moderator, and the audience all composed of robots.

Lewis: That is a serious question. That is a version of the poll I was trying to take. I assume it was something like that that you were . . . Just to get some sense of the audience: Do you think that at some finite time, in the future, this panel could be entirely virtual? Do you understand the question? Imagine that you really are who you are, but we are all completely artificial. How many think we will get there? . . . It looks like maybe a third think so. How many think not? It is about one-thirds to two-thirds.

Question: I have a two-year-old and a computer. I am quite certain that the two-year-old is conscious and quite certain that the computer is not. However, the two-year-old is not fully conscious and the computer shows bits of consciousness at times. It seems to me that there is something motivating the two-year-old that is not present in the computer. Until we get some sense of where that comes from, we are not going to make a whole lot more progress on the AI stuff. Consciousness seems to me to be an interesting source. I think this question of materialism is key. Do you believe that consciousness arises out of material events? Or, do you believe that material events arise out of consciousness?

Knuth: Well said — that's the best summary of the mysterious gap at the center of our knowledge that I've heard yet.

Lewis: I hope you weren't hoping for an answer to that question.

Veloso: How could we answer that question? On the other hand, let me tell you something. I do believe that your own experience may be what makes you claim that your child is conscious and your computer is not. If you would have little robots around, and if you would interact with them, the outcome of those interactions could surprise you. I just think that we have to move one step ahead and think that robots can live around us and we care for them, pet them, or say hi. Maybe they never answer, but we don't know. And then our experiences may be different and so also our attitude toward these things that we create.

Kapor: First, just to echo, that is a really deep mystery. I think the kindergarten of that mystery—which is probably resolved as a sort of postdoctoral fellow, or beyond, for me—goes through psychology. This is to say that one of the differences between the two-year-old and the computer, as far as I am concerned, is that the two-year-old has some kind of self sense, some representation of the self to itself; and that my Windows 98 machine kind of doesn't.

Barbara Grosz: This reminds me of a joke about a physicist, a minister, and a computer scientist having a debate about which of their professions was most important and fundamental. The physicist said that his profession understood the order in the universe. The minister said that God had created order out of chaos. The computer scientist laid claim to creating chaos.

My question, inspired in part by what Manuela just said, and also by what Don said, is about interaction becoming more important. As we look at computer systems today, comparing them with 30 or 40 years ago, there is much more emphasis on interaction with people and among the computer systems. Guy made a reference to Genesis where God creates a companion for Adam thinking he shouldn't be left alone. I am wondering whether you think that having more than one creature is important, in fact, for the evolution of spirituality, consciousness, or whatever this whole piece is; and, if then they have to be creatures of the same sort or they can be creatures of different sorts?

Veloso: That is a very good question. This will be my last comment. I really believe that we can increase our spirituality and our knowledge of ourselves, and our knowledge of our origins, by trying to create little intelligent creatures, trying to create intelligent artifacts, and interact with them.

If you think about the history of science, at the beginning we thought that the earth was the center of the universe. We were very disturbed by knowing that we were not. After all, the sun was there. How could we be going around the sun? We always think that we are the center of everything. It has been through science that we have increased our knowledge of the world. Really science has probably forced us to know more about ourselves.

I do believe that the goal of AI is to know more about ourselves, about the world, about how to interact. If God exists (as I do believe), the creation of physical artifacts will never contradict that existence. It will just, actually, make it even more visible.

How, I don't know. But I am not afraid of pursuing the AI goal, because I do believe that knowing more about myself and knowing more about the world can never lead me to the conclusion that God doesn't exist. I don't think that I would get to that end. Just the opposite.

Lewis: I want to thank all the participants very much for their contributions. Thank you all for being here.

Notes on the Panel Discussion

Page 208, *The Hacker's Dictionary*: Guy L. Steele Jr., Donald R. Woods, Raphael A. Finkel, Mark R. Crispin, Richard M. Stallman, and Geoffrey S. Goodfellow, *The Hacker's Dictionary* (New York: Harper & Row, 1983). Version 4.0.0 of this dictionary, edited by Eric S. Raymond, was published as *The New Hacker's Dictionary*, 3rd edition (Cambridge, Massachusetts: MIT Press, 1996); it features an introduction and cartoons by Guy Steele. The dictionary entries themselves can be found online at, for example, `earthspace.net/jargon/`.

Page 215, They defined it: Allen Newell, Alan J. Perlis, and Herbert A. Simon, "Computer Science," *Science* **157** (1967), 1373–1374.

Page 216, my little robots that play soccer: See Manuela Veloso, Peter Stone, and Kwun Han, "The CMUnited-97 robotic soccer team: Perception and multiagent control," *Robotics and Autonomous Systems* **29** (1999), 133–143; Peter Stone and Manuela Veloso, "Task decomposition, dynamic role assignment, and low-bandwidth communication for real-time strategic teamwork," *Artificial Intelligence* **110** (1999), 241–273; Manuela M. Veloso, Enrice Pagello, and Hiroaki Kitano, *RoboCup-99: Robot Soccer World Cup III* (Berlin: Springer, 2000) = *Lecture Notes in Computer Science* **1856**; Manuela Veloso, Elly Winner, Scott Lenser, James Bruce, and Tucker Balch, "Vision-servoed localization and behavior-based planning for an autonomous quadruped legged robot," *Proceedings of the Fifth International Conference on Artificial Intelligence Planning Systems* (Breckinridge, Colorado, April 2000).

Page 217, a really nice article: Paul Halmos, "Innovation in mathematics," *Scientific American* **199**, 3 (September 1958), 66–73, especially page 69.

Page 218, a little novelette: Donald E. Knuth, *Surreal Numbers* (Reading, Massachusetts: Addison–Wesley, 1974).

Page 219, a book by Dorothy Sayers: Dorothy L. Sayers, *The Mind of the Maker* (London: Methuen, 1941). The excerpts quoted appear on pages 141 and 186–187.

Page 220, this is the point: Subsequently I found very similar views expressed nicely by George Buttrick: "The Creative Mystery, Whom men in agelong faith have called God, is not the death of meaning, but its only home. A dead certainty is just that: dead. Knowledge that is cut and dried is just that: cut and dried. . . . Surely this Mystery, in which the mind already stands, provides vistas for the mind's adventure, more exciting and truer to the facts than the foreclosure of agnosticism or the confines of secularism." [*Biblical Thought and the Secular University* (Baton Rouge: Louisiana University Press, 1960), 58.]

Page 220, Thank goodness for mathematics: See Knuth's introduction to Jerry Slocum and Jack Botermans' *New Book of Puzzles* (New York: W. H. Freeman, 1992), 6–7.

Page 226, "serendipitous creativity": Gordon D. Kaufman, *In Face of Mystery: A Constructive Theology* (Cambridge, Massachusetts: Harvard University Press, 1993).

Page 230, *The Matrix*: A 1999 motion picture written and directed by Larry and Andy Wachowski. See *The Art of The Matrix*, by Spencer Lamm (editor), Andy Wachowski, Larry Wachowski, Steve Skroce, Geof Darrow, and Phil Oosterhouse (New York: Newmarket Press, 2000).

Page 232, slightly weird conjecture: Guy L. Steele Jr., "Comments on Hofstadter," *Synthese* **53** (1982), 219–226. [An invited paper presented at the conference on Matters of the Mind, University of Missouri, St. Louis, 28–30 October 1981.]

Page 234, shouldn't be left alone: Genesis 2:18.

INDEX OF BIBLE REFERENCES

INDEX

Stein, Lynn Andrea, vi.
Steinberg, Don, 37.
Stenger, Werner, 89.
Stockmeyer, Larry Joseph,
173–174, 200.
Stone, Peter, 236.
Stone, Sumner, 136.
stone cutting, 102.
stratified sampling, 29.
Strong, James, 57–58, 84.
Exhaustive Concordance,
57–61, 141, 163.
style, 101, 106, 116, 118, 122,
130.
sunsets, 222–224.
Super K, 171–175, 188, 192,
202.
surreal numbers, 175–176, 200.
Surreal Numbers, 153–154,
218–219, 237.
Sussman, Gerald Jay, 226, 227.
Sutherland, Norman Stuart, 185,
203.
syneídēsis, 75.

T (the MBTA subway), 7, 148.
Talmud, 162.
Taoism, 13.
taste, varieties of, 121.
tax code, 47.
tears, 96, 126–127, 139.
televangelists, 160.
Templeton, John, Foundation,
vi, ix.
TEX, iv, 17, 23, 37, 46, 72, 87,
92, 94, 133–134, 149, 154,
190, 208.
text reconstruction, 82.
textual problems, 40, 79–82.
*The Art of Computer Program-
ming*, 37, 55, 83, 91–92,

94, 157, 168, 187, 209–210,
218.
Volume 4, 149, 151–152, 157.
theía manía, 197.
theologians, 5, 9, 16–17, 20, 36,
61–62, 140, 144–145, 158,
167, 174, 181, 234.
theology, 139.
computers and, vi, 19.
theós, 89.
thumbs, 229–231.
Tillich, Paul Johannes, 66, 86,
149–150, 162, 164.
Tischendorf, Lobegott Friedrich
Konstantin von, 89.
Titus, Book of, 32, 44.
Today's English Version, 140.
Tolkien, John Ronald Reuel, 106.
Tolstoy, Leo Nikolaevich, 161.
top-down causality versus
bottom-up causality, 198.
transcendental meditation,
222–223.
translation of languages, 53–89.
as educational tool, 77–78.
goals of, 68, 71, 78, 80.
translations of the Bible, 10, 56,
see Annotated Scholars
Version, Bishops' Bible,
Cotton Patch Versions,
Dead Sea Scrolls Bible,
Douay Version, Jerusalem
Bible, King James Version,
Knox's translation, Living
Bible, New English Bible,
New Jerusalem Bible, New
Revised Standard Version,
Revised English Bible,
Revised Standard Version,
Septuagint, Today's English
Version, Tyndale, Vulgate.

whiteout, 118, 122.
Whitman, Walter, 128, 136.
Widener Library, 94.
Wigner, Eugene Paul, 146, 148,
    163.
Williams, Robert, 100–101.
Wilson, Colin St. John, 22.
Windows operating system, 234.
Winkler, Phyllis Astrid Benson,
    124, 219.
Winner, Elly, 236.
wisdom, 160.
women's liberation, 62–64, 69,
    101.
Wong, Allen Quan (= Wong
    Ging Quan), 104–105.
Wong, Jeanyee, 117–118, 135.
Woods, Donald Roy, 236.
word of God, 118, 153–154,
    174, 191.
worst-case estimates, 45, 52.
Wronker, Lily Cassel, 101, 135.

Y2K crisis, 27, 50.
Yale Divinity School, 140.
Yao, Andrew Chi-Chih, 205.
Yao, Frances Foong Chu,
    220–221.
yin and yang, 38, 52, 220.

Zachrisson, Bror, 134.
Zakariya, Mohamed, 136.
Zapf, Hermann, 65–67, 95–96,
    99, 121, 125, 134.
Zapf–von Hesse, Gudrun, 95,
    100.
Zen, 13.
Zeno of Elea, 211.
zero knowledge, 28.
Zigány, Edit, 111.
Zurek, Wojciech Hubert, 165.